Conversations with William F. Buckley Jr.

Literary Conversations Series
Peggy Whitman Prenshaw
General Editor

To Gregory Larkin,
with Best wishes
Bill McL

Conversations with William F. Buckley Jr.

Edited by
William F. Meehan III

University Press of Mississippi
Jackson

www.upress.state.ms.us

The University Press of Mississippi is a member of the Association of American University Presses.

Copyright © 2009 by University Press of Mississippi
All rights reserved
Manufactured in the United States of America

First printing 2009

∞

Library of Congress Cataloging-in-Publication Data

Buckley, William F. (William Frank), 1925–2008.
    Conversations with William F. Buckley Jr. / edited by William F. Meehan, III.
        p.   cm. — (Literary conversations series)
    Includes index.
    ISBN 978-1-60473-224-5 (alk. paper) — ISBN 978-1-60473-225-2 (pbk. : alk. paper)
1. Buckley, William F. (William Frank), 1925–2008—Interviews. 2. Journalists—United States—Interviews. 3. Novelists, American—20th century—Interviews. I. Meehan, William F. II. Title.
    PN4874.B796A5 2009
    070.92—dc22

                                                        2008044438

British Library Cataloging-in-Publication Data available

Books by William F. Buckley Jr.

God and Man at Yale: The Superstitions of Academic Freedom. Chicago: Regnery, 1951.

McCarthy and His Enemies: The Record and Its Meaning. (With L. Brent Bozell Jr.). Chicago: Regnery, 1954.

Up from Liberalism. New York: Putnam, 1959.

The Committee and Its Critics. (With others). New York: Putnam, 1962.

Rumbles Left and Right: A Book about Troublesome People and Ideas. New York: Putnam, 1963.

The Unmaking of a Mayor. New York: Viking, 1966.

The Jeweler's Eye. New York: Putnam, 1968.

Odyssey of a Friend: Letters to William F. Buckley Jr.: 1954–1961. New York: Regnery, 1987.

Did You Ever See a Dream Walking? American Conservative Thought in the Twentieth Century. (Ed.) Indianapolis and New York: Bobbs-Merrill, 1970.

The Governor Listeth: A Book of Inspired Political Revelations. New York: Putnam, 1970.

Cruising Speed: A Documentary. New York: Putnam, 1971.

Inveighing We Will Go. New York: Putnam, 1972.

Four Reforms: A Program for Today. New York: Putnam, 1973.

United Nation's Journal: A Delegate's Odyssey. New York: Putnam, 1974.

Execution Eve—And Other Contemporary Ballads. New York: Putnam, 1975.

Airborne: A Sentimental Journey. New York: Macmillan, 1976.

Saving the Queen. Garden City: Doubleday, 1976.

A Hymnal: The Controversial Arts. New York: Putnam, 1978.

Stained Glass. Garden City: Doubleday, 1978.

Who's on First. Garden City: Doubleday, 1980.

Atlantic High: A Celebration. Garden City: Doubleday, 1982.

Marco Polo, If You Can. Garden City: Doubleday, 1982.

Overdrive: A Personal Documentary. Garden City, Doubleday, 1983.

The Story of Henri Tod. Garden City: Doubleday, 1984.

Right Reason. Garden City: Doubleday, 1985.

See You Later Alligator. Garden City: Doubleday, 1985.

The Temptation of Wilfred Malachey. New York: Workman Publishing, 1985.

High Jinx. New York: Doubleday, 1986.

Racing through Paradise: A Pacific Passage. New York: Random House, 1987.

Mongoose, R.I.P. New York: Random House, 1987.

On the Firing Line: The Public Life of Our Public Figures. New York: Random House, 1989.

Gratitude: Reflections on What We Owe to Our Country. New York: Random House, 1990.

Tucker's Last Stand. New York: Random House, 1990.

In Search of Anti-Semitism. New York: Continuum, 1992.

WindFall: The End of the Affair. New York: Random House, 1992.

Happy Days Were Here Again: Reflections of Libertarian Journalist. New York: Random House, 1993.

A Very Private Plot. New York: Morrow, 1994.

Brothers No More. New York: Doubleday, 1995.

The Blackford Oakes Reader. Kansas City: Andrews and McMeel, 1995.

Buckley: The Right Word. New York: Random House, 1996.

Nearer, My God to Thee: An Autobiography of Faith. New York: Doubleday, 1997.

The Lexicon: A Cornucopia of Wonderful Words for the Inquisitive Word Lover. New York: Harcourt, 1998.

The Redhunter: A Novel Based on the Life of Senator Joe McCarthy. New York: Little Brown, 1999.

Let Us Talk of Many Things: The Collected Speeches with New Commentary by the Author. Roseville, Calif.: Prima, 2000.

Spytime: The Undoing of James Jesus Angleton. New York: Harcourt, 2000.

Elvis in the Morning. New York: Harcourt, 2001

Nuremberg: The Reckoning. New York: Harcourt, 2002.

The National Review Treasury of Classic Children's Literature. Wilmington, Del.: ISI Books, 2002.

Getting It Right. Washington, D.C.: Regnery Publishing, Inc., 2003.

The Fall of the Berlin Wall. New York: Wiley, 2004.

The National Review Treasury of Classic Children's Literature: Volume Two. Wilmington, Del.: ISI Books, 2004.

Miles Gone By: A Literary Autobiography. Washington, D.C.: Regnery Publishing, Inc., 2004.

Last Call for Blackford Oakes. New York: Harcourt, 2005.

The Rake: A Novel. New York: Harper Collins, 2007.

Cancel Your Own *Goddam Subscription: Notes & Asides from* National Review. New York: Basic Books, 2007.

Flying High: Remembering Barry Goldwater. New York: Basic Books, 2008.

The Reagan I Knew. New York: Basic Books, 2008.

Contents

Introduction

Although he will always be recognized as dashing public intellectual, polite controversialist, consummate sailor, accomplished harpsichordist, skillful debater, *Firing Line* host and *National Review* founder, admired lecturer, and of course principal architect of the American conservative movement, William F. Buckley Jr. might be appreciated above all as a literary figure. Producing about 350,000 words for publication a year, Buckley was never at a loss for what to say or how to say it. He wrote over 7,000 columns, articles, reviews, introductions, forewords, obituaries, and more, in addition to publishing fifty-seven books, including eighteen novels.

My initial encounter with Buckley as novelist is the library science textbook example of serendipity. I was browsing the recent acquisitions shelves in Morris Library at the University of Delaware one sunny Friday afternoon in the spring of 1984, when *The Story of Henri Tod* caught my eye. It was a few months after I had been introduced to *National Review*, so my curiosity about the book was aroused. I learned, from scanning the publisher's promotional copy, that it was a Cold War spy novel featuring Blackford Oakes, heralded as leading man in four previous works. My interest sufficiently piqued, I settled into a chair and opened to page 153 where I met Oakes who, riding a train in Germany and eyeing an attractive female passenger, pens an overture to her so cleverly imaginative that I checked the book out and spent the weekend with it. I discovered that in Buckley's wilderness of mirrors the Americans are the good guys and that Oakes was a character worth getting to know. The writing, moreover, was magnetic and the unfamiliar words dazzling, so I purchased the preceding novels and read them too. The result, a decade later after completing a dissertation on Buckley's prose fiction style, was the formation of an important relationship with Buckley as his bibliographer.

Buckley was fifty years old when he added novelist to his literary repertoire and attained instant acclaim on the fiction bestseller list with *Saving the Queen*. The success was due, in part, to the perspective he offered readers of spy novels. Buckley intended in the Oakes novels, he explains in the *Paris Review*, to "celebrate the Cold War" by filling a void he perceived in American literature and by distinguishing himself from other novelists in the genre. "I was determined to avoid one thing," Buckley adds, "and that was the kind of ambiguity for which Graham Greene and to a certain extent Le Carré became famous. There you will find that the agent of the West is, in the first place, almost necessarily unappealing physically. Then, at some dramatic moment there is the conversation or the moment of reflection in which the reader is asked to contemplate the difficulty in asserting that there *is* a qualitative difference between Them and Us. This I wanted to avoid."

Buckley leaves no doubt in his debut novel that Oakes differed from the conventional spy character, as the omniscient narrator illustrates when the Queen meets Oakes at a dinner she is hosting at Windsor Castle: "The Queen smiled and suddenly her eyes deglazed and she actually looked at the person she was addressing. She found herself most agreeably surprised by a young man of poise, with extraordinarily attractive features, blue eyes, dark blond hair, and an ever-so-slightly mischievous expression." From the outset, it is obvious that *she* pursued Oakes who, undercover as a researcher, ultimately penetrated more than the royal archives. Sales of the book in England were meager as a result, but *Saving the Queen* was a sensation everywhere else, as was Oakes. "I made Blackford Oakes such a shining perfection to irritate, infuriate the critics," Buckley tells "Tex" McCrary. "And I *scored!*"

Whenever the topic of Buckley's fiction arises when I am in gatherings where he is better known as a leading conservative, someone usually will want to know if Oakes shares his creator's political leanings. I brought this up with Buckley in my 1996 interview with him: "[Oakes is] libertarian," Buckley clarifies, "only in the sense that he's generally antistatist; he reads *National Review*. He is conservative in the sense that he thinks the values of the West are worth a nuclear deterrent, and devotes his life to corollary propositions . . . I can't remember that in any of the books I had him simply expatiate in general on any political policies. These aren't political books in the sense that *National Review* is a political magazine."

Buckley adapted for stage performance his second novel, *Stained Glass*, which won the American Book Award for Best Mystery, and he talks with Tom Augst about the rewarding challenge of writing a play. "By the time I sat down with the script a couple of months later to look at it again and rewrite it," he says, "I found I had achieved a perspective that I didn't have the very first night I started in . . . So it's fair to say the missing perspective began to crystallize—the idea of communicating with an audience exclusively through spoken words, without the reliance of nonspoken words which all novelists rely on very heavily."

Buckley departed, momentarily, from the spy genre in novel number eleven, *Brothers No More*, while later creating fictional accounts of the familiar figures James Jesus Angleton in *Spymaster*, Elvis Presley in *Elvis in the Morning*, Joe McCarthy in *The Redhunter*, and Ayn Rand in *Getting It Right*. When the *American Enterprise* wanted to know how he chose Presley as the subject for a novel, Buckley explains, "Well, I didn't set out to write about Elvis Presley. My goal was to chronicle a young American who goes left. In doing so, I wandered into the late fifties—and Elvis Presley is everywhere. He was an enormous cultural presence." Similarly, Buckley conveys to Kathryn Jean Lopez that he wrote *Getting It Right*, which describes the early days of the libertarian and conservative movements, "Because I wanted to write a story about politics, sex, and legendary American figures."

Buckley, whose third language is English after Spanish and French, was known for what Joseph Rago calls his "O.E.D. vocabulary." When I asked Buckley in our 1996 conversation if he had a philosophy of language, he elaborated on the subject that had generated applause and ridicule:

> The only philosophy of language that I have is that I won't, except in very exceptional circumstances, suppress an unusual word if the word flashes to my mind as exactly appropriate . . . The way I rationalize it is that word exists because there was what the economists would call, a "felt need" for it, i.e., no other word around did what this particular word does. Therefore, the eventuation of that word enriches the choices that you have. So, why do you want to be a party to diminishing the choices that you have, when you're dealing with a language which you worship for its beauty? . . . If you suppress a particular word, let's say "velleity"—something you desire, but not ardently—if you suppress that word, you diminish the choices by which people can express and distinguish between something they absolutely want and something they would like in the sense they would like an extra sweater. I don't want to be a party to that.

Each of us, Buckley maintains, has a distinctive working vocabulary; his just happens to contain around a thousand unusual words. Buckley is quick to point out, however, that he once passed around at a *National Review* editorial meeting a list of over twenty words, from John Updike's *The Coup*, whose meaning he did not know, while his five colleagues at the table were familiar with all of them. Buckley deployed an unusual word—chiliastic—on *Nightline*, when he and Ted Koppel were talking about the end of *Firing Line*, after its thirty-three year run. The ABC host had some fun with his guest: "Nobody ever says to you when you use one of these words, 'By the way, what the hell does chiliastic mean?'"[1]

Besides the unusual word, another notable aspect of Buckley's writing is the use of foreign words and phrases, which also irritates the critics as well as readers. "It's an old complaint, the use of foreign words," Buckley writes in response to a letter from a *National Review* subscriber in 1988.[2] "However, delicately used, they do bring little piquancies and with them—well, *aperçus*, which, because they are extra-idiomatic, give you a fresh view of the subject. As if, in a gallery, you could rise—or descend—ten feet, and look at the picture from that fresh perspective." What is more, he believed foreign words have a "special incantatory sound." And therein might be the key to his language. Buckley composes for a refined ear, so the prose is a delightful blend of rhetorical elegance, idiomatic phrasing, and grammatical solecisms, usually facilitated by an expertise with the comma. "Language is an aesthetic as well as an analytic tool," Buckley points out, "and to slur language is as painful to the well-tempered ear as to slur music."

Buckley's analogies to music are understandable, since it was a central part of his personal life and one of his familiar topics. His early schooling in the family home, Great Elm, in Sharon, Connecticut, consisted of formal piano lessons, while later at Wallack's Point, in Stamford, and at his Manhattan apartment, he regularly hosted performances by a musician or diva. Over the years, though, it was Bach and the harpsichord Buckley grew to treasure. In a self-interview in 1989 for the *New York Times*, "Buckley, Why on Earth? . . . ," he describes his solo harpsichord performance of Bach's F Minor concerto with the Phoenix Symphony Orchestra: "It was fun finding out that a lapsed amateur can, if he is willing to spend lots and lots of time on the problem, manage to draw on a lifetime of devotion to a composer and play creditably for eight and one-half minutes one of his beautiful concertos."[3]

For all the prose he generated, Buckley did not enjoy writing. He acknowledges his unease on those mornings he awoke knowing he had to produce an article but nevertheless turned anxiety into motivation. "If your living depends on writing a piece of journalism every day, and you find writing painful work," he comments in the *Paris Review*, "you're obviously much better off developing the facility to execute it in an hour rather than ten." Buckley further relates the story of learning out of necessity, at the age of fifteen, to touch type. He describes his penmanship as "sort of malformed," the reading of which prompted his father to have delivered a typewriter along with the message never again to send home a handwritten letter. A few years later as chairman of the *Yale Daily News*, Buckley goes on to say, he was still writing by hand a first draft of his articles before typing a second, but by the time he turned "twenty-three it wouldn't occur to me to write anything by hand." Buckley typed with astonishing speed, able to write a column in about twenty minutes.

Although Buckley might not have liked writing, he looked forward to finishing an assignment. "I get pleasure out of *having* written," he admits in *Bookviews*. And to help him complete the task as quickly as possible, Buckley exploited technology for its practicality. "It's sheer sloth," he shares with Peter Robinson in a *Forbes ASAP* interview.[4] "If a computer can save me ten minutes spent on research, so that I can do an editorial exercise in twenty minutes instead of half an hour, then I'm simply jubilant, I am excited to see technology happening. But my own interest is quite utilitarian." He embraced WordStar in 1981 and, with Quarterdeck's DesqView instead of Windows, depended on this software the rest of his career.

Buckley's favorite topic, aside from his syndicated column and articles for *National Review*, was sailing. He wrote more for periodicals devoted to sailing and yachting than for any other category of publication, and two of his four sailing books registered his best sales. In addition, the longest section of his memoir, *Miles to Go: A Literary Autobiography*, pertains to sailing. So it makes sense for this collection to include a conversation about the sport Buckley took up at the age of fourteen. Although his four trans-oceanic sails demanded much of him and his crew, life on a sailboat for Buckley was supposed to be fun. Buckley competed in a few ocean races, but he preferred recreational cruising. Jeff Hammond, who accompanies Buckley on the final cruise aboard his schooner, *Cyrano*, reveals one of the features of a Buckley cruise: BWT or Buckley Watch Time, which means setting watches one hour ahead. "There are two great advantages to BWT," Buckley suggests. "First, cocktail hour comes one hour sooner. Second, you get an extra hour of sleep before the sunlight hits you in the eye." Sailing, however, was not a pointless activity; it meant meaningful time with family and friends, providing pleasures that could not be matched. "I would never be a single sailor," he declares to Peter Robinson, aboard Buckley's thirty-six-foot sloop, *Patito*. "Zero appeal in that. Things like this should be shared."[5] Sailing also summoned in Buckley an appreciation for natural wonders, and his sailing literature contains a salute to nature not seen even in the novels where, he notes, "there's not a lot of time spent describing exteriorities."

Any discussion of Buckley as a literary figure naturally drifts into his role as a commentator, and the interviews with *Playboy* and the *Civil Liberties Review* explore a range of issues relevant to a full understanding of Buckley, as does the *Wall Street Journal* interview, with its coverage of more recent topics such as the George W. Bush presidency. These conversations confirm that Buckley's analysis was unique, guided by *recta ratio*; his observations over the years might be summed up with this comment to *Playboy*: "I happen to be more adventurous than some conservatives."

Buckley was an unwavering Catholic his entire life, finding at an early age the calming allure of the Latin Mass and the significance of his faith. Buckley devoted many column inches to criticism of Rome, but he followed the golden rule when it came to talking about religion. "I am, by nature," he discloses to Michael Cromartie in an interview about *Nearer, My God: An Autobiography of Faith*, "indisposed to bring up religious matters uninvited. I just don't do it." What is more, when *Vanity Fair's* Proust Questionnaire asked Buckley in 1993 what he wishes he could do better, he replied, "Pray."[6]

It might come as a surprise to discover that Buckley also did not spend time talking politics when he was, so to speak, off-duty. "It's not the kind of thing that interests me very much," he reveals to Brian Lamb on the television program *Booknotes*. "You see, there are other things to talk about." Perhaps that explains why Buckley's remarkable gift for friendship famously crossed political and religious lines, embracing those who held opposing views. "You can disagree very pointedly with somebody and still have an enormous bond of friendship," he assures Lamb.

In a span of three years in the 1960s, Buckley ran for mayor of New York, launched *Firing Line*, and appeared on the cover of *Time* magazine. He was, in other words, a familiar man about town with the qualities of a wonderful interviewee: raw intelligence, vigorous wit, and healthy sense of humor combined with verbal flair and genuine civility. When *Jock* magazine came knocking in 1969 and asked for some thoughts about the connection between sports and the quality of life in New York, Buckley had to confess that he knew nothing about it. So they agreed to solicit "his impressions of the sporting scene," in which Buckley reflected, "trained athletes are cool under stress, and know how to drive down the middle of the road, and avoid falling off bridges."[7] *Playboy Fashion* magazine wanted to know in 1982 what he thought about sartorial matters. As an aside towards the end of the interview, Buckley mentioned that he had "discovered the world's most comfortable shoe" but noticed that the price had gone up.[8]

Interviewer: Well, you do pay a price for fashion. But don't you think there's a difference between being a fashion plate and being fashionable?
Buckley: Most definitely. I remember an occasion when I gave a speech at a University of California campus during the Vietnam war. I was advocating a not terribly popular position at the time. Yet I wasn't booed. In fact, they listened to me very, very dutifully, with great concentration.
Interviewer: You mean they didn't agree with what you were saying, yet they were mesmerized by your personal style?
Buckley: Yes. I suppose, in that sense, I have always been fashionable.

Such self-assurance never made anyone uncomfortable, for it sprang from the heart of a man full of exuberance. Buckley always remembers, moreover, a primary inspiration, connected with his summers as a teenager in Camden, South Carolina. "Yes, I was greatly influenced by my father's own beliefs, which are thought of as Southern in character: honor, patriotism, truthfulness, courtesy," he tells Scott M. Morris, in an unpublished interview conducted in 1996 for the *Oxford American*, when asked about the bearing of Southern values on his life as a commentator.[9]

Buckley's life as an author spanned nearly six decades. One year after graduating from Yale, Buckley in 1951 entered the literary—and public—scene with a flourish as the author of *God and Man at Yale*, a critique of his alma mater. Buckley did not change his mind about the "superstitions of academic freedom" at Yale, but he later wondered about the quality of the writing in his first book. "I was twenty years old in those days," he explains to Alan Westin in the *Civil Liberties Review* almost three decades after the book's publication, "and I'm sure there isn't a paragraph in that book I wouldn't weep at the reading of. But, it would be less in what I said than in the way I said it."

After brief postings in the CIA and at *American Mercury*, Buckley in 1955 founded *National Review* and, from that moment on, seemed never to stop working until he passed away, at home sitting at the computer. Buckley worked at such remarkable pace because he feared boredom, a trait to which he attributes his fast-moving plots. He shed some light on this personal trait when he appeared on *Charlie Rose* marking the publication of *Happy Days Were Here Again*.[10]

> **Rose:** How about writing for you, writing novels? I mean, it always amazed me that you were able to create Oakes and be successful at it. What does that say about—does it say that you, a former CIA operative, just had a capacity to tell a story and that's what made you successful as a spy novelist?
> **Buckley:** Well, I suppose it probably has to do also with an individual threshold of boredom. I get bored very easily.
> **Rose:** So you want to move the pages along for your own—
> **Buckley:** That's right. So you're sitting there clacking away, and some people— that lovely Southern lady can write about the wisteria for seven pages . . .
> **Rose:** Eudora Welty?
> **Buckley:** Yes, and I love her for it, but I can't do that. I don't have those skills. So therefore, I've got to have action and words.

On a more lighthearted note, Buckley told *Time's* James Carney, in "10 Questions for William F. Buckley" in 2004, that his productivity was due to "The fear that the enemy will write more than I do."[11]

Buckley shifted from cruising speed to overdrive by organizing his life around deadlines, which he found liberating. "The people I pity," he states to Doug Anderson in *ElectriCity*, "are not the people who have deadlines, they're the people who *don't* have deadlines." Adhering to timelines allowed Buckley to host for thirty-three years the television show *Firing Line*, while delivering across the country about seventy lectures a year. The discipline also came in handy when he ventured into writing novels. Instead of abandoning any of his other obligations, Buckley simply arranged his calendar. He set aside February and March, in Switzerland, where he wrote 1,500 words a day from about 5:00 P.M. to 7:00 P.M., after devoting the morning to administrative business and the early afternoon to skiing, and before taking part in social engagements usually coordinated by his wife, Pat.

For audiences who knew Buckley through his decades on the lecture circuit, he "presents the crowning event of their day," in the words of Doug Anderson. A Buckley speech was an occasion surrounded in mystique. For some audiences, he was their dream walking, and it was Buckley himself they came to *see* rather than hear. "For all Buckley's contributions to conservative ideas, his most striking contribution is to the conservative personality," David Brooks reasons in the foreword to *Let Us Talk of Many Things*, Buckley's collected speeches. "He made being conservative attractive and even glamorous. One suspects that more people were inspired by his presence at these events than were converted by the power of mere logic."[12] His fans will never forget the evening with their guest of honor but, in the years to come, Buckley's contribution as literary figure might be his lasting triumph. "Buckley is one writer whose words have stimulated curiosity, scorn, legal action, reaction, reform, respect, and affection," Samuel S. Vaughan convinces in the introduction to *Buckley: The Right Word*. "They have helped to educate and elect Presidents. His language continues to generate exasperation and admiration for the man behind them."[13]

The fifteen interviews in this collection are reprinted as they appeared originally, the texts unedited except for the gentle correction of obvious typographical oversights, so some repetition unavoidably occurs. While interviewers often ask identical or similar questions, Buckley's answers display a consistency that scholars will value. The interviews are arranged chronologically according to the times they were conducted.

My editing the volume is due to Buckley's biographer Sam Tanenhaus who, when asked by the publisher for the name of someone capable of the task, mentioned me. I eagerly undertook the assignment and unexpectedly turned it into a protracted effort that leaves me indebted to Seetha Srinivasan, director of the

University Press of Mississippi. Editor Walter Biggins offered suggestions that unified the collection, and cheerfully fielded my questions while managing the publication process. My research was facilitated greatly by receiving access to Buckley's magazine files at *National Review*. I am grateful, as ever, for the assistance of Linda Bridges, Dorothy McCartney, and John Virtes, as well as for the help from the late Tony Savage in the early phase of my work. Finally, I express my gratitude for a Valdosta State University Faculty Research Grant and thank the copyright owners for permission to reprint their interviews.

WFM

Notes

1. *Nightline*, December 14, 1999.
2. William F. Buckley Jr., "Notes & Asides," *National Review*, April 29, 1988: 19.
3. Buckley, "Buckley, Why on Earth? . . . ," *New York Times*, Arts & Leisure Section, October 1, 1989: 27, 30.
4. Peter Robinson, "*ASAP* Interview: William F. Buckley Jr.," *Forbes ASAP*, October 10, 1944: 60–69.
5. Ibid.
6. "Proust Questionnaire with William F. Buckley Jr.," *Vanity Fair* (September 1993): 250.
7. "Athletes Are Cool Under Stress . . . ," *Jock* (October 1969): 34–35.
8. "A Conversation with William F. Buckley Jr.," *Playboy Fashion* (Spring/Summer 1982): 28–31.
9. Scott, untitled, unpublished interview, 1996.
10. *The Charlie Rose Show*, September 20, 1993.
11. James Carney, "10 Questions for William F. Buckley," *Time*, April 12, 2004: 8.
12. David Brooks, Foreword, *Let Us Talk of Many Things: The Collected Speeches*, by William F. Buckley Jr. (Roseville Calif.: Prima Publishing, 2000), xx.
13. Samuel S. Vaughan, "What's It Like to Edit William F. Buckley Jr.?" *Buckley: The Right Word*, edited by Samuel S. Vaughan (New York: Random House, 1996), xvi.

Chronology

1925	Born in New York City, November 24.
1938	Attends St. John's, Beaumont, Old Windsor, England.
1943	Graduates Millbrook School, New York. Attends University of Mexico. Drafted into U.S. Army.
1946	Honorably discharged, 2nd Lieutenant, U.S. Army. Enters Yale University.
1947	Appointed instructor in Spanish, Yale University.
1949	Elected chairman, *Yale Daily News*.
1950	B.A. with honors, Yale University; selected Class Day Orator. Marries Patricia Austin Taylor. Reappointed instructor in Spanish, Yale University.
1951	Publishes *God and Man at Yale*. Joins the Central Intelligence Agency.
1952	Appointed associate editor at the *American Mercury*. Son Christopher Taylor Buckley born.
1954	Employed in father's business Catawba Corporation.
1955	Founds *National Review*, first issued November 19.
1962	Begins syndicated column "A Conservative Voice," distributed by George Matthew Arnold Services, Inc., and renames column "On the Right."
1965	Joins Washington Star Syndicate, Inc. Runs for mayor of New York, receiving 13.4 percent of vote.
1966	Launches *Firing Line*. Receives honorary L.H.D., Seton Hall University.
1967	Appointed lecturer in municipal government, New School for Social Research. Featured on cover of *Time*, November 3. Receives Best Columnist of the Year Award. Receives honorary L.H.D., Niagara University.
1968	Receives Distinguished Achievement Award in Journalism, University of Southern California.
1969	Appointed to Advisory Commission on Information, U.S. Information

Agency. Receives Emmy Award for *Firing Line*. Receives honorary
L.H.D., Mount St. Mary's College; honorary LL.D., Saint Peter's College; honorary LL.D., Syracuse University; honorary LL.D., Ursinus
College.

1970   Man of the Decade Award, Young Americans for Freedom. Receives
honorary D.Sc.O., Curry College.

1971   Receives honorary LL.D., Lehigh University; honorary Litt.D., Saint
Vincent College.

1972   Introduces *Firing Line* as Public Broadcasting Service program. Receives honorary LL.D., Lafayette College.

1973   Appointed Public Member, U.S. Delegation to the 28th General Assembly of the United Nations. Appointed Froman Distinguished Professor, Russell Sage College. Receives honorary LL.D., St. Anselm's
College; honorary Litt.D. Fairleigh Dickinson University.

1974   Receives Cleveland Amory Award, *TV Guide*. Receives honorary LL.D.,
St. Bonaventure University; Receives honorary Litt.D., Alfred University.

1975   Sails *Cyrano* from Miami to Gibraltar.

1976   Publishes first novel, *Saving the Queen*. Named Fellow, Sigma Delta
Chi, the Society of Professional Journalists.

1977   Receives Bellarmine Medal.

1978   Receives honorary LL.D., University of Notre Dame.

1979   Receives Americanism Award, Young Republican National Federation.

1980   Sails *Sealestial* from St. Thomas to Marabella. Receives Carmel Award
for Journalism Excellence, American Friends of Haifa University. Receives the American Book Award for Best Mystery for *Stained Glass*.

1981   Receives New York University Creative Leadership Award. Receives
honorary LL.D., New York Law School; honorary L.H.D., College of
William and Mary.

1982   Receives honorary Litt.D., William Jewell College.

1985   Receives Lincoln Literary Award, Union League. Receives honorary
L.H.D., University of South Carolina; honorary LL.D., Colby College.
Sails *Sealestial* from Honolulu to Majuro.

1986   Receives Shelby Cullom Davis Award.

1987   Receives honorary Litt.D., Albertus Magnus College; honorary Litt.D.,
College of St. Thomas; honorary Litt.D., Bowling Green State University.

1988   Joins Universal Press Syndicate. Receives honorary L.H.D., Converse
College.

1989   Receives Lowell Thomas Travel Journalism Award. Receives honorary

Litt.D., Coe College; honorary Litt.D., St. John's University (Minnesota). Performs solo harpsichord, Stamford Chamber Orchestra and Phoenix Symphony Orchestra.

1990   Receives Julius Award for Outstanding Public Service, University of Southern California School of Public Administration. Performs solo harpsichord, North Carolina Symphony Orchestra and Yale Symphony Orchestra. Retires as editor of *National Review*. Sails *Sealestial* from Lisbon to Barbados.

1991   Receives Presidential Medal of Freedom. Receives Honorary Litt.D., Grove City College.

1992   Receives Gold Medal Award, National Institute of Social Sciences. Receives honorary L.H.D., University of South Florida. Performs solo harpsichord, Connecticut Grand Opera and Orchestra.

1995   Receives honorary L.H.D., Adelphi University.

1996   Receives Adam Smith Award, Hillsdale College.

1999   Tapes final *Firing Line* show, December 14. Receives Clare Booth Luce Award, Heritage Foundation.

2000   Final public speech, Allen County Lincoln Day Dinner (Fort Wayne, Indiana), April 12. Receives Henry Salvatori Award, Claremont Institute. Living Legend Award, Library of Congress. Receives L.H.D., Yale University.

2002   Receives Lifetime Achievement Award, Phillips Foundation.

2004   Sells *Patito*. Relinquishes ownership of *National Review*. Receives Alexander Hamilton Award, Manhattan Institute; Mightier Pen Award, Center for Security Policy; Benjamin Franklin Award, Year's Best Book in Autobiography/Memoirs, for *Miles Gone By*, Publishers' Marketing Association.

2005   Celebrates *National Review*'s fiftieth anniversary, National Museum of Buildings, Washington, D.C., October 6. Celebrates eightieth birthday, Pierre Hotel, New York City, November 17. Receives American History Award, Union League Club. Receives L.H.D., Hillsdale College.

2006   Lifetime Achievement Award, American Society of Magazine Editors.

2007   Wife Patricia Taylor Buckley dies, April 15.

2008   Dies in Stamford, Connecticut, February 27.

Conversations with William F. Buckley Jr.

Playboy Interview: William F. Buckley Jr.

David Butler / 1970

Playboy: It's already a cliché to say that the sixties were a remarkable decade. Looking back, what event or development stands out in your mind as most important?

Buckley: The philosophical acceptance of coexistence by the West.

Playboy: Why "philosophical"?

Buckley: Because a military acceptance of coexistence is one thing; that I understand. But since America is, for good reasons and bad, a moralistic power, the philosophical acceptance of coexistence ends us up in hot pursuit of *reasons* for that acceptance. We continue to find excuses for being cordial to the Soviet Union; our denunciations of that country's periodic barbarisms—as in Czechoslovakia—become purely perfunctory. This is a callousing experience; it is a lesion of our moral conscience, the historical effects of which cannot be calculated, but they will be bad.

Playboy: Among the reasons cited for a *détente* with the Soviet Union is the fact that the money spent on continuing hot and cold wars with the Communist bloc would be better spent for domestic programs. With the 150 billion dollars we've spent in Vietnam since 1965, according to some estimates, we could have eliminated pollution throughout the country and rebuilt twenty-four major cities into what New York's Mayor Lindsay has said would be "paradises." Do you think our priorities are out of order?

Buckley: When I find myself entertaining that possibility, I dismiss my thinking as puerile. But first let me register my objection to your figures: It's superficial to say that the Vietnam war has cost us 150 billion dollars. It has cost us X dollars in excess of what we would have spent on military or paramilitary enterprises even if there had been no war. That sum I have seen estimated at between 18 and

3

22 billion dollars a year. Now, suppose I were to tell you that if Kerenski had prevailed in Russia in 1917, we would at this point have a budget excess sufficient to create the city of Oz in Harlem and everywhere else. The correct response to such a statement, for grownups, is twofold. First, we are not—unfortunately—in a position to dictate the activity of the enemy; we cannot ask him please to let down because we need money for Harlem. Second, there are no grounds for assuming that the American people would have consented to spending the kind of money we're spending on the Vietnam war for general welfare projects. They might have said, "No, we'd rather keep the money and do what we want with it." I suspect they *would* have said just that, and with justification: The bulk of the progress that has been made in America has been made by the private sector.

Playboy: With reference to the first part of your answer: At the strategic-arms-limitations talks, aren't we actually asking the Russians to let down their guard if we let ours down?

Buckley: Yes, we are. And, ideally, there would be massive, universal disarmament. But we don't live in an ideal world. The fact is that the Soviet Union is prepared to make remarkable sacrifices at home in order to maintain its military muscle abroad. It is prepared to do so in a world that has seen the United States pull out from dozens of opportunities to imperialize. We have walked out of twenty-one countries—I think that's the accepted figure—that we've occupied in the past thirty years. The Soviet Union has walked only out of Austria, for very complicated reasons. Under the circumstances, one must assume that the arrant armament expenditures by the Soviet Union—for instance, 20 billion dollars to develop its ABM system and its MIRVs—have to do with the attraction of a first-strike capability. There is only one known explanation, for instance, for the known "footprint"—the configuration—of the MIRVs the Soviet Union has been practicing with. Those missiles are exactly patterned after our Minuteman installations. If the Soviets intended their MIRVs only as a deterrent to an American first strike, they would aim those missiles at American cities. But they aren't being fashioned that way. Now, I don't think the collective leadership of Russia would dream of making a first strike for so long as we are in a position to inflict insupportable damage in a second strike, whatever the urgings of their Dr. Strangeloves, who are not without influence. But, manifestly, America is not preparing for a first strike. If we were, we would be aiming our weapons not at Russia's population centers but at her military installations—and we're not.

Playboy: The best information available—from hearings of the Senate Foreign Relations Committee at which Deputy Secretary of Defense David Packard appeared—is that we are well ahead of the Soviet Union in the development of MIRVs, and it's generally conceded that we conceived the system. Doesn't this suggest both that the threat posed by the Russian MIRVs is less than you imply and that their MIRVs may have been developed as a defense against ours?

Buckley: The question of who conceived the system is immaterial. Who makes it operational is what matters. It is only a happy coincidence that Jules Verne was a non-Communist. On the question of whose MIRVs are more advanced, *a)* your information is, unhappily, incorrect and *b)* it is irrelevant to the question of whether MIRVs are designed for offensive or defensive purposes.

Playboy: MIT professor Leo Sartori, writing in the *Saturday Review,* implies that some of our ICBMs are aimed at Russia's missiles rather than at her cities. Doesn't this indicate that the U.S. is prepared—to the point of overkill—for a massive first strike against the Soviet Union?

Buckley: Look. The intellectual, attempting to evaluate the military situation, tends to fasten on a frozen position. He says, "Assuming apocalypse were tomorrow, how would the two sides stand?" But it is the responsibility of the military to understand how military confrontations actually work—which means that you cannot prepare for Tuesday by being absolutely prepared for Monday. In a world in which it takes between four and eight years to develop what is actually intended as a first-strike *defensive* system, you may, in the course of preparing for that system, find yourself temporarily with a first-strike superiority. A caricature of what I'm talking about is the sudden apprehension by Darryl Zanuck when he was filming *The Longest Day*—on the Normandy invasion—that he actually found himself in command of the third largest military force in the world. Presumably, he would not have used it even to attack Otto Preminger. You need to ask yourself the subjective question: Do I know people in the United States whose hands are on the trigger, who are actually conspiring to opportunize on the temporary military advantage? It seems plain to me that the recent history of the United States ought to be sufficient to appease the doubts of the doubters. In fact, we have had such superiority even at moments when the enemy was at its most provocative— and yet we haven't used it.

Playboy: Hasn't it been authoritatively asserted that U.S. superiority is over-whelmingly beyond the defensive or offensive necessity of any conceivable threat from another nuclear power?

Buckley: That's a military judgment and I don't feel qualified to pronounce about it. I feel confident only to make an elementary philosophical point. I tend to believe that what the lawyers call "an excess of caution" is not something we should penalize the military for. I *want* an excess of caution, because I understand a mistake in that direction to be apocalyptic in its consequences. Now, if you say, "I can establish that we are spending money to develop a redundant weapon," my answer is: Go ahead and establish it. Meanwhile, I would rather side with the cautious, the prudent people. And here I find myself wondering how it is that Robert McNamara—who, for some reason, tends to be rather beloved by the liberals—how come *he* didn't object to the technological-military evolution that nowadays strikes so many people as untoward. And, again, why have we so drastically reversed our attitudes concerning what was for so long considered the liberal thing to do? During the fifties, the great accent was on defense. The military-industrial complex—as you know—used to be called the "Arsenal of Democracy." Now, all of a sudden, when you talk about ABMs, the same people who encouraged us to spend 50 billion dollars—yes, 50 billion dollars—on defense during the fifties object to spending an extra five billion dollars on defense in the sixties.

Playboy: You seem to delight in reminding people that liberals are capable of changing their minds in the light of changing circumstances. Why?
Buckley: Quite apart from the fact that delightful pursuits are delightful, it is important for any ideological grouping to confront historical experience. For one thing, it makes the ideologists less arrogant; or it should. That ought to be a national objective, after we eliminate poverty.

Playboy: Ten years ago, wasn't there more reason than there is now to believe that the Russians wanted to bury us, militarily as well as ideologically?
Buckley: That is an exercise in ideological self-indulgence. How do you account for the anomalies? Such as the crash program the Soviet Union has developed in ABMs and MIRVs.

Playboy: One can only repeat that the U.S. is developing these systems as furiously as Russia is; and many observers feel that the Soviets have, therefore, just as much reason to suspect our intentions as we do theirs. But we'd like to return to your observation that the United States has walked out of twenty-one countries in the past thirty years and ask this: Doesn't the fact that we've also walked *into* Vietnam and Santo Domingo, tried to walk into Cuba at the Bay of Pigs, and attempted to control many other countries through quasi-military, CIA-type operations leave us open to the charge of imperialism you impute to the U.S.S.R.?
Buckley: Of course. But we are always at the mercy of the naïve. Imperialism suggests the domination of a country for the commercial or glorious benefit of oneself. The Soviet Union began its experience in imperialism not merely by jail-

ing and executing people who disagreed with it but by systematic despoliation. In Czechoslovakia, for instance, they took one, two, three billion dollars' worth of capital goods and removed them physically to the Soviet Union. Far from doing anything of the sort, we did exactly the contrary; we sent our own capital goods to places like France and England and Spain and Latin America. I can't think of any country that we've "dominated" or "imperialized"—in the sense in which you use those words—that is worse off as a result of its experience with America than it would have been had we not entered into a temporary relationship with it.

Playboy: One could argue that South Vietnam is such a country.

Buckley: South Vietnam? My God! Above *all*, not South Vietnam. Not unless one is willing to say that South Vietnam would be better off satellized by North Vietnam—and derivatively by Asian communism—and consigned to perpetual tyranny. Put it this way: I will assent to the proposition that South Vietnam has been harmed by America's efforts during the past five years only to somebody who would say that France was harmed by the efforts of the Allied armies to liberate it during the Second World War.

Playboy: We won't say that, but we will agree with the increasingly popular opinion that our adventure there has been a disaster—to us, as well as to South and North Vietnam—from the beginning. Yet you said recently that "the indices in Vietnam are good," which is something even McNamara and Westmoreland stopped saying three years ago. Why?

Buckley: Because the indices *are* good, right down the line: First, there is the prestige of Thieu and our increased identification with him. A week or so after the 1968 Tet offensive, Professor J. Kenneth Galbraith gave it as the conventional wisdom that Thieu's government would fall within a matter of weeks. I predict that in the next election, he will get a significantly greater vote than he got the last time. Second, there is a lower rate of infiltration from the North. Third, the area controlled by the good guys is now much greater than it has ever been. The fourth positive index is the introduction in South Vietnam of a nonregular army, the equivalent of a militia, which makes it possible for people simultaneously to till their land during the day and yet be part of a large constabulary. Still another indication is the relative rise in South Vietnamese casualties and decrease in American casualties, which shows that they are beginning to shoulder even more of the human burden of the war.

Playboy: How do you feel about Thieu's suppression of dissent among his political opposition—even moderate Buddhists and Catholics who have done nothing more subversive than suggest consideration of a postwar coalition government?

Buckley: I am not in a position to judge whether Thieu suppresses more or fewer people than he should suppress in order to achieve his goals. I know that my own countrymen were prepared to take tens of thousands of innocent Japanese and throw them in jail during World War Two. And I know that moral-political revulsion over that act didn't come until years later—when we recognized that what we had done to the nisei was, in fact, historically unnecessary. But it remains that a man who was tempered by four centuries of parliamentary experience—Franklin D. Roosevelt—thought it an altogether appropriate thing to do. I am not, under the circumstances, confident that I can authoritatively advise Thieu what is the right kind of suppression to engage in during a civil war.

Playboy: Then it *is* a civil war and not a case of Communist expansionism exported from Russia and China?

Buckley: Yes, it is a civil war, provided one is prepared to define any war as a civil war if one finds a significant number of collaborationists within the indigenous population. There are South Vietnamese Communists, even as there were Norwegian quislings, Northern Copperheads, and French appeasers. General Pétain was sentenced to death for obliging the Nazis less effusively than the Viet Cong have done the northern imperialists. If the "civil" insurrection in Vietnam had depended on its own resources, it would have lasted about as long as the insurrection of the Huks in the Philippines.

Playboy: You frequently use the fact that Thieu has fired 1,200 civil servants to demonstrate what you consider his opposition to corruption. But weren't many of those firings really intended to get rid of his political opponents?

Buckley: I didn't think to ask Thieu when I was over there. I assume it is because they were corrupt—at least the ones I'm talking about. I don't know how many he has fired for opposing his policies. I don't know how many officials Lyndon Johnson fired because they opposed *his* policies, or exactly how many FDR did—plenty, I assume. Incidentally, I thought John Roche made a rather good point when he said that the critics of Thieu fail to account for the fact that he moves about without any difficulty at all—without bodyguards or any other protection—throughout South Vietnam. And they fail to point out that he has done something no tyrant *ever* does, which is to arm the citizenry. The very first thing he did, when he became president, was to ask Westmoreland to increase the arming of the people. In Cuba, if you're caught with an unlicensed rifle, you're liable to be executed.

Playboy: Your satisfaction with the relative rise in South Vietnamese casualties indicates that you believe in Vietnamization. If, as Presidents Johnson and Nixon have claimed, we have a moral and legal commitment to defend the South Vietnamese, why are we now disengaging?

Buckley: We're not disengaging. We have a moral and legal commitment to give aid to the South Vietnamese in resisting aggression, pursuant to the protocol that extended the SEATO treaty to that area. We did not specify in SEATO the nature of the aid we would give. It is Nixon's strategy to arrive at a realistic formula: indigenous manpower and external material aid, precisely the way the Soviet Union and China have been handling the situation in behalf of North Vietnam. I advocated such a formula five years ago. Allowing for the cultural lag, it is time for its adoption.

Playboy: Do you feel it was wrong, then, to send our troops in the first place?

Buckley: No, we had to. The South Vietnamese were not prepared to defend themselves.

Playboy: In other words, though it was right to send them in when we did, it's right to withdraw them now. Are you saying that everything we've done there has been correct?

Buckley: Not at all—there are plenty of things we've done wrong. We shouldn't have stopped the bombing of the North and put the restrictions on it that we did. And, above all, I continue to believe that Japan is the key to that part of the world and that we may very well wish, before this decade is up, that she had the defensive nuclear weapons the nonproliferation treaty denies her.

Playboy: Do you think that if America remains steadfast in Vietnam—with or without the support of our allies in Asia or Western Europe—the Communists will be less likely to test our commitments elsewhere in the world?

Buckley: It's hard to say. In order to answer that question, you have to ask yourself: What is the point of view of the enemy? I have always maintained that the Soviet Union has been delighted over our experience in South Vietnam. It has cost them very little. But, at the same time, the Soviet Union has to reckon with the psychological realities. The psychological realities in the case of Vietnam are that America isn't prepared to do this sort of thing two or three times a decade. We did it in Korea and we're doing it in South Vietnam. If the Soviet Union decides to mount a challenge—let's say in the Mideast—it will probably have to reckon with the fact of a shortened American temper. The shortened American temper could result in one of two things. It could result in isolationism, which would please the Soviet Union dearly and encourage it; or that shortened American temper could result in our saying, "Since we cannot afford protracted, graduated South Vietnam–type resistances, we're going to go back to another kind of resistance. We're going to knock the hell out of you."

Playboy: Do you think that bellicose attitude *will* develop—and can you imagine it resulting in a nuclear strike by the U.S., say, over Berlin or in the Mideast?
Buckley: Only if the Soviet Union is capable of a miscalculation on an order that is unimaginable, on the basis of our historical experience with a society that on the one hand is ideologically rabid but on the other appears to have a positively Rotarian instinct for survival.

Playboy: Critics of the war point to the alleged massacre at My Lai to prove our indifference to the lives of Vietnamese civilians. How do you react to that incident, as it has emerged in the press?
Buckley: If, indeed, there were no extenuating circumstances in the case—if everything that Captain Medina has said is proved wrong, for instance—then either we have a case of collective hysteria or we face the appalling alternative that what happened there expresses a trend within America. I find it extremely difficult to indulge that conclusion, for the reason that if it were so, we would have had many more such incidents.

Playboy: In January 1967, ten Marines were court-martialed on charges resulting from the murders of a farmer, his mother, his sister, his three-year-old son, and five-year-old niece and the gang-rape of his wife. From the beginning of 1966 through October 1969, twenty-seven soldiers were convicted by U.S. courts-martial of murdering Vietnamese civilians; and since March 1965, twenty-one sailors and Marines have been so convicted. The speculation is that most such crimes by U.S. military personnel against civilians in Vietnam go unreported. So it would seem that there *have* been many other such incidents, though perhaps on a smaller scale.
Buckley: They are either so routine as to go unremarked—like, say, the incremental murder in Manhattan—or so spectacular as to be unbelievable. It took the most extraordinary coordination of ineptitudes to fail to bring the My Lai incident to light. Here we have a Pulitzer Prize–winning story—I predict that it will get the Pulitzer Prize—and yet the two newspaper people who had the story couldn't interest anybody in it for months. Editors wouldn't buy it precisely because they couldn't believe that kind of thing could have been committed on such a scale.

Playboy: Do you think there should be or will be extensive war-crimes trials of American servicemen and policy makers, conducted either by the United Nations or by us?

Buckley: No. There shouldn't be and there won't be. The whole Nuremberg Doctrine, I continue to believe, is an elaboration of the crime of losing wars. It was, for one thing, obviously and intrinsically contaminated by the presence on the tribunal, in the capacity of judges, of the principal massacre-maker of the twentieth century, namely, the representatives of Stalin. America is not about to invite the United Nations to preside over trials of American soldiers. Those people who have been guilty will be punished, most of them, by America. I grant that we have a technical problem of how to reach out and get some of those individuals who apparently ought to be defendants, but my guess is we're going to crack that problem.

Playboy: Do you see a moral difference between what is alleged to have happened at My Lai and the aerial bombardment of free-fire zones where, it's generally granted, some civilians almost always get killed?

Buckley: Of course. It's a difference explicitly recognized in Thomistic doctrine, where the whole definition of a just war was arrived at. If, in order to achieve a military objective, someone gets killed, that is on one scale of morality—on the permissible scale in warfare. If, however, someone is killed simply for the sake of killing him, unrelated to any military objective, that's different. Nobody would have thought twice about My Lai if there had been a machine-gun nest there and we had plastered the village from the air, resulting in an identical loss of life.

Playboy: But, of course, there wasn't a machine-gun nest there. Most critics of the war put little trust in those who decide which villages and which other targets are legitimate military objectives. Do you?

Buckley: I trust that somewhere along the line there is a constant monitoring of the criteria that are used by people who have that kind of authority. In the specific case of Lyndon Johnson, I am informed that only he *personally* could authorize the bombing of certain targets where considerable civilian carnage might have resulted. I believe that he took that kind of meticulous concern not merely out of political considerations but because he was always very sensitive to the notion that he was an indiscriminate killer.

Let me digress at this point: A few months ago, in Hawaii, a professor informed my audience that we had dropped one and a half times as many bombs on a very small area of Vietnam as were dropped on Germany throughout World War Two.

That statistic, he claimed, proves that we are committing genocide in Vietnam. I read the figures differently. It seems to me that if we have dropped that many bombs and killed as few people as we have—there are an awful lot of live Vietnamese left, no matter how you look at it—it must mean that an enormous effort is being made to drop bombs where people *aren't*.

Playboy: According to official sources, several hundred thousand North and South Vietnamese civilians have been killed by American bombing raids. In view of those statistics, do you think the bombing has been justified?
Buckley: It depends on whether there was an alternative, less bloody means of achieving the military objective. How many of those dead would be alive today if the North Vietnamese had desisted from infiltration as their principal technique? And if historical contexts interest you, bear in mind that we killed about as many German civilians in the course of a couple of raids over Dresden as we have killed Vietnamese in the five years in Vietnam.

Playboy: For all our bombing—precise or indiscriminate—we have not yet won the war. Do you think North Vietnam could successfully have resisted the most powerful military nation on earth for this long if it didn't have the support of most Vietnamese, North and South?
Buckley: There are both extensive and succinct ways to answer that. The succinct way is for me to ask you: Could Nazi Germany have triumphed over France without the overwhelming support of the French? My answer is—obviously—yes, Germany could, and did. The South Vietnamese situation is one in which the critical weapon was terror. I have great admiration for my countrymen, but I haven't the *least* idea whether or not we would have the stamina to resist an enemy that had strung up an equivalent number of our elite in the public squares. Roughly speaking, what the South Vietnamese suffered during the high period of terror from 1959 to 1963 would be the equivalent of, say, three million of our politicians, teachers, doctors, engineers, and civil servants being executed. How we would behave under the circumstances I don't know. I tend to reject the ethnocentrically arrogant assumption that we Americans are uniquely valiant. I think it's not at all impossible that years from now, people will think of the South Vietnamese resistance through this entire period as one of the truly heroic historical efforts.

Playboy: Weren't many of the South Vietnamese elite, during this same period, jailed or killed by the Diem regime?
Buckley: What you're saying is: Did Diem and the rest of them go to lengths they

needn't have gone in order to effect what they wanted to effect, which was the independence of Vietnam? My answer is—I don't know. A very good argument may
be made that they didn't go to great enough lengths. In fact, such an argument
could appropriately be engraved on Diem's tombstone.

Playboy: That sounds like an endorsement of political imprisonment and assassination.
Buckley: In time of war? Of course. The detection and shooting down of
Admiral Yamamoto was one of the triumphs of American intelligence during
the Second World War, and it gets described at least once every ten years in the
Reader's Digest. You do remember, don't you, how Walter Pidgeon almost assassinated Hitler at Berchtesgaden? Do you remember the political prosecutions during the Second World War, when the New Deal decided that [pro-Nazi authors]
George Sylvester Viereck and Lawrence Dennis should be put behind bars, so that
we could get on with the war? I think we overdid it. I hope the South Vietnamese
aren't as jumpy as we were.

Playboy: Is your claim that the leaders of South Vietnam have been motivated by
a desire for independence consistent with their near-total reliance on the U.S.?
Buckley: Of course they've depended on us. They are waging war not against an
autarchic aggressor that is satisfied to use its own resources but against an aggressor that—from the very beginning—has been armed by great powers, namely,
Red China and the Soviet Union. The South Vietnamese didn't have a *rifle factory*
in 1954. As far as I know, neither do they now. And neither did the North Vietnamese.

Playboy: Since you applaud the fact that we rushed to the assistance of the besieged South Vietnamese government, do you also think we should oppose any
war of national liberation that happens to have Communist support?
Buckley: No, I wouldn't be willing to make that generality. I'd want to know
where it was, what the surrounding situation was, how important it was to either
Russia or China at the moment—in short, what the consequences might be. I
would like to note that neither of those countries has ever supported a *real* war
of national liberation—in lower-case letters—that is, a war in which the objective really *was* national liberation. When the Communist powers get involved, the
point is *never* national liberation, always satellization. Now, it seems to me that
the United States position ought to be to support whatever elements in a particular country are heading in the better of the apparently available directions.
John Stuart Mill says that despotism is excused as a temporary arrangement,

provided the purpose of that despotism is to maximize rather than minimize freedom.

Playboy: Isn't the idea of despotism maximizing freedom a contradiction in terms—at least in practice?
Buckley: No. Lincoln put it well when he argued that it could not have been the intention of the framers of the Constitution to sacrifice all future prospects for freedom in order to celebrate constitutional punctilio.

Playboy: Isn't it true that most indigenous Communist movements in Southeast Asia are motivated more by nationalism or by economic needs than by ideological communism?
Buckley: No, it isn't. Most troops simply do what they are told. Intermediaries interpret the formulation that will most inspire a particular group of soldiers to act enthusiastically in obedience to orders—whether that's a matter of telling them that their kamikaze raids will instantly elevate them into the heavenly spheres, to live forever after in glory, or that they will become large landholders, or whatever. But the people who are directing the drives in that part of the world are, in my opinion, genuinely committed to a Communist vision. The general Western assumption has been that time erodes that vision; but it is, nevertheless, true that there is a fundamentalist Marxism-communism rampant in China today. It may be inevitable that time will overcome that ideological pretension, but that is not the kind of thing around which one writes a foreign policy for the here and now.

Playboy: It is also part of liberal orthodoxy—based on his longstanding animosity toward China—that Ho Chi Minh would probably have reached a Titoist accommodation with Peking had he succeeded throughout Vietnam. Do you think that might have happened?
Buckley: I have no doubt that Ho Chi Minh would have preferred to be the master of Vietnam rather than merely the surrogate in that area for Mao Tse-tung. But we have to recognize that Ho Chi Minh is dead and that it was foreseeable even six or seven years ago that he would be dead in due course, since he was an old man even then. The usefulness of Ho to Mao had to do with the veneration of Ho as an individual figure, which veneration would not and did not flow to his successor. In Chinese, Vietnam means "farther South," a fact that suggests the ancient Chinese attitude toward the area: that it was never really licensed as a separate territory—the same feeling they have toward Tibet.

Playboy: Considering your hard-line view of China, how do you feel about Nixon's recent diplomatic overtures to Peking?

Buckley: I don't really see why our attitude toward Red China ought to be different from our attitude toward the Soviet Union. The principal international leverage we have at this particular moment has to do with the Russian-Chinese feud. It strikes me as supremely intelligent to constantly advertise to the Soviet Union that, just as we were prepared to side with the Soviet Union in order to effect a victory over Hitler, so are we prepared to understand the potential desirability of a flirtation with Red China in order to contain the Soviet Union. Or the other way around. This strikes me as simply a return to traditional diplomacy.

Playboy: Do you think that we should—and will—recognize Red China?

Buckley: I think we should not recognize her—and that it is unlikely that we will. For one thing, it becomes increasingly apparent that all of the old arguments for recognition of Red China are meaningless. The old arguments were, first, "You can't ignore a nation of 800,000,000 people." But it has gradually become manifest that we are hardly ignoring a country by failing to recognize it. As a matter of fact, we are sort of *super*recognizing it. The easy thing to do is to recognize; if you *don't* recognize, you're giving it very special attention. Point two: The notion that if we recognize Red China, we would then be able to transact some differences with her—to talk about them—has been discredited by experience. We've had hundreds of meetings with Red China: we are probably having one tonight. So we go ahead and have the meetings anyway. Number three: We have discovered from the British experience that the mere fact of having an active consulate or an ambassador in Red China has no effect at all in terms of a thaw. The English have not been able to show that they've accomplished a single thing— even concerning the protection of their own citizens—that they might not have accomplished if they hadn't had their people there. Number four, and finally: It was Lyndon Johnson who said that he would agree to give passports to Americans who wanted to visit Red China—journalists and so on. What then happened, of course, was that Red China refused to grant visas. So that we are therefore left with no adverse practical consequences of a diplomatic nature having to do with the recognition of Red China, but purely with symbolic consequences. And those consequences, in my judgment, argue against recognition.

Playboy: So far, you haven't disagreed with any aspect of President Nixon's foreign policy. One critic has suggested that you may feel a sense of obligation to him for appointing you to the advisory commission of the USIA.

Buckley: Oh, for God's sake. The point is that when I look around the world to-day and ask myself what it is that I truly care about in international affairs that Nixon has let me down on, I don't come up with anything. On the other hand, I acknowledge that there may be a feeling of restraint deriving not from my appointment to the commission but from the fact that I have seen him once or twice privately. I have discovered a new sensual treat, which, appropriately, the readers of *Playboy* should be the first to know about. It is to have the president of the United States take notes while you are speaking to him, even though you run the risk that he is scribbling, "Get this bore out of here." It's always a little bit more difficult to be rhetorically ruthless with somebody with whom you spend time. For example, I find it more difficult to be verbally ruthless with Hugh Hefner after meeting him as my guest on *Firing Line* and seeing him on a couple of other occasions. Beyond that, if I'm kind to Nixon, it's also because I think he needs to be protected from that part of the right whose emphasis is unbalanced in the direction of the paradigm.

Playboy: Is Nixon conservative enough for you?
Buckley: My ideal conservative president would be one who would strike out for certain radical reforms that, in my judgment, would greatly benefit America and augment human freedom. But such a president cannot be elected—at this time— and couldn't get his programs through Congress. It is also true, I think, that the paramount need of this highly divided society at this particular moment is for conciliation; and Nixon—who is making gradual progress while attempting to fortify the bonds of common affection—is a good president from the conservative point of view.

Playboy: Do you think that Vice-President Agnew served the purpose of conciliation when he referred to the leaders of last October's Moratorium as "an effete corps of impudent snobs"?
Buckley: No, he served other purposes. There *are* other purposes to be served, such as isolating the sources of discontent and the agitators and merchants of it. Some presidents do that kind of thing adroitly, some don't. At a moment when we needed reconciliation after Pearl Harbor, I think it was wrong for FDR to call those who were against the war "the New Copperheads." But history appears to have forgiven him.

Playboy: To many liberals, Agnew's attacks on the media late last fall brought to mind the Chinese emperors who executed messengers bringing bad news. Do you think that the press is as objective as it professes to be?

Buckley: When Mr. Nixon in November said that North Vietnam cannot defeat or humiliate the United States, only Americans can do that, he meant that if the American people refuse to back an enterprise that—in the judgment of the men they elected to write their foreign policies—is essential to the good health of this country and of this century, then one must face two alternative explanations for their failure to do so. One is that they have run out of stamina. The other is that they have been constantly hectored into taking an erroneous position because they are insufficiently aware of the dimensions of the problem. He would obviously prefer the latter explanation to the former, as would I. He tends to feel that the majority of morally alert people in America have, for the most part, heard only a single side on the Vietnam issue—in the universities as well as in the press. He is absolutely correct. It is almost impossible, you know, to work your way through Yale or Harvard or Princeton and hear a pro-Vietnam speech. This is a pure caricature of academic freedom.

Playboy: Aren't campus conservatives free to speak—and don't they, often and at length?
Buckley: Well, you must mean students, because there are very few conservative professors. At Princeton, for example, 65 percent of the faculty voted for Humphrey in 1968, 7 percent for Dick Gregory, and 7 percent for Nixon. And it's the professors I'm talking about; their capacity, at a college, is to instruct.

Playboy: Then you're suggesting that the faculty allows its political bias to creep into every course.
Buckley: Constantly. In any course in the humanities or social sciences. And not only in their teaching but in the books they assign. It seems to me that the entire academic community collaborated in the demonstration of academic bias when Walt Rostow and Dean Rusk went around looking for an academic post after they left Lyndon Johnson. What kind of a demonstration do you need beyond that? Here are two people whose academic credentials are absolutely first-rate. But all of a sudden, you find MIT—that paragon of academic freedom and scientific devotion—saying that they assumed Walt Rostow had "forgotten" what he knew about economics as the result of his stay in government. That was one reason given by a senior faculty member; even James Reston made fun of it. You will notice nobody at Harvard went around saying that Galbraith "forgot" what he knew about economics as the result of his service for John Kennedy. Though I don't know. Maybe they hoped he had.

I think the health of any university is damaged by this monopoly of opinion. I spoke at the University of Minnesota a few months ago. A professor—a very distinguished historian—stood up and said that there are fifty professors of history at the university and one Republican, himself; that is, the ratio is fifty to one. Now, how much real political dialog is the typical student at the University of Minnesota going to be exposed to, under the circumstances? And if he is *not* subjected to a true dialog, then he tends to think dialog is unnecessary, that what you need is asseveration. Placard justice: "Hey, hey, LBJ—how many kids did you kill today?"

Playboy: Don't you think most students get the pro-Vietnam argument from their fathers?
Buckley: That's unrealistic. Students are terrific snobs. I was one myself, though I had no right to be with my own father. The fact is that unless your father is right up with the academic vernacular—unless he's read Douglas Pike as recently as last week—you tend to feel that he's not equipped to discuss serious intellectual matters with you. In any case, I think that this hegemony of thought within the colleges is something that—perhaps without even knowing it—Agnew is scratching up against.

Playboy: In his speech on TV news, the vice-president's avowals of distaste for censorship, coupled with his allusions to the power of the FCC to withhold broadcasting licenses, struck many liberals as hypocrisy. How do you feel about it?
Buckley: I think they were entitled to think of it as at least potentially hypocritical. I find absolutely mysterious the way in which the debate was ultimately joined. My devoted friend Frank Stanton, who emerged as the spokesman for the victims of this pogrom—or intended pogrom—didn't, for instance, pause to remark that Congress has *already* withheld total freedom from the industry. The whole equal-time provision is an effort by the Congress of the United States to say to the networks and television and radio stations, "Certain freedoms you don't have." The FCC finds as much in the fairness doctrine every year as the Supreme Court finds in the First Amendment.

Playboy: So it was really unnecessary for Agnew to refer to licensing?
Buckley: It may be that Agnew's speech will serve some sort of a maieutic function—that it will tease out of the system a public policy concerning the tendentious limits to which an individual station owner may go. Such a policy would be a refinement of the fairness doctrine, which was not only accepted but applauded by liberals as recently as four or five years ago. In any case, *I* would like to say: Let any radio or TV station owner do what he wants. If he wants to put only Benjamin Spock on from midnight to midnight, let him do it. But make

it as hard as possible for him to achieve monopoly status—by licensing pay-TV, which is precisely the way to wed the individual eccentric with his individual network or station.

Playboy: What was your reaction to the vice-president's blast at the liberal *Washington Post* and *New York Times?*
Buckley: If the press is so easily intimidated as to feel threatened by three speeches by the vice-president of the United States—if all those effete snobs are moral pygmies after all—then I ought to be even more worried about the press than I am. Mr. Agnew is not Mussolini; for better or worse, he cannot close down the *New York Times.* To sum up: I think what Mr. Agnew was attempting to say to the American people was that, particularly in New York, the networks and the commentators tend to reflect a single point of view—they look and act like the Rockettes—and that it is necessary for people to escape from the assumption that that is the only point of view. I think he has done an extremely useful service. Of course, it isn't just Mr. Agnew who came to such a conclusion: The identical conclusion was arrived at a few weeks earlier by Theodore White, who is a renowned liberal, on my television program. Agnew was simply accenting the obvious; and the obvious, when it has been taboo to state it, tends to hurt. *Ce n'est que la vérité qui blesse,* as Mr. Agnew would put it.

Playboy: How would you feel if Agnew were to become president?
Buckley: I have been persuaded for several years that the office of the president is so staggeringly complicated that nobody can, by conventional measurement, be "a good president." That is to say that nobody can conceivably oversee the range of activities that, technically, the president is responsible for overseeing. Under the circumstances, whereas it is widely supposed that the president needs to be a man of more and more complicated attainments, I tend to feel that he needs to be less and less a man of complicated attainments. A hundred years ago, a president really had to run the post office, among other things. Today, what one needs most from a president is good will, a working intelligence, and sound character. The people who praise Harry Truman were willing to point this out at the time, incidentally, but were not willing to remember the thought when it looked as though Goldwater might be nominated by the Republican Party. Second, I do think that when a man becomes president, a transmogrification takes place; that which was theretofore inconceivable becomes somehow conceivable. Nobody could really imagine Harry Truman—even himself, as he subsequently confessed—as president, until all of a sudden, he *was* president. Allan Drury dwells on this in one of his books. On Monday, the man is just that vicious, sniping, polemical, Nixonite

vice-president; on Tuesday, he's inaugurated and suddenly things happen not only to his critics and to the people but also to him. In short, Agnew wouldn't sound like Agnew if he were president—and, in a sense, properly so.

Playboy: When you list good will, a working intelligence, and sound character as what we need most from a president, do you mean regardless of ideology?
Buckley: A man can't have a working intelligence, as distinguished from an abstract intelligence, without a reasonably sound "ideology"—a word I don't use much.

Playboy: By reasonably sound, you mean reasonably conservative.
Buckley: Yes. Conservatism is the politics of reality.

Playboy: Do you think the administration is using Agnew in an attempt to wrest away some of the support for George Wallace in the South?
Buckley: I hope so. Anybody who can take the nine million votes that went to George Wallace, baptize them, and rededicate them to a hygienic conservatism certainly has my best wishes. It would be as though Adlai Stevenson had addressed the Communist Party and urged them to desert and follow the Democratic Party.

Playboy: Kevin Phillips, in *The Emerging Republican Majority*, argues that Republicans can strengthen their current national advantage by building an alliance of heretofore solid Democratic voters in the South, already conservative citizens in the traditionally Republican heartland states, and middle-class whites everywhere who are disenchanted with costly Democratic social engineering. Do you think this so-called Southern strategy is a correct one for the Republican Party?
Buckley: Any strategy is correct that isn't practiced in such a way as to persecute the people who do not acquiesce in the goals of the winning party. Kevin Phillips is saying that a single politics, in fact, can, given the foreseeable future, appeal to the majority of the American people. If it follows that that particular appeal is at the expense—indeed, has as its intention the persecution—of people who do not agree with it, then one would have to renounce it. But in all the criticism I have seen of Mr. Phillips's book, I have never seen that made plain. Of course, I start on the heretical assumption that Southerners are people and that, under the circumstances, it is not immoral to appeal to somebody merely because he is a Southerner. If you're going to appeal to Southerners by promising to re-enslave the black people, then I consider that to be immoral, but I don't see any suggestion of this in Mr. Phillips's book. I think, actually, that the horror Mr. Phillips has inspired in such people as George McGovern derives not

from any moral abhorrence of the thesis but out of a recognition by a very shrewd professional—which Senator McGovern is—that Mr. Phillips has the clue to how to stitch together a winning majority. Franklin D. Roosevelt, McGovern's patron saint, found such a clue, which remained operative for an entire generation.

Playboy: Whatever the intention of Phillips's Southern strategy—which you seem to be endorsing, with some qualifications—its effect is clearly to exclude blacks from "the emerging Republican majority." And we note that in citing the West's acceptance of coexistence as the most significant development of the sixties, you apparently downgrade the importance of the black revolution, which many consider the milestone of the decade. Why?

Buckley: I think that the important philosophical fight in the area of American black-white relations was won by Abraham Lincoln, who insisted on the metaphysical fact of human equality. This was the great achievement of the American nineteenth century. The next milestone, as far as the Negroes are concerned, will come when whites turn to—and seek out—Negroes as a result of their individual achievements. This has come in some places and will come in others, but it is going to take time. It is certainly open to speculation whether all of the activities of the past fifteen years have significantly accelerated that emancipation.

Playboy: Do you think the black struggle in the past fifteen years has *retarded* that emancipation?

Buckley: America has, lately, given herself over to the promulgation of unrealizable goals, which dooms her to frustration, if not to despair. Voegelin calls it the immanentization of the eschaton—broadly speaking, consigning that which properly belongs to the end of life to the temporal order. That can lead only to grave dissatisfactions. The very idea of "Freedom now" was an invitation to frustration. *Now* means something or it means nothing. When months and then years went by and the kind of dream that Martin Luther King spoke about in 1963 in Washington didn't come true, a totally predictable frustration set in. It is one thing to engage in great ventures in amelioration; it is another to engage in great ventures in utopianization.

Playboy: Couldn't it be argued that the career of Martin Luther King—even if it didn't create freedom—inspired a sense of dignity in the masses of black people?

Buckley: It could. It could also be argued that the dignity was already there. What Dr. King inspired was more nearly self-assertion, which sometimes is and sometimes isn't the same as dignity.

Playboy: Your belief that black Americans had dignity before the appearance of King strikes us as less important than the fact that millions of blacks themselves didn't think so.

Buckley: Look. There was anti-black discrimination pre-King, there is anti-black discrimination post-King. If dignity is something that comes to you only after you succeed in putting an end to discrimination, then the blacks didn't have dignity then and don't have it now. If dignity is something that comes to you by transcending discrimination, then I say they had it then even as they have it now. What some blacks—and a lot of whites—now have, which is distinctive, is a greater tendency to self-assertion. I am trying to insist that that isn't the same as dignity.

Playboy: In an *Atlantic* magazine interview on the occasion of your unsuccessful candidacy for membership in the Yale Corporation two years ago, you made the unluckily timed crack: "It was only a very few years ago that official Yale conferred a doctor of laws on Martin Luther King, who more clearly qualifies as a doctor of lawbreaking." A few weeks later, Dr. King was assassinated. Did you regret the publication of your quote? And do you think of Martin Luther King as a pernicious force in American history?

Buckley: I regret but am philosophical about the fact that there is a lead time in journalism, so that you sometimes find yourself reading something that is inappropriate the day you read it, which, however, was altogether appropriate the day you wrote it. *Look* magazine's cover, after JFK's assassination, had on it, "Kennedy Could Lose." As regards what I wrote, I think it was correct. I wrote it a couple of days after Dr. King threatened massive civil disobedience if the forthcoming demands of his poverty marchers were not met. I don't want to answer your question about whether he will be seen as a good or a bad force in history, because I don't know. He was clearly a bad force on the matter of obeying the law. His attempt to sanctify civil disobedience is at least one of his legacies; if it emerges as his principal legacy, then he should certainly be remembered as a bad force. If, on the other hand, his principal legacy emerges—the wrinkles having been ironed out by the passage of time—as a spiritual leader of an oppressed people whom he urged on to great endeavors, then he will be a great historical force.

Playboy: Could you yourself ever justify breaking a law?

Buckley: Yes. I would justify the breaking of a law that, by more or less settled agreement on the separation of powers since the time of Christ, is ontologically outside the state's jurisdiction. For instance, when the government of Mexico, beginning a government or two after the overthrow of Diaz, forbade Mexicans to attend church, hundreds of thousands of them did so anyway, in underground churches. It seems to me that this is an excellent example of justified breaking of the law, against which there could be no reasonable recrimination.

Playboy: Then it depends on the individual's idea of the character of the government as well as of the laws.
Buckley: No, it doesn't. I didn't say the individual's idea and I didn't say the character of the government. I said the settled idea of the separation of powers and I said the character of the law, not of the government. Scholars, secular and religious, have agreed for two thousand years that the state has no business interfering in the traffic between man and his God; any attempt to do so breaks the legal bond that the government has over the individual. I assume, of course, that we are talking about free or relatively free societies. If we're talking about totalitarian societies, the essential relationship of the subject to the slavemaster ought to be mutinous.

Playboy: Since you have referred to the religious justification for lawbreaking: Do you think a young man has the right to use the fifth commandment—thou shalt not kill—as justification for refusing induction into the armed forces?
Buckley: The fifth commandment obviously is not a proscription against taking another man's life under any circumstances. Moses led a pretty robust army even after he came down from Mt. Sinai. The rendering should have been, "Thou shalt not murder." I am not correcting God—He had it right. The imprecision was King James's.

Playboy: You said that the essential relationship of subject to slavemaster ought to be mutinous in totalitarian societies. Aren't there degrees of unfreedom—and isn't there a point at which the erosion of freedom must be resisted, perhaps by civil disobedience?
Buckley: There is a point at which an individual citizen rejects his society. He has at that point several options. One is to leave. The society ought not to hinder his doing so. A second is to agitate for reform. The society ought to protect his right to do so. A third is to drop out. The society ought to let him alone, to the extent it is possible to disengage reciprocating gears. A fourth is to disobey the laws or to revolutionize. In that event, the society ought to imprison, exile, or execute him.

Playboy: You've identified what you consider the utopianism of Martin Luther King's call for "Freedom now" as a negative aspect of the civil rights revolution. Do you see any positive aspects to that revolution?

Buckley: Yes, several. I supported Dr. King in Montgomery. I very much believe in voluntary boycotts. If Woolworth isn't going to let you sit down and buy a Coca-Cola, then, goddamn it, don't patronize Woolworth. I certainly believe in equal access to public accommodations, and I have always opposed the denial to anyone of any constitutionally specified right, by reason of race, color, or creed.

Playboy: Including the right to vote?

Buckley: Yes.

Playboy: But you have argued, haven't you, for limiting the franchise?

Buckley: Yes. I think too many people are voting.

Playboy: Whom would you exclude?

Buckley: A while ago, George Gallup discovered that 25 percent or so of the American people had never heard of the United Nations. I think if we could find that 25 percent, they'd be reasonable candidates for temporary disfranchisement.

Playboy: How would you find them?

Buckley: Ask the Ford Foundation where they are. Incidentally, there's an interesting paradox here. I think that as power is centralized, one can make less of a case for extending the vote. In the ideal world, where power is decentralized—in my kind of a world—one wouldn't have to know what the United Nations was in order to assess intelligently the local situation and express yourself on it.

Playboy: You didn't include the school-desegregation decision of the Supreme Court in your list of the beneficent results of the civil rights movement. Why?

Buckley: When *Brown vs. Board of Education* was passed, we at *National Review* called it "bad law and bad sociology." I continue to think it was lousy law, historically and analytically. There are, unfortunately, increased grounds for believing that it was also bad sociology. Coerced massive integration is simply not working at primary and secondary school levels, and I notice that, for instance in Harlem, the voters don't list integrated schooling as among their principal demands. What they want, and should have, is better education. The superstition that this automatically happens by checkerboarding the classroom is increasingly apparent to blacks as well as to whites. Meanwhile, in the total situation, you are taking very grave risks in jeopardizing the good nature of the white majority.

Playboy: Could your concern for the good nature of the white majority be interpreted as acquiescence to their prejudice?
Buckley: The word prejudice becomes a little strained, used in that way. Look,
95 percent of the white people who live in Washington are Democrats, political
liberals who give speeches in favor of integration and vote for politicians who
favor integration—and then take their children out of the public schools when
Negroes enter those schools. If you call them prejudiced, they reply that that isn't
it, but that they want for their children a better education than they will get at the
public schools in Washington.

Playboy: If every school in the country were integrated by law in the next two
years, wouldn't you have a generation twenty years from now that was relatively
free of race prejudice?
Buckley: I fear not. There is still anti-Italian prejudice in Jewish sections of New
York and anti-Jewish prejudice in Italian sections of New York, and they've been
going to school together for more than twenty years. It may be, ages hence, when
the final sociological report is stapled and submitted, that we will discover that it
all had something to do with numbers. It may be that a school that has 10 percent
Negroes will be successful and a school that has 30 or 40 percent Negroes won't
make it; either the whites will pull out or racial antagonisms will disrupt the
school. Meanwhile, the things to stress and restress are better education and better job opportunities for Negroes.

Playboy: How should black demands for better education be met—or do you
think they shouldn't be met?
Buckley: The discussion so far has been within the context of the existing
system. I have always been attracted to the twin notions that what we need are
many more private schools and that public schools ought to approximate private
schools as closely as possible, which means that public schools ought to have the
same rights as private schools. These are among the reasons why I am so strongly
attracted to the so-called voucher plan, which would work this way: A parent
would be given a voucher for five hundred dollars—or whatever it costs to educate
a child—which the parent would then take to any school, public or private, close
to home or distant, where he wanted to matriculate that child. The school would
get its money by cashing in these vouchers. The virtues of the plan are the virtues
of the free-enterprise system—concerning which, incidentally, you are strangely
uncurious. Specifically, it gives freedom of choice to the parent, whether he's rich
or poor. Under the voucher plan, schools would become more competitive; they
would strive to serve their customers—namely, the students.

Playboy: How much do you think remains to be done to improve black job opportunities?

Buckley: Plenty. I am convinced that the truly important way for the Negro to advance is economically. We should, first, deprive labor unions of their monopolistic privileges. In fact, I'd do that anyway, even if no Negroes existed. But when we know that those privileges are being exercised in part to prevent Negroes from getting jobs in certain industries, the very least the government ought to do is act in *those* cases. Second, we should encourage preferential hiring in situations where there isn't unemployment. It's unrealistic to think that you can refuse to hire a white in order to make room for a Negro if there is wide unemployment. Point three: A revival of the whole apprenticeship idea would be extremely useful at this point. It would involve, among other things, modifying—and preferably repealing—many of the minimum-wage laws. I digress to say that the minimum-wage laws are, of course, the great enemy, especially of teenage Negroes. Professor Milton Friedman has shown that there was approximately a 100 percent relative rise in Negro teenage unemployment after the last increase in the minimum wage. Further, I would like to see somebody draw up a sophisticated table of tax deductions given to individuals who hire Negroes as apprentices, the idea being to teach them a profitable trade—in construction, in electricity, in plumbing, in newspaper offices, wherever.

Playboy: Beyond increasing job opportunities, what else can be done to eliminate poverty in America? Specifically, are you in favor of President Nixon's welfare-reform proposals?

Buckley: We are eliminating poverty in this country faster than any society ever has. There is a downward-bound graph that begins with about 50 percent of the population poor at the turn of the century and dips to the present, where there are about 9 percent poor, using the same indices. So my first comment is that I don't want anything to interfere with the direction of that graph, which the overhead costs and economic strategy of many social-welfare programs tend to do. Now, it may be that the curve is asymptotic, that it will never quite close. The residual poor will, of course, have to have some kind of a relief program, even as they do now. I myself would buy the Moynihan plan, or the Nixon plan, or the New Federalism—whatever you call it—as a substitute for all existing measures. It may well come down to a matter of American know-how moving in on a congeries of welfare systems to make welfarism both more manageable and an instrument that itself might break the so-called vicious cycle that everybody agrees has discredited the existing system.

Playboy: What sort of program—if any—do you favor for eliminating hunger?
Buckley: I'm attracted to the notion of giving out four basic food materials, free, to anybody who wants them. The cost, according to one economist, would come to about a billion dollars a year. The idea is that these ingredients would be available at food stores to anybody—you, me, Nelson Rockefeller—because it simply wouldn't be worthwhile trying to catch anyone who was taking the free food and didn't need it. With such a plan, you could officially and confidently say that the residual hunger in America was simply the result of people not knowing how to utilize these materials.

Playboy: What are they?
Buckley: Powdered skim milk, bulgur wheat, soybeans, and a kind of lard. You can make very good bread out of them, for instance. This bulgur wheat, incidentally—which is a staple in the Mideast—is not much liked by Americans and yet Alice Roosevelt Longworth loves it, considers it a delicacy.

Playboy: Do you agree with those analysts who feel that—in part because of the black revolution and because of federal "handout" programs—the general electorate is moving to the right?
Buckley: There are all sorts of conflicting indices. The Moynihan plan that we just talked about is left by orthodox conservative standards; if it had been proposed by Franklin Delano Roosevelt in 1933, it might have gotten even *him* impeached—and yet the people seem willing to accept it. But looking at the broad indications, I do feel that there is a move to the right. I've always believed that conservatism is, as I said a while ago, the politics of reality and that reality ultimately asserts itself, in a reasonably free society, in behalf of the conservative position. An excellent example was the race riots of the mid-sixties. Even the participants discovered that those Gadarene experiments were futile.

Playboy: Mayor Daley's celebrated order to the Chicago police to maim looters in the rioting that followed the assassination of Martin Luther King confirmed the feeling of many young people—black and white—that American society places a higher value on property than on human life. Do you think looters should be shot?
Buckley: I reject the notion that a property right is other than a human right—that is, it's not an animal right or a vegetable right. The commitment of the state to the individual is to protect the individual's freedom and property, property being one of the things that materialize from the exercise of freedom and, therefore, in many senses, are the fruits of freedom. So I elect a mayor to protect me and my

property effectively, with graduated responses to various conditions. If theft is an aberration—as it is, for instance, in the Scandinavian countries—I would consider a mayor who orders his men to shoot thieves to be absolutely barbaric. But if theft reaches near-epidemic conditions, a different response is indicated. I wish there were something in between simply shouting, "Hey! Come back!" and shooting somebody in the leg. Unfortunately, I fear that when that in-between thing is discovered, liberals are going to come up with elaborate reasons for not using it—mace being an excellent example.

Playboy: Mayor Daley's shoot-to-maim order, and his handling of demonstrators at the Democratic Convention that same summer, struck many observers as proof of an authoritarian and ugly aspect of America's turn to the right. If you had been mayor of Chicago, would you have handled the protesters as he did?
Buckley: No. I've been pretty well satisfied that it was a basic mistake not to open up Lincoln Park. You simply can't require people to evaporate—incorporealization not being a typical human skill. But with the exception of his ruling on the use of the park, and the workaday tactical errors, I think Daley's resoluteness was justified. Obviously, the excesses of his police were *not* justified, but a lot of Americans were glad the demonstrators got beaten up. They were glad for the commonplace reason—there's a little sadism in all of us—but they were also glad because they knew goddamn well that the chances of the demonstrators' breaking the law with impunity were overwhelming. It was sort of a return to posse justice. If you knew absolutely that Abbie Hoffman and the boys were never going to spend a night in jail—which was a good guess at the time—then people figured, "What the hell, beat 'em up. At least get *that* satisfaction out of it."

Playboy: Is that the way you felt?
Buckley: No. But I understand the feeling.

Playboy: Liberals Carl Stokes and John Lindsay were both reelected mayor last year. Do these elections contradict your general thesis of a move to the right?
Buckley: No, they don't. Lindsay's reelection is certainly a special case. A perfectly reasonable assumption is that if there had been a runoff between him and Procaccino, even Procaccino might have beaten him. I don't think one can conclude very much of an ideological nature from the event in New York City. In the matter of Stokes, it seems to me that there are a great number of people who practice, for reasons that I applaud, an inverse racism; many Cleveland whites voted for Mr. Stokes precisely because he is a Negro. The idea is that, among other things,

it is a good investment in conserving America to remind a population that is always being urged toward cynicism that it *is* possible to rise up the ladder. But I think that Stokes is one of the four or five truly brilliant politicians I've ever run up against, so I'm prejudiced in his favor.

Playboy: Would you practice this kind of inverse racism?
Buckley: Yes. I think there's a very good argument for voting for a Negro because he's a Negro—until such time as it becomes simply redundant to make such a demonstration. I wouldn't vote for a Jew because he was a Jew, because it seems to me that the time has long since passed when it was necessary to demonstrate that a Jew can rise as high as he wants to. This is not the case with the Negro.

Playboy: Haven't you used this argument to suggest that America should have a black president?
Buckley: Yes, I have. I would take great pleasure in the pride that would come to the black community if there were a Negro in the White House. I think it's worth working for.

Playboy: The possibility of a black American president seems remote in a decade that is opening with a widespread crackdown on such militant black groups as the Black Panthers. Do you think there is a campaign to exterminate the Panthers?
Buckley: No. But I think there should be. I mean, obviously, to exterminate the *movement*, even as I favor the extermination of Ku Klux Klanism, though not necessarily Ku Kluxers.

Playboy: Why?
Buckley: Because I am persuaded that the Panthers have solemnly registered their basic goals, which are to rob people, by category, of their rights to life, to liberty, to freedom; and because they are arming themselves for that purpose. Any organization caught—as the Panthers have been caught time and time again—with caches of machine guns and grenades and Molotov cocktails is presumptively guilty of non-Platonic ambitions. Every state in the Union forbids that sort of stockpiling of arms.

Playboy: Where have the Panthers indicated that their basic goal is to rob people of their rights?
Buckley: In their literature. Read it. I don't carry it around. It is as thoroughly impregnated with genocidal anti-white racism as ever the Nazis' was with anti-Semitism. And it makes no difference to the Panthers where on the left-right

spectrum the white politician stands. On the death of Bobby Kennedy, the Black Panthers' national newspaper ran a photograph of him lying in a pool of his own blood in the Ambassador Hotel with the head of a pig replacing the head of Mr. Kennedy. The rhetorical totalism suggested here, combined with the doctrinal genocidal passions, suggests to me that whatever was the appropriate attitude toward Goebbels in, say 1930, is appropriate, in 1970, toward the Black Panthers.

Playboy: Doesn't the publication of such a picture, however repugnant, come under the protection of the First Amendment?

Buckley: It does, formalistically; which is why I included actions—the Panthers' stockpiling of weapons—among the reasons why I think their extermination as a movement is desirable. But I would like to note that it is a naïve liberal assumption to think that the Bill of Rights protects every manner of written or spoken dissent. In the heyday of McCarthyism, Professor Samuel Stouffer from Harvard did one of those *Travels with Charley* bits around the country to discover the extent to which the Bill of Rights was an article of practical faith held by the American people. He found out that something like 75 percent of us didn't believe that members of the Communist Party should enjoy *any* rights. Needless to say, he wrote a horrified book about his findings. Now, it is extremely easy for people with an ideologized knowledge of American history to suppose that this is something new, let alone that it is impossible to compose a theoretical defense of it. But it is apparent to me that the profoundest studies of what, for instance, Thomas Jefferson or Abraham Lincoln meant by freedom was a freedom that was severely limited, even theoretically, in the right it absolutely granted to anyone to call for the persecution, let alone the liquidation, of others. When Jefferson said, "Those who wish to dissolve the Union or to change the republican form of government should stand undisturbed as monuments of the safety with which error of opinion may be tolerated where reason is left free to combat it," I am convinced by such scholars as Harry Jaffa that he meant not that we should grant freedom to the enemies of freedom because they are entitled to it but that we should grant freedom to the enemies of freedom because we can afford to *indulge* them that freedom. Accordingly, it becomes a practical rather than a theoretical consideration whether, at any given moment in American history, a particular group of dissenters whose dissent is based on the desire to rob other people of their freedom ought to be tolerated.

Playboy: Are we at such a moment in history—when we can't afford that freedom to a few hundred out of 200,000,000 Americans?

Buckley: Quite possibly. I don't think the Panthers are in a position to take over the country, any more than the Klan was. But the Klan deprived particular people in particular places of their effective freedom. So have the Panthers, by the use of the same weapons: intimidation and, it is now alleged by one or two grand juries, both murder and conspiracy to murder. So I say: Let's do to them what I wish we had done to the Klan fifty years ago.

Playboy: When you say that we should not tolerate a group of dissenters such as the Panthers, what do you propose we do about them?

Buckley: Society has three sanctions available for dealing with dissenters of this kind. There is the whole family of social sanctions; if they don't work, we then have legal sanctions; if the legal sanctions don't work, we are forced to use military sanctions. As an example of the social sanctions, I give you what has happened to Gerald L. K. Smith, the fierce anti-Semite. Would Smith be invited to join the sponsoring group of the Lincoln Center? If he gave a thousand-dollar contribution to the President's Club, would he be admitted as a member? No. Gerald L. K. Smith has been effectively isolated in America, and I'm glad that he has been. After such an experience as we have seen in the twentieth century of what happens—or what can happen—when people call for genocidal persecutions of other people, we have got to use whatever is the minimal resource available to society to keep that sort of thing from growing. If the social sanctions work, then you have the Jeffersonian situation, in which libertarian rodomontade is onanistically satisfying—a society in which the least possible force is the effective agent of that society's cohesiveness. I would like to see people like Bobby Seale and Eldridge Cleaver treated at least as badly as Gerald L. K. Smith has been. But no: They get applauded, they get invited to college campuses, they get listened to attentively on radio and on television—they are invited to Leonard Bernstein's *salons*—all of which makes rather glamorous a position that, in my judgment, ought to be execrated.

Playboy: They also get jailed, exiled, and even shot.

Buckley: Cleaver was jailed for committing rape, which Gerald L. K. Smith hasn't done, so far as I know. And he was wounded after a shoot-out with Oakland police. Huey Newton was convicted of voluntary manslaughter. A gang of them are up now for murder and conspiracy to terrorize. Now, I'll grant you this: I have not been satisfied that the killing of Cleaver's buddy in that particular battle in Oakland—the young man who walked out of the house in his shorts and T-shirt—was justified. The policeman who killed him may have panicked, as others of us have done, with less tragic consequences, to be sure. But he wasn't acting on orders from J. Edgar Hoover, whose sins, if there are any, are explicit rather than implicit. But to return to my point, if I may, about the attention lavished on such people: The same, to a certain extent, was true of George Lincoln Rockwell, who got an extensive ventilation of his views in this magazine. For as long as that kind of thing happens, you encourage people to consider as tenable a position that in my judgment ought to be universally rejected as untenable. The whole idea of civilization is little by little to discard certain points of view as uncivilized; it is impossible to discover truths without discovering that their opposites are error. In a John Stuart Mill–type society—in which *any* view, for so long as it is held by so much as a single person, is considered as not yet confuted—you have total intellectual and social anarchy.

Playboy: On the other hand, by publishing an interview with a George Lincoln Rockwell, one might encourage him to expose the untenability of his views and thus help discredit both himself and his philosophy, even among those who might previously have been sympathizers.
Buckley: I acknowledge the abstract appeal of the argument, but I remind you that it can be used as an argument for evangelizing people in Nazism, racism, or cannibalism, in order to fortify one's opposition to such doctrines. The trouble is that false doctrines *do* appeal to people. In my judgment, it would be a better world where nobody advocated tyranny; better than a world in which tyranny is advocated as an academic exercise intended to fortify the heroic little antibodies to tyranny.

Playboy: If the evils of a particular doctrine are so apparent, what harm is there in allowing someone to preach that doctrine?
Buckley: What is apparent to one man is not necessarily apparent to the majority. Hitler came to power democratically. It's a nineteenth century myth to confide totally in the notion that the people won't be attracted to the wrong guy. George Wallace, not Nixon or Humphrey, got the highest TV ratings. Take, once more, the Panthers. There are, I am sure, hundreds of thousands of Americans who would like to hear a speech by Eldridge Cleaver. One reason they would like to do so is because they like the excitement. Another is that they like to show off. People like to show their audacity, their cavalier toleration of iconoclasm—it's the same kind of thing, in a way, as shouting, "F--- Mayor Daley" in a loud voice in the middle of a park in Chicago. Moreover, the views expressed by Eldridge Cleaver, et al., have not been proscribed by settled intellectual opinion, because, thank God, we have not experienced in America the kind of holocaust that Caucasians visited against the Jews in Germany. I contend that it is a responsibility of the intellectual community to anticipate Dachau rather than to deplore it. The primary respon-

sibility of people who fancy themselves morally sophisticated is to do what they can to exhibit their impatience with those who are prepared to welcome the assassination of Bobby Kennedy because that meant one less pig. Their failure to do that is, in my judgment, a sign of moral disintegration. If you have moral disintegration, you don't have left a case against Dachau. If you don't have that, what *do* you have? Make love not war? Why?

Playboy: Do you think that a more concerted police attack should be launched against the Panthers?
Buckley: I would support a full legal attack, with the passage of new laws, if necessary, as we have done in other areas. For instance, I don't think we have enough legal weapons against people who push heroin. People who are practiced in the profession of trying to halt the flow of heroin see themselves as engaged in a losing fight—primarily because by the time the agent can gain entry to the home or apartment where he suspects there is a stash of heroin, it has been flushed down the toilet. The so-called no-knock provision of the president's new crime bill was written precisely to overcome that problem. Now, I know—everybody knows— that that provision is capable of abuse. But I think a libertarian ought always to ask himself: What is the way to maximize liberty?

Playboy: In what way does the no-knock law maximize liberty?
Buckley: Directly. In *Manchild in the Promised Land*, Claude Brown identifies heroin as the principal problem in Harlem—*not* housing, *not* education, *not* discrimination, *not* the absence of economic opportunity. Heroin. If the heroin traffic in Harlem were brought under control, we would see—in his judgment— a dramatic drop in crime and a lessening of those restrictions on freedom that accompany a high crime rate.

Playboy: Would you disagree with former attorney general Ramsey Clark's contention that eliminating poverty is the key to reducing crime?
Buckley: I would. Drug abuse and crime both have to do with the state of the ethos; and the ethos is not a function of poverty. Consider Portugal or Ireland: Poor people don't necessarily commit crimes.

Playboy: A few minutes ago, you referred to the moral disintegration of some Americans. Would you make that a general indictment—applicable not only to those who tolerate the Panthers but to most Americans?
Buckley: Yes. The most conspicuous attribute of the twentieth-century American is his self-indulgence. In a marvelous book called *The Odyssey of the Self-Centered Self*, Robert Fitch traces the principal concerns of civilization through the past

two hundred or three hundred years; our concerns were, he says, first predominantly religious, then predominantly scientific, then humanistic—and today are essentially egocentric. I think that ours is an egocentric society. The popular notion is that there is no reciprocal obligation by the individual to the society, that one can accept whatever the patrimony gives us without any sense of obligation to replenish the common patrimony—that is, without doing what we can to advance the common good. This, I think, is what makes not only Americans but most Western peoples weak. It comforts me that that also was the finding of Ortega y Gasset.

Playboy: How does the increasing social awareness and involvement of young people fit into your thesis?

Buckley: I don't say that somebody who spends the summer in Mississippi trying to bring rights to black people is primarily self-centered, although such a case could be made concerning some young people and by using less intricate psychological arguments than, for instance, the liberals fling around to prove that we are all racist. I'm talking about the general disease of *anomie*, which is the result of people's, by and large, having become deracinated, suspended from any relationship to the supernatural and prescinded from the historical situation. A lot of them retreat and think about themselves, even *exclusively* about themselves—the drug people—the dropouts, formal and informal. Certain others venture into utopianism, which, as I've said, necessarily and obviously breeds frustration and despair, conditions that some of them prefer even to drugs. But the lot of them, I think, fail to come to terms with the world, fail to come to terms with the end of life. They have absolutely no eschatological vision, except a rhetorical sort of secular utopianism. A related phenomenon: When I was last on the Johnny Carson show, he announced to his mass audience, "Well, after all, the reason the Soviet Union arms is because *we* arm," the implicit axiom being that there is obviously no difference between them and us. What makes it possible for the man who has the largest regular audience of anybody in the United States— not excluding the president—to say blandly something like that is wave after wave in the intellectual offensive against epistemological optimism, against the notion that some things are better than others and that we can know what those things are.

Playboy: Do you think this moral relativism is at least partially a consequence of the decline in religious belief?

Buckley: Yes. In orthodox religious belief. It's a commonplace that there is no such thing as an irreligious society. The need for religion being a part of the nature of man, people will continue to seek religion. You see the Beatles rushing off to listen to the platitudinous homilies of that Indian quack, Maharishi-what's-his-name, but they'd rather be caught dead than reading Saint Paul. Young people who have active minds tend to be dissatisfied with the ersatz religions they pick up, and yet so formal is the contemporary commitment to agnosticism—or even to atheism—that they absolutely refuse to plumb Christianity's extraordinary reservoirs of rationality. I doubt if you could get one of these kids, however desperately in search of religion—who will go to any guru, who will even talk to Joan *Baez* and attempt to get religion from *her*—to read *Orthodoxy* by Chesterton or any book by C. S. Lewis.

Playboy: Perhaps orthodoxy—lower case—is at fault. Many young people would say they think Christ was a great man; they might even know a good deal about Him. But they are appalled by Saint Paul's horror of the body and of sex.
Buckley: I'm sure that among the vast majority of students, the knowledge of Christ is superficial and that the *only* thing they know about Saint Paul is that he was "anti-sex." In fact, Saint Paul's anti-sexuality was, I think, a mode by which he expressed the joys of asceticism, the transcendent pleasure of the mortification of the flesh. By no means is this distinctive to Christianity. In fact, Christianity in its formal renunciation of Manichaeism took a position concerning the flesh that is far more joyful than, for instance, that of the Buddhists or of a number of other religions.

Playboy: One of the reasons many people have difficulty accepting your religion, Roman Catholicism, is that they have been convinced by experts that there are soon going to be more people on the globe than the earth can support, yet the Church does its not-inconsiderable best to prevent the spread of birth-control information. Do you also take a serious view of the population problem?
Buckley: Yes, I do. I think it is the second most important problem in the world, after ideological communism.

Playboy: Then the Church's position on birth control distresses you?
Buckley: No. It is not established by any means that the influence of the Church is very direct on the matter of the increase in population. It happens that the birth rate is the greatest where the Church has no influence: India, for instance, or Nigeria. It is impossible to establish a correlation between the birth rate in Latin America and the prevailing religion on that continent. The Catholic position on birth control is, therefore, something against which we agonize rather more theoretically than practically.

Playboy: What do you think we can do, then, to keep the population down?
Buckley: Get people to stop reading *Playboy.*

Playboy: What's the real answer?
Buckley: Well, the real answer is to make sure that people who don't want more children and who have no religious scruples against the use of abortifacients or prophylactics are aware of how they can get and use them. My own assumption is that we are moving toward the discovery of a chemical that will prevent conception, that will be generally dispensed—perhaps in the water supply—and can be readily neutralized by any woman who desires to do so.

Playboy: Should the U.S. volunteer birth-control information and devices to such overpopulated nations as India?
Buckley: They don't need any more information. They can get it from the *Encyclopaedia Britannica.* As to giving them the pill—sure, if they ask for it.

Playboy: Do you have any other sexual opinions that might shock your bishop?
Buckley: I didn't give you a "sexual" opinion. I don't know that giving free pills to India is heretical. Would American rabbis object to free pork for India? Heresy? I don't think so. I happen, for example, to favor the legalization of private homosexual acts committed between consenting adults and of prostitution. The second is the more important. Legalizing prostitution would provide a ready outlet for pubescent lust and greatly facilitate the hygienic problem, pending the domination of the appetite and the restoration of morality. Also, it would cut down the profits and power of the Mafia, the existence of which enrages me.

Playboy: How else would you combat the Mafia?
Buckley: By making gambling—but not gambling debts—legal.

Playboy: Advocating the legalization of gambling, prostitution, and homosexual acts between adults puts you in agreement with most liberals. Do you also agree with them in the area of censorship? Would you defend the right of the state to, say, stop performances by Lenny Bruce?
Buckley: I'm troubled by that problem. By the way, do, please, try to remember that the conservative opposes unnecessary legislation. I've written about the censorship dilemma. Obviously, a perfectly consistent, schematic libertarianism would give you an easy answer—let anybody do anything. Including cocaine vending machines. But a libertarianism written without reference to social universals isn't terribly useful. Here, I think, is where the science of sociology becomes useful. If sociology suggests that societies don't survive without the observance of certain common bonds, certain taboos, then we can maintain that

in the long run, we diminish rather than increase freedom by protecting people who violate those taboos. Having said that, let me add that I'm perfectly well aware that this particular argument can be abused by people who want a narrow conformity. But once again, let's reach for an example: When *Salvation,* the rock musical, was produced in New York City, the reviewer for *Time* magazine listed the things that it takes to make a successful rock musical nowadays. It has to be dirty, anti-American, and anti-religious. Under the last category, he said: It will no longer do to attack Protestantism, because Protestantism has become so etio-lated as to have no potential for shock. You can't shock anybody by making fun of the dogma of the Bishop of Woolwich. Second, it can't be anti-Jewish, because the playgoing community on Broadway tends to be heavily Jewish and the Jewish people hold that certain things should be held in reverence. For instance, no jokes about Dachau or Buchenwald can be made in New York City. Therefore—attack the Catholics!

There's still a certain amount of awe in the Catholic religion, but the Catholics are a politically unorganized group in New York City and you can get away with ridiculing them. So, the writer gives the audience the iconoclast's thrill, but safely: They're not going to lose at the box office. Now—should society in general defer to the specially pious concerns of significant groups within that society? We ex-tend certain protections against public affronts. For instance, the courts recognize a limit to what a storekeeper displays in his window. But what about his shelf? Or the stage? Is it right to have laws forbidding, let us say, a comedy based on what happened at Dachau? I know all the theoretical arguments against it, but there's a tug inside me that says that a society perhaps has to maintain the right to declare certain kinds of aggressions against the venerated beliefs of the people as taboo. This is a codification of grace, of mutual respect.

Playboy: Would you admit that the tug inside you to ban certain kinds of irrever-ence may be irrational?
Buckley: Yes—absolutely. But there is a place for irrationality. Many of the con-ventions of any society are irrational. The obsequies shown to the queen of En-gland, for example, are utterly irrational. Oakeshott [Michael J., a British econo-mist and political theorist] has made the demonstration once and for all that rationalism in politics—which may be defined as trying to make politics as the crow flies—is the kind of thing that leads almost always and almost necessarily to tyranny.

Playboy: Can you give us a specific way in which society might suffer from a comedy—however tasteless and debased—about what happened at Dachau?
Buckley: Yes. You can hurt a people's feelings. A people whose feelings are hurt

withdraw from a sense of kinship, which is what makes societies cohere. Moreover, a society so calloused as not to care about the feelings of its members becomes practiced in the kind of indifference that makes people, and the society
they live in, unlovely.

Playboy: But if a taboo has to be maintained by force of law, is it still a taboo?
Buckley: It depends. Some taboos are codified, some aren't. Some laws protect
what isn't any longer taboo. I don't think Lenny Bruce would be arrested today in
New York, the movement having been in the direction of permissiveness in the
past four or five years. The question really is: Do we—or do I, I guess—approve of
the trend, and I'm not so sure that I do. A society that abandons all of its taboos
abandons reverence.

Playboy: Doesn't society abandon something even more precious by attempting
to preserve that reverence by force?
Buckley: Again, it depends on the situation. If you have a society that is cor-
porately bent on a prolonged debauch—determined to wage iconoclasm *à
outrance*—then you've got a society that you can't effectively repress. I mean,
you have a prohibitive situation. But if you have a society—as I think we still
do—in which the overwhelming majority of the people respect their own and
others' taboos, the kind of society that, say, forbids a lawyer from referring to
Judge Marshall as a nigger, or Judge Hoffman as a kike, then it isn't much of an
exertion on the commonweal to implement such laws as have been on the books
in New York for generations. My final answer to your entire line of questioning
is ambiguous: If you ask simply: Does the individual have the absolute right to
do anything he wants in private contract with another party? then my answer
is: No, only the presumptive right. A sadist cannot contract to kill a masochist.
John Stuart Mill reduces the matter of sovereignty to the individual's right
over himself. The state hasn't the right to protect you against yourself—which
is a good argument against my being required to wear a helmet when I ride my
Honda.

Playboy: Doesn't Mill's dictum against the state's right to protect you from yourself also argue for the abolition of most drug laws?
Buckley: Does it? Take heroin. Except under totally contrived circumstances,
there is no such thing in America as a person inflicting purely on himself the consequences of taking heroin. If a man goes that route, he deserts his family—if he
has any; he becomes an energumen who will ravish society to sustain the habit,
and so on. Most important—as far as I'm concerned—he becomes a Typhoid

Mary of sorts. I know that I'm using a metaphor, but I can defend the use of this particular metaphor. We know from serious studies that heroin users desire to communicate the habit to other people and often succeed in doing so.

Playboy: Do the same arguments apply to marijuana?
Buckley: Not really, or not so severely. The first and most obvious thing to say about marijuana is that the penalties for using it are preposterous. But I don't believe that it ought to be legalized yet; the consequences of its use have not been sufficiently studied. It seems crazy to me that in an age when the federal government has outlawed Tab, we are wondering whether we ought to legalize marijuana. Now, it may be that marijuana is harmless, although at this moment, I am persuaded by those scientists who emphatically believe the contrary. It may be that we would be much better off persuading everybody who now drinks whiskey to turn on instead. But we don't *know.* Some scientists say that middle-aged people who take marijuana risk special dangers because they have gradually concatenated their own quirks, latent and active, into a moderately well-adjusted human being. Psychotropic drugs can shatter that delicate equilibrium. Conversely, it is speculated that marijuana can keep some young people from making the individual adjustments they need to make. Some scientists claim that prolonged use of marijuana wages a kind of war against your psyche, the final results of which are not easy to trace.

Playboy: Your attitude toward grass typifies your agreement with middle-class Americans on some issues. Are there any contemporary American middle-class values that you *dislike?*
Buckley: You'd have to make me a list of them. If ostentatious forms of material achievement are a middle-class value, I don't much like them, though I wouldn't go out of my way to evangelize against them; we all have our little vanities. I am told that in certain big corporations, it is unseemly for the junior V.P. to own a more expensive car than the senior V.P., and absolutely *verboten* for his wife to have a mink coat if the wife of the senior V.P. doesn't have one. But who *does* approve of Babbittry? Not even Babbitt. He merely practiced Babbittry. The middle-class values I admire are husbandry, industry, loyalty, a sense of obligation to the community, and a sense of obligation to one's patrimony. When Winston Churchill died, Rebecca West said that he was a great affront to the spirit of the modern age because he was manifestly superior. I said in introducing Clare Boothe Luce, when we did a TV program in Hawaii a few months ago, that her documented achievements are evidence of the lengths to which nature is prepared to go to demonstrate its addiction to inequality. It is a middle-class value

to defer, without animosity, to people of superior learning, achievement, character, generosity.

Playboy: To whom do you personally feel inferior?
Buckley: Millions of people, living and dead.

Playboy: Who among the living?
Buckley: To begin with, anyone who knows more than I do, which would be millions of people—or hundreds of thousands of people—right there. I also feel inferior to people who regulate their lives more successfully than I do, to people who are less annoyed by some of the petty distractions that sometimes annoy me, to people who are more philosophical in their acceptance of things than I am.

Playboy: Does that include Mrs. Luce?
Buckley: She's much more talented than I am.

Playboy: Norman Mailer?
Buckley: Much more talented than I am. Now, there are certain things in which I am Mailer's manifest superior. Politically, he's an idiot. And he's botched his life and the lives of a lot more people than I've botched, I hope. On the other hand, he's a genius and I'm not.

Playboy: Among other contemporaries, how about T. S. Eliot?
Buckley: You're talking about birds of paradise now. Like Whittaker Chambers. I make it a point to seek the company—intellectually, above all—of people who are superior to me in any number of ways, and I very often succeed.

Playboy: To whom do you feel superior—and why?
Buckley: To those who believe that they are the very best judges of what is wrong and what is right.

Playboy: Would you please name names?
Buckley: Would you please expand your printing facilities?

Playboy: As long as the discussion has become personal: To what extent has your feud with Gore Vidal developed into a publicity stunt from which you both have benefited?
Buckley: In my case, at least, to no extent at all. I don't see how one profits *a)* from being publicly libeled or *b)* from walking into a situation in which one pays legal expenses several times the value of anything one earned after industrious work preparing for television programs or doing an article.

Playboy: Would you care to add anything to what you said about him on the air during the 1968 Democratic Convention and in response to his subsequent comments about you?
Buckley: No.

Playboy: Why did you agree to appear with him in the first place?
Buckley: I agreed to appear in November of 1967 because I thought I could use the forum effectively to advance the conservative viewpoint. I was informed in April that Vidal had been selected to appear opposite me. My alternatives then were to break my contract or to proceed. I decided not to break the contract, even though Vidal was the single person I had named as someone I would not gladly appear against.

Playboy: You have been publicly active for nineteen years. How successful do you think you have been in advancing the conservative viewpoint?
Buckley: Very successful. That success has come primarily through the instrumentality of *National Review,* which has the second highest circulation of any journal of opinion in America. It repeatedly furnishes the reading public with the very best conservative thought, whether philosophical, critical, strategic, or social. It has had the effect of consolidating the conservative position, causing many people to abandon—however unhappily—their resolution to dismiss the conservative alternative as anachronistic, superficial, and inhuman. I don't say that *National Review,* or something like it, would not have been created had I not been around; it most certainly would have—in fact, I only midwifed it—but I'd say that the mere fact of having done so renders me, as midwife, very successful.

Playboy: Which failures of the conservative movement in the past ten to twenty years most distress you? The fact that Goldwater didn't get more votes than he did?
Buckley: No, not at all. It was a forgone conclusion that he wouldn't get many votes from the moment Kennedy was assassinated. It's very hard to explain to militant pro-Goldwaterites like myself that in a strange sort of way, an inscrutable sort of way, voting against Goldwater was explainable as a conservative thing to do. The reason I say that is because a nation convulsed in November of 1963 as ours was reached for balm, for conciliation, for peace, for tranquillity, for order. To have had three presidents over a period of fourteen months would have been dislocative beyond the appetite of many conservatives. Now, this doesn't mean that I side with those conservatives who voted against him—I happen to

be more adventurous than some conservatives—but I can respect their point of view. In any case, that was not by any means my idea of the great disappointment of the sixties. That was the failure, on the whole, to verbalize more broadly, more convincingly, the conservative view of things. The conservative critique has been very well made, but it hasn't got through with sufficient force to the opinion makers. It is still hard as hell to find a young conservative with writing talent. That distresses me deeply. Most of the people who write the really finished essays in the college newspapers are liberals, New Leftists. I don't know exactly why and I'm vexed by it, but there were only a dozen—or fewer—conservatives in the sixties who have become writers of some achievement.

Playboy: Personally, what do you expect to do during the next five years? Do you plan any more political candidacies?
Buckley: There was a lot of pressure on me to run against Goodell. By the way— I haven't told this before to anybody, but what the hell—I had decided back in 1967 to run against Bobby Kennedy in 1970. I reasoned that Johnson would be re-elected and that Bobby would go for president in 1972. He was, in 1967—as, indeed, later—the symbol of left opposition to Johnson. I resolved to challenge his politics in the senatorial race. When he died, I abandoned any idea of running for senator in 1970. Along came Goodell—and the pressures on me to challenge him. The principal moral allure was that it was something I deeply wanted *not* to do. Quite apart from the sort of inertial disadvantages of running against Goodell, and the gruesome prospect of campaigning, I had to face the fact that I would automatically be stripped of those forums to which I had gained access. No more thoughtful television programs, no more columns—because it has now been more or less agreed among American editors that they won't carry a column written by a practicing politician. I think of Galbraith's adage: The senate is a good place to be if you have no other forum. If I were senator from New York, it isn't at all clear to me that I'd have more influence than I have today, with my various outlets.

Playboy: Did running in the 1965 mayoral race in New York strip you of those forums?
Buckley: Yes and no. In the first place, it was a local contest and I never wrote about it in my columns. The television series was postponed precisely on account of my running. Another thing: It was sometime after 1965 that many newspaper editors reached their decision to embargo writer-politicians. They faced the problem directly when Senator Goldwater, a columnist, ran for president, lost, resumed his column, and ran for senator in 1968.

Playboy: How would you feel about running for a seat in the House?
Buckley: God, no. Not unless I can have all the seats simultaneously.

Playboy: If there were a conservative administration in this country—say, if Ronald Reagan became president—would you be tempted to accept a high post in the administration?
Buckley: No. In the first place, I don't like it much. In the second place—

Playboy: Don't like what much—Washington?
Buckley: That's right.

Playboy: Cabinet meetings?
Buckley: I don't much like any kind of meetings. Besides, I have no reason for supposing that I'm a skillful administrator; I may be or I may very well not be. But the kind of thing that I am practiced in requires considerable freedom of expression, and freedom of expression is obviously something you need to be very continent about when the point of the thing is to advance the collective endeavor.

Playboy: With or without your own involvement in an official capacity, are you optimistic about the conservative movement in America?
Buckley: I am, mildly. There has been some encouraging de-ideologization of politics in the past twenty years. When I went to college, Henry Wallace was still able to grip a lot of people with hopped-up visions like the nationalization of the steel industry. We've watched the experience of England since then and studied nationalized industries elsewhere, and *no* one will go to that parade anymore, no one except the types who squat in the fever swamps of ideology. The collapse of the poverty program as a federal enterprise strikes me as significant. It strikes me as significant, too, that Patrick Moynihan got up at an A.D.A. meeting a year or so ago and said, Let's face it, gang, conservatives know something intuitively that it takes us liberals years of intellectualizing to come up with—namely, that the federal government can't do everything it wants to do. Peter Drucker, who is certainly not considered a conservative fanatic, says now that the only things the government has proved it can really do competently are wage war and inflate the currency.

We've seen what's-his-name, that nice guy Kennedy sent down to South America to screw things up—Richard Goodwin—predict in *Commentary* that the great struggle of the seventies will be over the limits of state power. Which is exactly what conservatives wanted to fight about in the thirties. We've seen Arthur Schlesinger call a couple of dozen Kennedy types into his apartment for a daylong "secret" seminar—nobody was supposed to know about it, but *I* knew about it—in which they reconsidered their enthusiasm for executive power, because executive power, it turns out, can be administered by the likes of Lyndon Johnson! These are pretty encouraging indices. They suggest to me that there is a wide concern over the survival of the individual in the machine age and over the limits of federal and executive power. They may, in turn, stimulate a curiosity about the ontological role of the state. That is conservative territory, but admittance is free.

Playboy: Even if you don't intend to run for office again, do you plan to keep writing?
Buckley: Yes. We've kept an alternative landing field in operation, you see. When the liberals fly in, thirsty, out of gas, they'll find it in full working order—radar OK, bar open, Coca-Cola and coffee on the house. We know it's necessary to assimilate the experience of the modern age. Cardinal Newman said in a related contest—between the logical positivists and the conservatives—that one of our great challenges is constantly to incorporate new experience, so as not to leave ourselves with a piece of brittle lace, the touching of which would cause it to crumble.

Playboy: Don't most dogmas, theological as well as ideological, crumble sooner or later?
Buckley: Most, but not all.

Playboy: How can you be so sure?
Buckley: I know that my Redeemer liveth.

"I Fear the Attrition of the Law's Prestige": A Conversation with William F. Buckley Jr.

Alan F. Westin / 1978

From *The American Civil Liberties Review*, March/April 1978. © American
Civil Liberties Union. Reprinted with permission of the publisher.

CLR: I don't know whether anyone has ever compiled a complete Bill Buckley
box-score on civil liberties, but I do know—from having reviewed your positions for this interview—that you are not a prototypical American conservative. On some issues, you share positions taken by civil libertarians (or they share
yours)—as in your support for decriminalization of marijuana, your condemna-
tion of the FBI agents who bugged Martin Luther King Jr. and tried to intimidate him through the recordings, your opposition to most state censorship of the
arts and expression, your belief that police ought not to concern themselves with
"victimless" crimes, and in your views on international human rights. On many
other issues, though, your views do not coincide with civil libertarian positions,
as on abortion, government aid to parochial schools, amnesty, capital punishment, ERA, and the rights-of-the-accused decisions of the U.S. Supreme Court.
On still other issues—such as court-ordered wiretapping for particular crimes—
I suspect your views are the same as those of a minority of card-carrying civil
libertarians.

What I'd like to do in this Conversation, is to bring out the substance of your
positions on a wide range of civil liberties and civil rights questions, and explore
the assumptions about society and liberty that underlie your stands. To begin, let
me evoke a few Buckleyite orientations. What is your view of the *Bakke* case?

Buckley: An employer who surveys the application forms of half-a-dozen candidates for an opening and quietly gives the advantage to the black candidate is,
in my opinion, doing the right thing. But what he did could not stand the test
of universalization. You could not take that discreet preferment and write legislation about it, ordaining it, as the people at the University of California in effect did, as the Act of Reverse Discrimination Designed to Atone for White Men's

Oppressions During Four Centuries. I believe in the establishment of two or three medical schools at which students would be bound, as students at West Point are bound to spend time in the Army, to spend time in the ghettos. But what the University of California did cannot be the law. I say this without the slightest enthusiasm for the Court using the *Bakke* case to interfere with the admissions processes of universities, especially private universities.

Incidentally, that expresses my attitude also toward laws to outlaw smoking on planes or trains. For heaven's sake, keep government out of this domain. Let the airlines, the restaurants, the bus companies, and the steamships handle the problem. The authority of the state should extend only to airless public places like elevators, subway cars, and lunar modules.

CLR: But as to *Bakke*, don't you believe it should be legally permissible for a university to adopt *voluntarily* and *openly*, not by subterfuge, programs that take into account the university world's prior discrimination against blacks? That is, to take a goal of preferring some black students in the marginal pool of applicants?
Buckley: Not a university supported by public funds.

CLR: How do you regard legislation to prohibit the use of federal Medicare funds to finance abortions? Does it bother you that this operates basically against poor women and becomes class legislation?
Buckley: I am opposed to any taxpayer funds being used for feticide, when this is unnecessary to protect the mother's health. Actually, not very much money is involved, only fifty to sixty million dollars to be paid to abortion clinics. Abortions are cheaper than color TVs, and getting cheaper all the time. If we assume that roughly half the American people are in favor of subsidizing abortions, then the philanthropic resources of half the American people could be stimulated to come up with fifty million dollars for abortions for those who can't finance the couple of hundred bucks required.

I take this view because both my religious convictions and my reading of a growing body of scientific evidence lead me to the judgment that a fetus is as much of a human being as a day-old baby, and, as a life, is entitled to as much legal protection. Those of us who believe that the fetus is human, like those who believed that the Negro was human and fought for civil rights, cannot do less than to advocate such a view as public policy, especially where taxpayer funds are concerned. As for the Supreme Court's original pro-abortion ruling in 1973, this was verily the *Dred Scott* decision of the twentieth century. The court had no business entering this sphere and preempting state legislative judgment; it was entirely beyond the competence and the authority of the Justices.

CLR: Most of our readers probably recall that you became something of a "civil liberties" activist by working for the retrial and release of Edgar Smith, who had been convicted of murdering a fifteen-year-old girl in New Jersey in 1957. After one of the longest stays on death row in American history, Smith was released in 1971, in part because of your championing of his cause. Why did you campaign for a convicted criminal?

Buckley: During the course of our correspondence, which was considerable— he wrote me over 2,900 pages of letters between 1964 and 1971—I became convinced that he had not been tried fairly, and that he could not have committed the murder in the time and under the circumstances alleged.

CLR: In 1976, though, he was charged in San Diego for an atrocious assault on a woman, and you helped the authorities apprehend Smith. Did this turn of events change your mind about the first case?

Buckley: I believe now that Smith was guilty of the first crime. However, there is no mechanism as yet perfected that will establish beyond question a person's guilt or innocence. There will be guilty people freed this year and every year. But for those who believe that the case of Edgar Smith warrants a vow to accept the ruling of every court as definitive, it is only necessary to remind ourselves that this year and every year, an innocent man will be convicted. Edgar Smith has done quite enough damage without underwriting the doctrine that the verdict of a court is infallible.

CLR: But if courts are less than fallible, doesn't that lend support to not imposing an irreversible penalty—death?

Buckley: Every punishment is irreversible, beginning with a day in jail.

CLR: More recently, you also supported reform of the marijuana laws.

Buckley: I think that laws that absolutely don't work should be looked at again. The old saw that the best way to repeal a bad law is to enforce it—which in this instance would put fifty million Americans in jail—is certainly a case in point here.

CLR: What do you think is responsible for the change in public sentiment about decriminalizing marijuana that we're witnessing today? Is it merely a matter of widespread usage, or does it strike a deeper chord of feeling about freedom in our society?

Buckley: During the late sixties and early seventies, the public mood changed to the extent of opposing jail sentences for marijuana users. In New York State, as in so many states, there were draconian penalties for smoking marijuana. That's changed now in New York State and many other states that have decriminalized marijuana.

What upset me about the evolution of the law until the decriminalization statute passed recently was that fewer and fewer people were being prosecuted under the law, but the law remained on the books. When that happens, you run the risk of the capricious judge, the literal-minded judge, or, if you like, the ignorant judge, who all of a sudden has a guy who has smoked a joint brought before him, he looks in the book, and says one to three years, well, I'll give him two, and off he goes to Attica. I saw that happen; twenty years, busted in some remote rural town. It's the lack of uniformity. My guess is that even before decriminalization you could walk into a police station in New York City dragging on a marijuana cigarette without getting arrested.

CLR: You're not impressed with the argument, which is often made, that if you remove that law, then you've opened the floodgates to softening other kinds of drug enforcement laws?

Buckley: Yes, I'm impressed, but less so than the people who try to impress me. Because they do it by saying that the drug culture is a comprehensive one. I don't think so. I think some places it's comprehensive, some places discrete. I know some people who smoke marijuana and that's all they do. It's also correct that some people smoke marijuana and find themselves on an escalating route toward the other stuff. The probability is that people who are going to experiment are going to experiment anyway, but I do think that the principal reason why Middle-America declines to encourage people to violate the law is because they feel that in doing so they're co-opted—all of a sudden they are members of the Woodstock Nation—and this they just don't want to do. The others, and I am on their side at this point, reject the use of individual victims for the sustenance of a legal chimera, and recoil against cynical uses of the law. Not because we are purer, but because we fear the attrition of the law's prestige.

CLR: What then would you favor in terms of reform of the marijuana laws?
Buckley: What's needed, as Dr. Nicholas Pace, president of the New York City Commission on Alcoholism, suggests, is something on the order of the Sacramento Citation-Diversion Program, which requires youths arrested for drug possession to attend a drug information study course, upon the completion of which their arrest records are wiped clean.

CLR: You wrote in your book, *United National Journal: A Delegate's Odyssey*, that, when you were appointed to the UN Human Rights Commission by President

Nixon, you thought you would "cajole, wheedle, parry, thrust, mesmerize, dismay, seduce, intimidate" in defense of liberty. Your book records a very different reality, though.

Buckley: Those who cherish illusions about the United Nations should never be permitted to sit in on a meeting of the Human Rights Committee or Human Rights Commission. I was struck by two things there: by the hypocrisy and by how quickly even I became used to it. The first few days I listened to this Cuban or that East German going on about the liberty in their country with indignation. How could anybody tolerate this? After a week, I didn't even notice what they were saying. And that's what really horrified me. It's like the charge one encounters about Germans who kept hearing rumors during the war about what was going on in the extermination camps, and after a while they just didn't notice the rumors.

The trouble with American representation at the UN, at least until Daniel Moynihan showed how to do it differently, was that we supinely accepted the most outrageous conduct of other governments and refused to attack their distortions about our own record. By the way, while I was serving in the UN, I attended a ninetieth birthday party for Roger Baldwin, who was then pressing for better UN protection of human rights in his work for the International League for the Rights of Man. Now, there is a lot about Roger Baldwin I have disagreed with, especially when he confused his social ideas with civil liberties. But when Baldwin rose to speak, a virile, poised, incorruptible man, the high commissioner, in a way, of the American human rights movement, I saw more authentic devotion to human freedom than I had heard expressed in three months with the Human Rights Committee of the United Nations. Then and now, the Baldwin position just doesn't get presented for the United States.

CLR: It seems interesting to me—especially if you look at the positions of liberals and conservatives on the United Nations over the past twenty years or so—that today more certified liberals find themselves in agreement with certified conservatives in dissenting from the United Nations' positions and values than has ever been the case since its founding. The disenchantment liberals feel about the UN as a result of the prevailing majority in the General Assembly, and the terminology on racism and human rights now in use, has brought this around full circle.

Buckley: No question about it. Human rights are at a very low ebb on this planet, in part because they are systematically violated by governments that seek to distract attention from these violations by pointing to violations of lesser countries.

CLR: Do you think the United States campaign for global human rights has been successful?

Buckley: Well, the Spanish have a word: *pujanza*. It is used to define a really brave bull who keeps charging you and keeps on charging, such is his desire to get you. He has pujanza. He turns around and charges you again, and charges again. American policy on human rights thus far lacks that quality.

CLR: What has been your reaction to President Carter's statements about human rights?

Buckley: Mr. Carter has recognized the existence of real heroes and genuine victims of systematic persecution. He has mentioned a few by name. He has actually visited with one, though as discreetly as if he had arranged to see a peep show. But in terms of policy, he has used no sanctions against the Soviet Union, only against relatively impotent Latin American nations. In the course of doing so—of ruling, say, against Uruguay, but not against the Philippines—Carter has stressed quite candidly the necessity of superordinating the national interest. Translated, that means the Philippines can hit back at us, Uruguay can't.

CLR: Do you believe Carter's attempts to point out Soviet violations cause diplomatic problems—as they did during the SALT talks—and that this will cause Carter's protests to diminish?

Buckley: What is unsure about Carter is where he will go from here. If Tito, in the period immediately ahead, should join his ancestors, and the Soviet Union were to touch off local disturbances, will we stand in the way of Russia's twenty-five-year-old dream of reacquiring effective power in Yugoslavia? Candidate Carter seemed to be saying, No; but then that was the same hour during which the president of the United States told us that Poland was already free—so maybe it was an off night.

CLR: I get the impression that you feel the American commitment to human rights advocacy abroad is ambivalent.

Buckley: Well, yes. Take the Kennedy Amendment in 1976. Senator Kennedy added a provision to federal law forbidding the sale of arms to Chile on the grounds that Chile is suppressing human rights. Senator Kennedy's patience, he reported, was exhausted. On the other hand, Senator Kennedy's patience is infinite in respect to the suppression of human rights in other countries. We have given more arms to Yugoslavia than to any country in the world, and they have been suppressing human rights in Yugoslavia since before Senator Kennedy began his lifelong study of ethics at Harvard University.

CLR: But does that mitigate the situation in Chile? Do you favor selective action on behalf of human rights?

Buckley: Now, you know, and I know, that Chile's salient offense isn't that it is torturing people. It is that the present regime overthrew the government of Salvatore Allende, and therefore incurred the undying hostility of the world's left-wing press. But in Chile, so far as the visitor is able to see and based on what he reads in wildly different sources, there is public order.

CLR: That may be so, but does "public order" excuse the use of torture, or are you convinced that the allegations against the Chilean government are fabricated?

Buckley: My rule is to presume the worst where there isn't a free press. In Chile, the press is free to reproduce criticism that originates from outside the country. This produces pressure which, in my judgment, has reduced torture and the suppression of human rights to the point of virtual insignificance by the unhappily low standards of the Third World nations.

CLR: In general, though, whom are we to believe when accusations of torture and violation of human rights are made?

Buckley: Only a free press, as I say, can do the job adequately. As a rule, where there is no free press, assume the worst. Not necessarily because the worst is true—but because that is the ethically cautious conclusion to reach.

CLR: Speaking of the press, I know that you would put limits on what can be openly stated. Your successful libel suit against the Reverend Dr. Frank Littell, for comments he made about you in his book *Wild Tongues,* is a concrete example. In *Wild Tongues,* Littell claimed that you were, "in America, the outstanding representative" of the fellow traveler function typified by Von Ribbentrop in Nazi Germany; that you, and your writings and TV shows, "frequently print new items and interpretations picked up from the openly fascist journals and have been important and useful agencies for radical right attack on honest liberals and conservatives"; and that you "never admit a mistake or apologize to the victims." The United States Court of Appeals found in your favor, but awarded little in damages, and the Supreme Court subsequently denied certiorari. The ACLU defended Littell, arguing that you are a public figure, in the sense in which that phrase is properly defined, and that Littell's comments were within the range protected by the First Amendment as a comment on the activities of a public figure. Why did you bring this suit against Littell, who had only a sliver of the public attention and media impact that you command, then and now?

Buckley: I think that whenever I say anything about someone which is not true—that he is the Molotov of America, that he makes his living by lying and cheating and passing along the propaganda of Communist journals, that he is totally unrepentant whenever he is proved wrong, and that he is thoroughly in sympathy with the historical acts of the Communist movement—that individual should be able to sue me, and *win*.

CLR: Don't you think this type of lawsuit exercises a serious chilling effect on political discourse?
Buckley: I think it *should* have a chilling effect on all libel. I am in favor of the libel laws. I believe that the libel laws ought to be a protection for anyone to use against people who show a reckless disregard for the facts. I think if I said, "Alan Westin is a son-of-a-bitch," I should be protected, because that is an opinion. But, if I said Alan makes his living by misrepresenting, lying, and serving as a transmission belt for the Communist line, I should be punished because that is reckless disregard of the facts.

CLR: Yet that kind of free-swinging comment is the very type of political polemic that characterized the newspapers of Washington's, Adams's, and Jefferson's day. It is a part of the tradition of political writing in America, and that kind of description of ideas and affinities is a part of free speech in our society.
Buckley: Well, it certainly should not be a part of free speech in our society. In the first place, until 1965 I would have won a summary judgment for libel. Then, in 1965, in *Sullivan v. New York Times*, though it dismissed a libel case against public officials, the Court said that proof of reckless disregard of the truth *could* be a basis for libel recovery. It did *not* take the Hugo Black position on libel, which is that no libel exists. There have been several striking cases after *Sullivan*, including *Goldwater v. Ginsburg*, and *Butz v. Saturday Evening Post*, which said it's actual malice to publish a defamatory statement in reckless disregard of the known truth, and when this is proved to the satisfaction of the Court, libel was committed and damages could be awarded.

CLR: Well, you'd have to review the words that were used to see if there was reckless disregard of the truth.
Buckley: In my case against Littell, God knows the judge attempted to help this guy come forward with the factual case. What really did Littell in was when he said, "I don't think Mr. Buckley is a fascist at all." The judge tried to alert him, as did his own lawyers, to the danger of what he was saying. But he said, "No, no, I think Mr. Buckley is a perfectly reasonable guy," and so on. And the judge kept saying, you know recovery for malice is permitted under *Sullivan v. New York Times*. You can say something unpleasant about someone because you want to,

because you just don't like him, but you can't say something about him that you know isn't true. He'd have had a much better chance if he had said, "I believe it, I believe it, somebody told me he really is a Nazi." I think then he would have had a better chance. I don't think he would have gotten off, but I think he would have had a better chance. The guy ambushed himself.

CLR: Are there other forms of speech which you think aren't protected by the First Amendment?

Buckley: I don't think anyone has the right publicly to mock my religion, and under the circumstances I believe that certain laws against blasphemy are understandable. It's much better when those things are regulated by social sanctions. If, let's say, there was a musical comedy based on life inside Buchenwald, it seems to me that the proper way to treat it would be to boycott it effectively. But I would not stand in the way of a civic ordinance that denied someone the right to produce such a musical at this particular moment in history.

CLR: How about pornography?

Buckley: Well, surely a society that allows the reduction of sex to its exclusive biological dimensions is no more commendable than a society that reduces wine to its alcoholic content.

CLR: But do you believe that the government should be telling people what they can or cannot see or read?

Buckley: I tend philosophically to be opposed to government censorship. But I also think that free speech, the moment it becomes licentious, becomes less than useful. And I think that many people are engaged in undermining the value of free speech precisely by abusing it in this manner.

CLR: Doesn't that position ignore the redeeming social value in various kinds of venturesome publications in the sexual realm?

Buckley: Look, there may be shadow cases. I grant ambiguity in most cases, but I think that anybody who says there's redeeming social value in something like *Deep Throat* or *Hustler* magazine is simply having us on. Now this is something very difficult to regulate, but I simply concede philosophically that it is possible at one and the same time to have a robustly free society and one in which certain categories of verbal offenses are not permitted. I think it is right for Congress, though it acts very unwisely most of the time, to forbid the use of the federal mails to transport obscene materials.

CLR: Do you limit your support of government prohibitions to sexual expression or would you also include political expressions that "abuse" freedom?

Buckley: Well, it is a naive liberal assumption to think that the Bill of Rights protects every manner of written or spoken dissent. Take the Black Panthers. Their basic goals were to rob people, by category, of their rights to life, liberty, and freedom. I don't think anybody has that right, or the right, for instance, to say that all Jews should be exterminated or all Negroes lynched or deported. I think there may be a good argument for letting them speak, because it might be more of a nuisance to shut them up than tolerate their expression. But I don't think they have a *right* to expression at all.

CLR: Does that lead you to oppose the ACLU's defense of the right of the Nazi party to hold a march in Skokie, Illinois?
Buckley: Yes.

CLR: Isn't your general support of prohibitions against aggressive speech an invitation to the kind of governmental suppression you philosophically oppose?
Buckley: The suppression of certain things is an aspect of the assertion of one's values—even as we suppressed the circulation of racist literature in Germany after the war. I think it was a correct thing to do because it had become blasphemous in the most realistic sense. Besides, if one in fact takes seriously the First Amendment to the Constitution, which says that Congress can't encumber the right of free speech, how is it that you permit a labor union to encumber the right of free speech?

CLR: I assume you're referring to your dispute with the American Federation of Television and Radio Artists (AFTRA)?
Buckley: That's right.

CLR: You brought suit against AFTRA because you didn't want to have to join AFTRA or pay dues to it in order to appear on radio or television. As I recall, you also objected to signing a form that forced you to obey union orders concerning when to strike and when to refuse to cross picket lines. But ultimately, the court of appeals ruled against you, didn't it, overturning a district court decision in your favor?
Buckley: Yes. The late Alexander Bickel, the AFTRA counsel, agreed that I would not have to be a member, though he would not agree that I would not be counted as a member of the union for bargaining-representation purposes. Technically, I am free to defy a picket line and to speak what I want to speak, which is a most significant victory.

CLR: But you still have to pay money equal to the dues of an AFTRA member?
Buckley: Yes, and that is an unworkable solution so long as they insist on a code

of fair practices for broadcasting stations which specifies that all performers shall be members of AFTRA. We submitted a letter from a broadcasting network stating they would not put me on the air unless they had a letter from AFTRA saying that my appearance on the air was authorized by AFTRA. We wanted a declaratory order to the effect that the code of fair practices, in and of itself, to the extent that it insists on full-scale membership, is illegal. In the first place, you never know the number of people who will simply not hire you rather than face an angry shop steward the next time negotiating time comes around. My position is that the burden should be on the station to show why it is not using the performer, not on the performer to prove he is usable. It's as though my responsibility was to come in with a copy of the Bill of Rights every time I went up to Central Park and made a speech, rather than the responsibility of the police officer, who denied me the right to speak, to show wherein he had that authority. And the matter of initiative is extremely important. For one thing, it's extremely important because it's expensive. . . . God, you're inscrutable.

CLR: I'm inscrutable?

Buckley: You're sitting there . . . I don't know whether you approve, disapprove, if you're horrified. . . .

CLR: I'm trying to draw out your views rather than debate each issue with you. Actually, I agree that someone like you can fight union threats much more easily than somebody at the lower level who runs afoul of shop stewards or union authorities and to whom agreement with AFTRA could be a major deterrent on his or her free speech. Tell me, though, do you see this as a right-to-work case?

Buckley: To the extent that it becomes necessary to communicate via truncation, the right to work is a shorthand way of saying the right-to-work-without-the-necessity-of-joining-a-private-organization. The free speech aspect of my case only accentuates that deeper aspect.

CLR: Turning to another issue, were you disappointed when the House Committee on Un-American Activities, later known as the House Internal Security Committee, was disbanded in the mid 1970s?

Buckley: No. I had years earlier proposed to call it the Committee on Communist Activities, and let other targets be ad hoc. I'm disappointed in the sense that we obviously haven't learned in this country how to keep pace with the technology of subversion while maximizing our freedom.

CLR: Do you believe the United States is currently in danger because of subversive activities?

Buckley: We're in grave danger to the extent that we fail to understand the destructive threat of Communism, and we haven't understood it because we have certain fixations that vague welfare state policies represent an adequate substitute for effective international anti-Communism.

CLR: But haven't the revelations about CIA and FBI misconduct illustrated the related danger of overzealous and all-encompassing security? What has been your reaction to these disclosures? I mean, about the intelligence community's massive domestic surveillance operations?

Buckley: I view it as abominable on the whole, but not very surprising. You get about one person who is genuinely corrupt in one hundred, and you'll find that so even in self-consciously incorruptible organizations. Remember Ralph Nader's assistant? The one who made the secret tape of Nixon's conversations public at a cocktail party? He had no right to do that. There's no excuse, either, for putting a bug under the mattress of Martin Luther King. But it is also true, I think, that where you have centralized power you have a temptation for courtiers who wish to please the king. Certainly one of the reasons why conservatives tend to feel secure in their insights against the accumulation of central power is that people tend to do that kind of thing.

On the other hand, I did not regard it as a simple mistake—such as everybody occasionally makes—when the FBI made six or seven hundred illegal entries into the offices of the Socialist Workers party over a period of thirty years. Over a period of thirty years, they couldn't find enough to charge them with double parking. In the light of such an experience, it is right to refine the legal restrictions against certain kinds of FBI activity.

Likewise, I regard it as shocking that officials of the FBI should have reported directly to Lyndon Johnson on the personal activities of Martin Luther King. It is shocking that the president of the United States has the power to acquire knowledge about the sex life of anybody. I don't know who voted Presidents Roosevelt, Johnson, or anyone else the right to act as peeping Toms.

CLR: Do you think that Congress has done a good job of investigating and reporting on intelligence abuses?

Buckley: The Church Committee Report deserves to be taken seriously. It would appear to have established beyond serious question that the chief executives, from Franklin Roosevelt on, have given very little thought to questions of law, let alone constitutionality, when dealing with intelligence activities and domestic security. What is missing from the Church Report is what logicians call an *a posteriori* look at the problem; for instance, a look that reasons from the facts back to the theory.

The facts during the late sixties were that the United States government was not fulfilling its primary responsibility to protect the people. There were tens of thousands of urban bombings, buildings burned, arson advocated, the civil rights of establishmentarian dissenters violated, civil disobedience was the rage, hijackings every week, military and diplomatic secrets published, and Soviet money promoting internal dissension.

It will require the integration of these conditions within a doctrine of proper self-defense by a free society, rather than a mere abstract affirmation of freedom from surveillance, to convince us that the Church Committee has done a complete job. But it certainly has shown us that the FBI and CIA appear to be as capable as any other bureaucratic agency of excesses—at the expense of the presumptive right of American citizens to privacy.

CLR: What are your views about current threats to privacy?
Buckley: I have a revulsion against anything that interferes with individual privacy, and I subscribe to a great deal of what you wrote about in *Privacy and Freedom*. But, like you, I also recognize that with the mechanization of crime, we have to enlist the aid of technology. That has to be done, obviously, with safeguards for innocent people, and this is one of the great creative reconciliations on which, unfortunately, the nation's liberals have not, in my judgment, done as much as they should. For example, how to protect your ultimate privacy against criminal assault, and at the same time protect those other privacies against random interference by pesky bureaucrats.

CLR: I still sense that you would accept the use of high technology in surveillance against people considered subversives. Would you see this as justifying COINTELPRO's activities against the Communist party?
Buckley: Yes, because that was counter-terrorist. For example, I think the Ku Klux Klan was a subversive organization, and in order to neutralize the head of the Ku Klux Klan, you resort to this kind of activity. I'm not prepared to say that that's worse than leaving him alone and waiting for him to lynch a Negro and hoping that you've got somebody around in a helicopter with an X-ray movie camera that will catch him up at it. Certain people, in the way in which they assault society, require that they be met in kind. I recognize that this is a dangerous thing, a dangerous cliché, but I nevertheless say it.

CLR: But when government agents move from the Klan to the Southern Christian Leadership Conference and other targets of this kind of government penetration and psychological warfare, didn't we have a very dangerous process?

Buckley: Well there's the left-right spectrum. Over here you have the Ku Klux Klan using violence; and over there you get the Black Panthers flashing a picture of Bobby Kennedy lying in a pool of his own blood, and saying "one less pig to worry about." You get the Symbionese Liberation Front. You get Bernadine Dohrn's outfit, and this spectrum stretches way on over past the NAACP or the John Birch Society.

So far as I know, the John Birch Society has never threatened to kill anybody, and I think it's ridiculous to snoop around, beyond subscribing to its publication, as I do to the NAACP's publication. If circumstantial evidence accumulates; if, let's say, the NAACP all of a sudden started to bloom through the newspapers of America with full-page ads the way the Fair Play for Cuba Committee did, on whose masthead was Truman Capote, Norman Mailer, and so on, that could trigger official interest. The Cuba Committee was being subsidized by Cuban funds in violation of the law, as was later revealed by a Senate investigation.

Now where should you draw the line? I think you should draw the line on the basis of an intelligent judgment as to the kind of thing particular organizations are up to. Let me give you a very concrete example. Am I being too loquacious?

CLR: No. Go right ahead.

Buckley: Let me give you a concrete example. Timothy Leary testified to the Justice Department recently. They wanted to know how he escaped from prison. He was in a maximum security prison, and all of a sudden he was free and in Algeria. But he was now reformed and repentant, and his decision was: I'm going to tell what happened. So he says there were five to six people involved in his escape, and he names them. Two of them are lawyers. One of them is a lawyer who is affiliated with the Communist party—he's usually there to spring bail or fight for a Smith Act defendant, or whatever. Another is not that kind at all; he's just a lawyer loosely identified with liberal movements.

Now the question: Is the Justice Department, with this kind of information in hand, entitled to look into some of the organizations with which this lawyer is affiliated, and find out whether there is a pattern there? Have they helped any other prisoners to escape? Is it in fact true? Could Leary be lying? You see here an example of the practical problems one meets on a day-by-day basis, which can only be met by the application of human intelligence. There's got to be some kind of position.

CLR: The example you give is one that originates with a specific investigation of a particular criminal act, and moves back to try and understand its sources. That, I think, would not trouble many people who regard themselves as civil libertarians. It is the dragnet surveillance of political groups that poses the hard problem; plus the fact that the police continually say they need to surveill nonviolent Group A because "violent" Group B draws recruits from Group A.

Buckley: But what about circumstantial evidence? What about my example of the Fair Play for Cuba Committee taking out $10,000 ads in the *New York Times*? Are you entitled to be suspicious? No, a keen nose for probabilities suspects that the money was coming from an undisclosed source—which in fact it was.

CLR: And that leads you, then, to say government should bug the headquarters of the Fair Play for Cuba Committee?

Buckley: That's right. If you also bug the headquarters of the Cuban liberation people who try to throw mortar shells at the United Nations building. It's a very complicated problem. Now, we do know that the Supreme Court acted on the question and attempted to set guidelines. We know that some of the bugs that were instituted by whoever—Nixon, Kissinger, let's leave that moot—pre-1970, were thought to be legal by every president of the United States up until the Supreme Court ruled they were not lawful. I favor the observance of guidelines, but I'm very suspicious of any guidelines that turn out to be absolutist in nature because I think the resulting inviolability would not be the presumptive freedom I'm in favor of.

CLR: Do you think the Congressional Oversight Committee concept is the right method for keeping the intelligence agencies in check?

Buckley: The new Oversight Committee is on the one hand desirable—we do need protection against capricious use of intelligence capabilities; on the other hand, it is an example of efforts by lawyers and jigsaw makers to pin down with exactitude the rules by which we govern ourselves in a spontaneous world substantially dominated by tyrants. If we go down, they are saying, it will be with punctilio.

CLR: Then you are in favor of continuing some covert operations?

Buckley: Yes. Are we in fact prepared to retreat from the inaugural ideal of JFK—that we "shall pay any price, bear any burden" and so on "to assure the survival and success of liberty," so that we will stop any clandestine efforts to help our friends in other countries help themselves? I do not think we should stop.

CLR: Let's shift to some entirely domestic issues. What are your current views on gun control?

Buckley: I was recently moving toward what might be called creeping acquiescence in the matter of gun control legislation. But a recent article in *The Public Interest* changed my mind. It found that there is practically no correlation between gun control and crime control. It is a pity, of course, because it would have been fun to end violent crime by simply scooping up forty million hand guns. But we shall have to come up with a more complicated way of dealing with the problem.

CLR: Don't you think stricter controls on the possession of hand guns would at least reduce the incidence of violent crime?
Buckley: I don't know for sure. But I am persuaded that there's another side to the argument. Suppose you've got, say, a seventy-year-old couple living in the Bronx. There have been some rather arresting stories about things that have happened to people in the Bronx, causing one couple recently to commit suicide as an act of desperation, having twice been mugged and tortured. Now, how would they look at a law that said they couldn't have a pistol by their bedside, let's say, after being mugged twice? In the first place, they'd probably disobey it.

CLR: But wouldn't stricter controls at least cut down on the accessibility of firearms for the average criminal and reduce the amount of accidental deaths caused by guns, as well as the crimes of passion where the presence of a gun at the wrong time is the key factor responsible for the shooting?
Buckley: The statistics show one misuse of a gun for every four thousand guns, which is a better ratio than in automobiles. I don't think that if one were to pass gun control laws, which would be respected by the law-abiding but not by the lawbreakers, that ratio would change, except in the wrong direction.

CLR: Let's move to a more general consideration of the courts and civil liberties. The Warren Court was a favorite target of yours. What are your thoughts on the Burger Court's behavior?
Buckley: I'm still very unhappy with the Supreme Court, for technical, moral, and political reasons. Technically, it seems to be plain that their workload is something like fifteen to twenty times the caseload they had twenty years ago, so that they can't give conscientious scrutiny to important cases. Morally, I'm dissatisfied because the Supreme Court has been accepted by the majority of the American people as a moral tribunal, which, I think, is shattering. The notion that the Supreme Court can say what the law *is* is acceptable to me; that they should say what the law *ought to be* horrifies me. And, politically, my impression of the Court continues to be that they seem to be prepared to rule with the notion

that they are sort of an arm of the legislature, notwithstanding what Frankfurter and a lot of other people wrote to the contrary.

It has settled into that posture, and that includes the conservatives of the Court, to the extent that they are willing to mitigate the passion for activism that characterized the Warren Court but are *not* willing to take it back substantially in a different direction. Ed Muskie, on my *Firing Line* program, pointing out the appalling ignorance of the American people, showed a poll that had been taken by his committee which showed that 65 percent of the American people believe that the Supreme Court is an arm of Congress. And I said, of course, it's the other way around.

CLR: You seem to be opposed to the practice of the judicially applied remedy. With something like school desegregation, what remedy would you suggest instead?

Buckley: It was not contemplated that the illegalization of compulsory segregation should lead to the illegalization of uni-racial schools if they merely reflected the incidence of residential racial patterns. One is left with the desire for effective legislation freezing the role of the courts past the point taken at *Brown v. Board of Education*, but short of the bureaucratizing of the judges, whose decisions in Richmond, Charlotte, and Detroit triggered the convulsion of 1972. But I think probably the bulk of the writing I have done in opposition to the Supreme Court's decisions have to do with criminal jurisprudence. At least, when I look for reforms, that's what I concentrate on.

CLR: What reforms would you recommend?

Buckley: Well, I judge the effective repeal of the Fifth Amendment, as presently used, to be the single most important procedural reform designed to rescue the adversary process from discredit.

CLR: But isn't protection from self-incrimination a major tenet of our legal process?

Buckley: We don't want to compel testimony, but somebody's refusal to testify ought to be a fact that can be commented on in front of a jury. Besides, illegal police practices would still be prohibited by the remaining amendments.

CLR: What are your views concerning the rights of defendants in other, earlier steps in the process of criminal procedure, for instance, the *Miranda* and *Mapp* decisions?

Buckley: Well, I certainly don't approve of *Miranda* or *Mapp*. I agree with the Chief Justice of California who said evidence is evidence irrespective of how it was secured. *Miranda* and its constellation have done more than anything since the invention of human verbosity to delay, prolong, and complicate criminal trials.

CLR: How would you remedy the situation?
Buckley: To prosecute the man who violates the Fourth Amendment. Send him to jail. But it takes a high form of irrationality, as it is practiced in America, to say that when the defendant is guilty, you punish him, but if he is guilty, and the policeman is also guilty, you release both of them.

CLR: The trouble with that view is that few if any such prosecutions of police took place between 1948 and 1962, and the Supreme Court was finally driven to use exclusion of illegally obtained evidence as the only visible tool to affect police behavior. However, to shift the focus a bit, how do you account for current failures of the American system of criminal justice to prosecute criminals speedily, and avoid plea bargaining, while also protecting the rights of the accused?
Buckley: There you must examine the role of the state. There is no plausible excuse for the state except to defend the individual. The individual having been violated, the state asserts the claims of the individual dead, maimed, or deprived. Obviously the claims of the innocent, mistaken for the transgressor, are as great as those of the victim, which is the reason for the adversary process. But the rhetoric of civil liberties during the past fifteen years has concerned itself almost exclusively with the claims of the accused, in disregard of the claims of the victim, and that is perversion. And it is indeed significant that the most prestigious civil rights organization in the country, or should I say the world, gave more attention in 1976 to the right of a Utah killer not to get executed, even though he wanted to be executed, than to the millions of people throughout America who, every day, are deprived of their life, liberty, and property by a criminal class that enjoys permanent predatory rights to mug, rape, and kill.

Why are things so bad? For one thing, the prisons are full, and there isn't any room for extra people. So when anybody who has done anything less than, say, torture his grandmother to death, comes before a judge, the judge tends to just shove the case to one side, grant continuance after continuance, and eventually the case, if not formally dismissed, sort of dies from attrition.

CLR: What do you think can be done to break this pattern?
Buckley: There is an urgent need to clear the decks. A good place to start is by easing away from judicial concern over so-called "victimless crimes." But since we know nothing about rehabilitation, and since we have irrefutable evidence

that recidivism is responsible for a huge percentage of crime, we are faced with a problem: How should we deal with a repeat offender found guilty of a second violent crime?

CLR: What sort of victimless crimes would you want to see decriminalized?
Buckley: I oppose expending heavy prosecutorial or police effort on combatting gambling offenses, or prostitution that does not create criminal acts. I also oppose prosecution of homosexual adults for engaging in consensual sexual conduct. I also favor protecting employment rights for homosexuals, but not in the kind of categorical way that has been proposed, as also for the ERA.

CLR: You mean a gay employment rights bill, as the ones proposed in Dade County, Florida, or New York City?
Buckley: Precisely. I believe in civil rights for homosexuals, but in doing so, I do not find myself committed to the proposition that there are no circumstances under which an employer ought to be allowed to discriminate against homosexuals.

CLR: What are some examples where you would consider it legitimate to take homosexuality into account in a hiring decision? Fire Department? School teacher?
Buckley: In the school setting, where the situation warrants it, as where you had a special class or a special school for slightly troubled young people. If you had a boy or a girl put into such a school because they couldn't adapt in a regular school, owing to psychological difficulties, I would insist upon calling for normality in that setting. Some years ago, there was a guy who had a camp for troubled boys, in Connecticut, with about fourteen or fifteen troubled children. He was a sort of lay psychologist, deeply beloved of all the neighborhood. He had wigwams for the boys, they made their fires, and one day, one of the boys came back home and said to his mother, "Why is Dr. so and so a pig?" Well, anyway it turned out that he was sodomizing the boys regularly. So he was brought to trial, and he insisted that this was part of his therapy. The local liberals supported him on the grounds that this was experimental therapy. He was sentenced and went to jail (for about three hours, as I recall), but that points up the kind of situation in which society has the duty to insist upon protection of troubled youngsters.

CLR: Let's turn for a moment to some underlying sources that you draw on for your beliefs about liberty in modern society. When you think about classic writings on liberty, whose ideas are central to your thinking about the individual and the state?

Buckley: I don't really think any single work is central, because there are none that strike me as having the ideal blend. The position I settled on about ten years ago is expressed as a presumption in favor of liberty for the private sector, and I tend to find excesses in the major theorists on that notion. I don't like the social contract people, for various reasons. It strikes me that there's a hard, despotic, and elitist thread in Plato. Rousseau is a schematic. John Stuart Mill is an epistemological pessimist. Sumner and Marx are Anarchists.

CLR: How about Burke?

Buckley: Well Burke is not primarily thought of as a philosopher of freedom. I think of him as a philosopher of order, a philosopher of the complete man, arguing for organic rather than abstract arrangements. I lean very heavily on him. But there isn't anybody who strikes me as having said everything that needs to be said about liberty in the mid-twentieth century, given our experiences.

CLR: If you think about recent writers who have dealt with dilemmas of liberty and the modern state, who are some of the people that you admire?

Buckley: Well, I admire James Burnham. I admire Robert Nisbet. I admire Russell Kirk. I admire Harry Jaffa. I admire, with reservations, Frank Meyer. I admire Whittaker Chambers, but, there again, it might be that in these people I have in mind certain passages in certain books. So there isn't anybody around of whom I can say, "This guy's analysis is exactly like my own." That is one reason why I edited a book for the Heritage Series on conservative thought.

CLR: I was interested in whether you would mention Ernest van den Haag, whom you quote often.

Buckley: I would include him especially for his pragmatic wisdom. He is interested in that which works, rather than that which is aprioristic.

CLR: Would you comment on some of your early books that dealt with civil liberties issues, so that our readers might get your present view of your previous writings? Let's start with *God and Man at Yale*. What do you think about that book in terms of academic freedom issues since the time that you wrote that, almost twenty years ago?

Buckley: As for *God and Man at Yale*, I'm sure there are passages in it which, for stylistic reasons among others, would be most embarrassing if reiterated right now. But I haven't changed my position that a college, to the extent that one focuses on the teaching part of a college, ought to be animated by certain values. The extent to which there are differences in what is taught there is an expression of pedagogical security, related to Thomas Jefferson's notions that those that disagree should be able to do so. The fact that they can state their disagreement with serenity, he said, is testimony to the resolution of free men. By which he meant that it's testimony to the fact that people reject what they say. They have made a precommitment to that which is right and that which is wrong. I would withhold any financial contributions or expressions of support, and would even campaign aggressively against any university I had attended that had more than a fair share of professors who taught error. A few for the purpose of piquancy, like Herbert Aptheker, would be all right. But only a few.

So I continue now as I did then to reject the theory of academic freedom as expounded by such as John Dewey and Henry Steele Commager. I have no apologies for stating that disagreement in my book although I am sure that the statement of it was extremely callow. I was twenty-three-years-old in those days, and I'm sure there isn't a paragraph in that book that I wouldn't weep at the rereading of. But, it would be less in what I said than in the way I said it.

CLR: I'd love to review some of your other books but probably we should return to the 1970s now. I'm curious to get your reaction to last year's Nixon-Frost conversations. Do you think it was proper for Nixon to reap such profits from recounting what most Americans believe to be a betrayal of his oath of office and a clear violation of the law?

Buckley: Is it implicitly charged that Nixon should have done it for nothing? He was not only deposed from office, losing salary and most perquisites. He was also disbarred. He is sued by every ideological ambulance chaser in the country. People who stumble into a pothole on the DMZ in 1990 will end up suing Richard Nixon. Is it really a valid cause of resentment that he should be paid money which could never begin to pay the cost of his endless fight to present his case to history?

CLR: I suppose that line of reasoning follows from your approval of Ford's pardon of Nixon.

Buckley: I called it an act of charity and prudence. I think that Nixon's conduct was punished. And, I call it an act of prudence for the reason that when Nixon went out, there were a considerable number of Americans, 25 or 30 percent is probably a safe figure, who felt that he'd been railroaded out of office. Indeed, he was guilty of certain infractions of the positive law, but those infractions were in no sense different from those of which his predecessors were regularly guilty. If it had gone to trial, it would have taken a year's preparation, during which there would have been a considerable mobilization of Nixon supporters, and he would have had the best trial lawyer available.

Imagine him with Edward Bennett Williams defending him, and the verdict, whether it went for or against him, would have left us worse off than we were by an act of presidential commutation which presupposes guilt. So, now you say he's guilty and we're not going to send him to jail. But, there would have been a highly divided and very nearly mutinous resentment by a great many people in America.

CLR: That interests me because, if I had my ideal scenario, I would have thought that bringing it out in a forum like the Senate, which would have allowed for confrontation, would have shown that what Mr. Nixon did in the cover-up was *not* what any president previously had done. In the case of Nixon, wasn't the ultimate crime that he engaged in the deception of the American people?
Buckley: You mean as far as I'm concerned?

CLR: Yes.
Buckley: Well, I'll tell you what offends me. You see, you are a sculptural polemicist, and so am I, and Edward Bennett Williams is worth a thousand dollars an hour on the free market, and he's worth it because, to quote Plato, "He can make the good case bad and the bad case good."

All I'm saying is that by no means would I—or Lloyd's of London—have given heavy odds on the conviction of Richard Nixon. I happen to think that Angela Davis was clearly guilty, on the basis of the evidence. She's been acquitted, so we consider her "innocent." I'm prepared to consider people who are acquitted "innocent." I think that's a civil obligation. But in my private mind, I think she's guilty. A lot of people would consider Nixon innocent if found guilty, and guilty if found innocent. But the historically adroit move by Ford, whether or not he knew it to be that, makes that question moot. I think it's exactly what Lincoln would have done. I think he would have had a deeper and more profound understanding of what he was up to, but I think that the instincts of Ford were sound. Sorry. I just don't see any way around that conclusion.

CLR: Actually, I happen to agree with you on that.
Buckley: You do?

CLR: Yes, I do. I agree about the inadvisability of having had a public trial of Nixon. For one thing, the length of time and the distraction from critical affairs that this would have meant in 1974–75 would have been very harmful to the country. . . .

If I may pursue a final line of questioning, since you have long preached the "politics of stability," could you in any way justify breaking a law?
Buckley: Yes. I would justify the breaking of a law that, let's say, forbade church

attendance. There is a point at which an individual can be forced to reject his society. He has at that point several options. One is to leave. The society ought not to hinder his doing so. A second is to agitate for reform. The society ought to protect his right to do so. A third is to drop out. The society ought to let him alone, to the extent it is able to disengage reciprocating gears. A fourth is to disobey the laws or to revolutionize. In that event, the society ought to imprison, exile, or execute him.

CLR: But didn't the United States emerge out of the ideas and actions of revolutionaries, and didn't they practice physical agitation with disruptions such as the Boston Tea Party?

Buckley: Simply because in the light of history we decide to interpret a particular historical act of civil disobedience as an act of heroism, we musn't forget that as of that moment, it was nevertheless an act of disobedience. It was proper that it should have been punished by the British. Look, a lot of the laws under which I labor are lousy laws, but so long as I live in a free society that is democratically governed, I have very little alternative except to obey these laws or to declare myself an exile from that society.

CLR: It is a liberal tenet that society can preserve its free and democratic condition by allowing competing points of view to be forcefully presented, in the classic John Stuart Mill assumption, that the good will win out in the long run. I doubt whether that idea thrills you.

Buckley: Exactly. What is apparent to one man is not necessarily apparent to the majority. Hitler came to power democratically. It's a nineteenth-century myth to confide totally in the notion that the majority won't be attracted to the wrong guy. The whole idea of civilization is little by little to discard certain points of view as uncivilized; it is impossible to discover truths without discovering that their opposites are in error. In a John Stuart Mill–type society—in which *any* view, for so long as it is held by so much as a single person, is considered as not yet confuted—you have total intellectual and social anarchy.

CLR: Does that include in private, too?

Buckley: If you ask simply, does the individual have the absolute right to do anything he wants in private contract with another party, my answer is: No, only the presumptive right. A sadist cannot contract to kill a masochist.

CLR: We've gone into quite a wide range of your views on issues of liberty, equality, and justice. I doubt whether anyone reading this Conversation would confuse you with a member of the ACLU National Committee. On the other hand, our discussion would also help them not to confuse you with a John Bircher, or the late J. Edgar Hoover either. It might also help them understand those points at which libertarians and civil libertarians are in agreement.

Is there a parting comment you'd like to offer?

Buckley: Yes. I thank you for your patience and hope you concur with me in the proposition that the reader should be indulgent on reading extemporaneous interviews which leave so much to be desired in the way of form, clarity, and precision.

Airborne Again

Jeff Hammond / 1978

From *Motor Boating & Sailing*, November 1978. © Jeff Hammond. Reprinted with permission of the author.

One wonders how it is that a man as busy as William F. Buckley Jr., a man who has a weekly TV program, who writes a thrice-weekly newspaper column, edits a fortnightly magazine, publishes one or two books a year, lectures extensively, and is the chairman of a large media company, among other things, ever finds the time to go cruising. But if we mortals stand in awe of Bill Buckley's prodigious output, to him it is simple.

"Deadlines," he says, "I have deadlines for everything. I find them liberating. Don't you?"

It's pure Buckley. Deadlines, the curse enslaving every editor, are liberating to the busiest one of all.

This summer alone Buckley has cruised the Bahamas, the Greek Isles, Long Island Sound, and as you read this he is in the South Pacific, cruising near Fiji. How does he find the time? Like so much of what he does, it is rooted in a basic philosophical approach.

"There is never a good time for a busy man to take a vacation. And since there is never a good time, he might as well take it whenever he wants."

And wherever he wants, in the case of Buckley. This time, Bill decided that a late spring cruise from Miami across the Stream to Cat Cay and Bimini would make for a soothing escape from the hurly-burly. It would be the last escape aboard *Cyrano* before he sold her. For the cruise, Bill and his wife Pat invited along four long-time friends and cruising companions. Although I had been across this stretch of water twenty-five or thirty times, it was my first sail with WFB, so a little orientation was in order.

Although Buckley travels fast, he by no means travels light. He arrived at *Cyrano*'s dock on Biscayne Bay with a cart piled high with suitcases, leather valises, attache cases, a typewriter, his sextant case—everything except a steamer trunk. It was a gangplank scene out of F. Scott Fitzgerald, and I felt negligent with only a small seabag in hand for the four-day cruise.

More orientation. When Buckley sails with his friends, their conversation is peppered with abbreviations and acronyms. Such as Bill's occasional reference to "BO." Buckley talking about BO? With some attentive listening, you learn that "BO" refers to the "Big One"—his 1975 transatlantic crossing.

Then there's BWT. Not a fancy sandwich, but "Buckley Watch Time." Aboard *Cyrano* it is held in even higher esteem than GMT. Upon stepping aboard, the Buckley regulars automatically move their watches one hour ahead.

To me, at least, it soon became apparent that BWT is the cause of all manner of confusion. When working our celestial sights, for example, ZT (Zone Time) must be converted to GMT, then all recalculated if someone forgets BWT has thrown everything off one hour. Anything done on shore, of course, like making a restaurant before closing time or an airport before flight time, must all be adjusted for Buckley Watch Time. About the only person on board who didn't know this was the new hand who helped with the cooking—dinner was never on time, (always exactly one hour late Eastern Daylight Savings Time).

Now, why would a man whose whole life's endeavor has been to clarify matters choose to obscure the time?

"There are two great advantages to BWT. First, cocktail hour comes one hour sooner. Second, you get an extra hour of sleep before the sun hits you in the eye." Who can argue with the logic of that?

Buckley has an intense interest in the discipline of celestial navigation. It is fitting. After all, his taste in music runs to Bach and he plays the harpsichord; he's a student of the classics, and he will quote St. Thomas Aquinas at the drop of a winch handle.

So the sea buoy off Key Biscayne had only just passed astern when Bill emerged from the companionway, sextant in hand. Throughout the cruise, he would practice and refine his technique of celestial, both ashore and aboard.

In mid-Gulf-Stream, a Loran-A fix placed *Cyrano* two miles west of Buckley's celestial LOP. But he was unfazed by this discrepancy. "It just proves you can't trust electronics."

Mrs. Buckley flashes a knowing wink, indicating she neither trusts electronics nor Bill's celestial.

"Oh ye of little faith," Bill says. "Continue to make fun and I'll set a course to windward."

And that is the ultimate rebuke aboard the genteel *Cyrano*. But a threat that has rarely, if ever, been carried out aboard the beamy, shoal-draft schooner, I might add.

If you have read Bill's book *Airborne*, then you know that his fondness for electronics rivals his feeling for Chairman Mao. And no wonder. Aboard *Cyrano*, electrical gadgets are as reliable as NOAA weather reports.

My first inkling that something was amiss was when two of the guests stepped aboard toting voltmeters. Now I certainly believe in being prepared for a cruise, and often bring rigging tools, a safety harness, a float coat, foul weather gear, etc. I've never thought of a voltmeter, but aboard *Cyrano*, it was a more common appendage than a rigging knife.

And no wonder. During the course of the cruise: the shore power cable wouldn't conduct electricity, the battery in the Whaler went dead, the Kenyon worked sporadically, and the radar—which had never worked before—inexplicably worked fine.

The marine environment aboard *Cyrano* was beyond the engineering capabilities of America's best electronics minds, but Buckley and his crew coped with rare resourcefulness. With all the dogged determination of Sherlock Holmes, they would track down the offending wire, not with a bloodhound but with a voltmeter. And if no reasonable solution surfaced, Buckley was amused and not a little proud: "This boat defies deductive logic!"

On that point, there can be no debate. For example, the winches on board are made by five different manufacturers, each requiring a separate handle. The accommodations are more than egalitarian. The owner's and guest cabins are roughly the same size and share a common head, while the crew's quarters are larger and have a private head. And then there were those three Winslow life rafts strapped down on the foredeck, just in case *Cyrano* ever stopped defying deductive logic.

Early on, I wagered one free haul-out that the rafts wouldn't work. It was a safe bet because: 1) they are Winslow rafts, and 2) they hadn't been inspected for several years. There were no takers. But then there were no believers, either. Mrs. Buckley, in particular, seemed to have great faith in the rafts, probably due to the fact they are not electrical. By and by, one was selected for a test.

When it inflated, I, too, began to believe that everything aboard defied deductive logic. There was merriment all around, not so much because a piece of equipment had performed its function, but because the Editor had been proven wrong.

But twenty minutes later the raft was flat. The manual pump was, of course, rusted solid and its inflation tube had rotted off. Leave it to Buckley to find a silver lining. He blew through the tube and pronounced it fit for service in mock delight.

It wasn't long before I discovered what was really in most of those suitcases that were lugged aboard. Like so many things with Bill Buckley, appearances are often deceiving.

The suitcases held mail—pounds and pounds of it. At odd hours during the cruise, WFB would disappear below to empty one after another of paperwork. And that, of course, is the real secret of how this busy man gets so much done—he works during vacation!

As *Cyrano* sailed through the indigo blue waters of the Stream, the ship's tape deck played classical music while Buckley addressed his Dictaphone ("My secretary requires Bach in the background when I dictate.") One by one, he answered letters from those high in the government, those formerly high in the government (and now in the slammer), and members of an aroused citizenry, like a doctor who took exception to *Airborne*:

> Dear Mr. Buckley: *Airborne* is totally without merit, except for its title which, although clever, is a misnomer, since a substantial part of the trip was under power, with barrels of fuel lashed on deck, no less. The book has no substance, no message, no entertainment, no value. Your publisher should be more discriminating.
> Sincerely yours,
> Louis E. Prickman, M.D.

> Dear Doc: Please call me Bill. Can I call you by your nickname?
> Cordially,
> WFB

One evening we anchored off the leeward shore of Gun Cay for dinner. As always, the food was superb, and as always, we ate by candlelight. However, I was never quite sure if that was out of a sense of romanticism or to conserve the ship's batteries.

At about 2000 hours, we hoisted anchor to make our way back to Cat Cay for the night. It was pitch black. The crew was fumbling in the darkened midships cockpit for something. Bill was aft on the wheel. All of a sudden I heard oaths the likes of which could never be uttered aboard *Cyrano*. Just as I was thinking, "No one on this boat would swear like that," I saw that, indeed, the obscenities were coming from another boat.

The one we were about to ram amidships. Bill put the wheel hard over, but a few seconds later *Cyrano*'s sixty tons crunched into a small, beautiful wood schooner. Her bobstay was carried away, her rail was cracked, and—we found out later—a bulkhead was moved about an inch to port.

The schooner had been anchored in the dark with no visible anchor light, a sitting duck for any boat making toward the Gun Cay beacon. We circled, traded insurance information, determined that neither boat was taking on water, and returned to Cat Cay.

The next day we saw what was nearly an identical schooner anchored in daylight off the southern tip of Key Biscayne. I sidled over to Bill and asked, "Do you think she's fair game?" The moment I said it, I regretted it. How would he take such an impertinent remark after the accident the night before?

Buckley turned toward me and flashed his famous smile. "Shall we give them a taste of our bowsprit?"

We docked overnight at the marina, on Cat Cay, which was crowded with Feadships, Bertrams, and Hatteras motor yachts. As we powered out in the morning, the docks of those grand yachts were lined with owners and guests waving cheerfully. I asked Bill if he always got this kind of adulation.

"Notice," he intoned, "that they're all clutching their insurance policies."

But if yachtsmen everywhere know Bill Buckley, so do Customs agents. Back in Miami, we tied up at midnight and a Customs inspector came on board and pleasantly recalls a run-in with WFB five years ago.

"Remember the time you were bringing in those Cuban cigars? That was when the government's policy was against Cuba and you were writing all those editorials against Castro. How could you do that? You, of all people?"

"Well, you see," said Buckley, "I didn't want the Communists to have them."

Although much has been written by and about Bill's sailing experiences, little has ever been written about Mrs. Buckley, who is aboard for most of his cruises. For those who don't read the New York society pages, just let it be said that Mrs. Buckley is one of the most fashionable and chic ladies around. Yet aboard the boat she is a willing and able crew, helping with the sails, docking, and any minor adversities, as well as a wizard in the galley. She is as good on a boat as any of the women I had crewed with to Jamaica or Bermuda and who, without exception, performed heroically on long, wet, miserable races.

I wanted to convey to her that observation, so I said at the end of the cruise that I'd be pleased to count her among my crew anytime, because I knew she'd come through when the chips were down.

"Aboard *Cyrano*, dearie," she told me, "the chips are always down."

People have asked what it is really like to cruise with Bill Buckley. Well, it's like it ought to be. It's also like being home on the range, where there's never a discouraging word . . . and never a dull moment.

Bookviews Talks to William F. Buckley Jr.

Ralph Tyler / 1978

From *Bookviews*, October 1978. Reprinted with the permission of R. R. Bowker LLC. Copyright © 1978.

William F. Buckley Jr. knows exactly what he'll be doing at 4:30 p.m. Swiss time next January 16. After a day recovering from jet lag, he'll be sitting down at his typewriter at the ski resort of Rougemont and beginning his third thriller starring Blackford Oakes, boyish cold warrior. Since it will take him approximately a month to write, and since it is bound to be a best seller—like the earlier accounts of Oakes's derring-do, *Saving the Queen* (1976) and this year's *Stained Glass*—it is only charitable to reassure grudging fellow authors that Buckley is miserable when he writes. That, he explains, is why he writes so fast: to get *on* with it.

"If it weren't for the fact, that I'm paid for it I would never write as much as the 350,000 words a year I average," he said. "Everyone has bills."

Perhaps he noted a glint of disbelief in *Bookviews*' eyes. The surroundings were Capuan: terraces carpeted with flowers fell away to the sapphire of a swimming pool and the agate blue of Long Island Sound. Even the scents that lingered on the Buckley veranda were choice: of ivy, salt air, geranium, and (from the goblets of iced tea Pat, his wife, had brought from the house) mint.

"Couldn't you imagine reducing your scale of living?" asked *Bookviews*, gazing across a sweep of lawn to a neighboring estate in the Stamford, Connecticut, compound the Buckleys call home when they are not in their Park Avenue apartment. Fearing it might have committed some form of *trahison des clercs*, *Bookviews* waited for the answer with trepidation.

"Do you mean, would I rather work hard and live well than not work hard and not live well? I would rather work hard and live well. I've got a puritanical streak that makes me work whether I like to or not, just as I exercise and watch my diet whether I like to or not."

His care has been rewarded; he'll be fifty-three on November 24 but his six-foot-one-inch frame, garbed at the moment in faded blue denim trousers and a darker blue Chemise Lacoste shirt with the ubiquitous alligator, was in athletic trim. He sails and skis and does not, in an interview, sit still for a moment. When the telephone rang, as it did frequently ("Crisis in the executive suite," he explained), he would leap up and bound into the house like a tennis ace returning a tricky serve. Even when the phone was temporarily silent, he seemed primed to move. Part of the torture of writing for him must be the need to sit at it for longish stretches. Thinking on his feet comes naturally to him; one reason, no doubt, why he is such a skillful debater. And debate, too, is a species of sport—zinging the telling argument into your opponent's far court.

"George Will said recently that for two mornings a week he was a happy man—those were the mornings he had his column to write. I write three columns a week ['On the Right,' syndicated in 350 papers], and those are the mornings I *don't* look forward to."

The phone rang again and he vanished. When he came back, he picked up the thread: "I get pleasure out of *having* written. I like to paint. I don't like writing, but there is a net satisfaction when it's done."

He writes his Blackford Oakeses during an annual Swiss ski holiday. To keep at them despite encroaching ennui, he maintains a rigid schedule. The mornings are devoted to his duties as editor of the *National Review* and to his column, the early afternoons are for skiing, from 4:30 to 7 p.m. he edits the previous day's work and then drives the narrative ahead, and the evenings "are for my wife's activities."

"I write every day without excuse. If you put in seven days a week at 1,500 words a day, in five weeks you have a book. Lots of people—Georges Simenon and Earl Stanley Gardner, for example—wrote much faster than that. Gardner dictated his work, didn't he? At least I can type."

Buckley says he takes longer over his essay and article collections that G. P. Putnam's Sons has been publishing every other year for nearly twenty years. The latest, out this month, is *A Hymnal: The Controversial Arts*, which Buckley spent more hours on than on *Stained Glass* and *Saving the Queen* together. The time is consumed trying to integrate the various pieces, only about 15 percent of which were written originally for *National Review*. "The difference between that and working on the novels," Buckley said, "is the difference between starting to do a mosaic *ex nihilo* and being given a number of pieces and instructed to do a mosaic. It's largely a negative exercise: you know you're going to eliminate 600,000 words. The creative part is developing what is left and determining how you are going to balance it."

A particularly amusing article in *Hymnal* is "The Selling of Your Own Books: A Bill of Rights." It tells about the affronts Buckley has suffered on talk shows trying to promote his books in the teeth of uninterested hosts. But of all the articles in the new collection, Buckley seems proudest of "At Sea," an excerpt from *Airborne*, his 1976 book on sailing, which appeared first in the *New Yorker*. "Many people who read it there were probably unfamiliar with me except as a stereotype. It was the most successful article I ever wrote in terms of letters from readers. I think it was because it deals with a father and son relationship [Christopher, the Buckleys' son and only child, was along on one of the voyages]. Everybody either is a father or has been a son, or is a daughter or a mother. I imagine that was it."

As a rule, said Buckley, the audience for his fiction is bigger than for his non-fiction—but *Airborne* was the exception. It went into eight printings in two months and topped 100,000 sales. At the time of the interview, *Stained Glass* was well entrenched on the best seller list at 80,000. Sales of his other books, he says, range from 30,000 to 50,000. Although, like other authors, he knows he has some readers who will read everything he writes, he tends, he says, to have discrete audiences: "some who read my fiction, some who read my nonfiction, some who watch me on television, some who read my magazine."

How did Buckley get caught up in thriller writing after decades of largely polemical nonfiction, starting with *God and Man at Yale* in 1951, with occasional ventures into reminiscence, such as his *United Nations Journal: A Delegate's Odyssey* (1974)? The suggestion he write a novel, says Buckley, came out of the blue from Samuel Vaughan, president of Doubleday Publishing Co., halfway through lunch at the Italian restaurant Buckley favors near the *National Review* offices in New York.

Vaughan, however, remembers it differently, but, as he told *Bookviews*, "publishers are as good at their kind of fiction as authors." Wine had flowed during the substantial lunch and there was no tape recorder to set the record straight. Here, anyway, is Vaughan's version:

"I had known Buckley for a long time and always found him fun to deal with. We never approached him to write a book for Doubleday as long as he was with a single publisher, but when he began writing for other publishers, we suggested lunch. Buckley informed us that when someone other than his regular publisher comes to him with an idea he likes, he's free to do it. I was prepared with two ideas for nonfiction books, but Buckley brushed them aside like crumbs from the table. So I asked: 'What would you like to write next that you are not now writing?' A novel, he said. What kind? I asked. Like Forsyth, he said. I thought of Galsworthy's *Forsyte Saga*, but it turned out he meant Frederick Forsyth, who wrote *The Day of the Jackal*. He wanted to write an entertainment, a thriller.

"I told him," Vaughan continued, "that I'd like to see a thriller about a CIA agent in the conditions of today, when he doesn't feel he has the appreciation behind him he used to have. Buckley took the notion and decided to put it back in time."

Buckley said he was wary after the lunch because he wasn't confident he could execute a novel and William Safire had just had a finished manuscript turned down as not good enough. "In fact what happened was Watergate; there was no big market for a pro-Nixon book," Buckley said. To protect himself against that kind of denouement, Buckley worked out a fail-safe contract. By its terms, he would write one hundred pages for one-third of his $36,000 advance; at that point either he or the publisher could call the whole thing off, but if they agreed to go ahead, he would be guaranteed the full advance for the completed manuscript, no matter what second thoughts Doubleday might have. As we now know, he needn't have worried.

The people at Doubleday gave him a few pointers, and he read *Writing a Novel* by John Braine, the English writer best known for his *Room at the Top*. "Barnaby Conrad told me the other day that he had read Braine's book, too, and found it more useful than any other book on novel writing."

What had he learned from it?

"The only thing I can remember is that Braine said readers will accept one major coincidence, but not more than one." The one Buckley allowed himself, he said, was to have both the hero of *Saving the Queen* and his antagonist, Peregrine Kirk, chosen to test their countries' planes at an air show.

Buckley appears to be having fun with the name Peregrine, since Peregrine Worsthorne, the London *Daily Telegraph* columnist who leans, if anything, even further to the right than Buckley, is the only well-known bearer of that name, redolent of snuff boxes and the quizzing glass. Similarly, he models the father of a Soviet spy in his second novel on his friend the late Vladimir Nabokov ("I told him I was going to do it"). Prankishly, too, he puts echoes of himself in his novels, as in this description in *Stained Glass* of one Razzia, "whose mannerisms were widely known and widely caricatured because of his depressing ubiquity. He was a syndicated columnist, a television host, an author, editor of his own magazine, and now announced he would also write novels!"

But Buckley isn't only playing games with his thrillers, although he assured *Bookviews* that, regardless of his puritanical streak, he sees nothing wrong with writing simply "for the sake of entertaining oneself and the reader." Both books are set in the iciest days of the Cold War in the 1950s and represent a vigorous defense of the CIA—under something of a cloud, at least among liberals, when the novels were written.

Buckley, however, denies he intended a CIA apologia, pointing out that the investigation of the agency by the Rockefeller panel, which forms a prologue and epilogue to *Saving the Queen,* only occurred after he had written the main body of the novel. The frame, therefore, is an afterthought. His real motive for using the CIA, he says, was to draw upon his own experience—"I lubricate better in reality." Buckley himself joined the CIA in October 1951, about the same time as Oakes, and underwent the training he describes in *Queen.* Unlike his hero, however, Buckley got out the following May, bored, he said, with being a deep cover agent, which meant that he had to occupy some apparently conventional walk of life. Whatever he did he did in Mexico, and that has a certain symbolic significance inasmuch as Buckley's father, a Texas lawyer turned oilman, was expelled from Mexico during a revolutionary upheaval four years before Buckley was born. The father's direct confrontation with revolutionists must have played at least some part in his abiding hatred for the left, which his ten children have by and large inherited.

For his first novel Buckley also made use of his experience at a Catholic boarding school in England he attended in 1938–39. "When we were on the way to my school I remember my father told the driver to stop near a crowd at the airport. There was Chamberlain with his umbrella, coming back from Munich with 'peace in our time.'" Oakes also attends a British boarding school, where he is cruelly thrashed.

So heartfelt is Buckley's description of the caning that *Bookviews* couldn't forego asking it if had happened to him. "I was never caned, but I probably should have been," he said.

The Buckley children had been happy being tutored at the family estate at Sharon, Connecticut, when Buckley Sr. got it into his head that they weren't speaking distinctly. "He was slightly idiosyncratic and hyperbolic and remarked that ten years had gone by since he had understood anything said by any of his ten children. He didn't think he should strain to hear what other people are saying. In his view, only the English knew how to open their mouths, so we were sent to school there."

In *Queen,* Oakes finally is avenged for his British thrashing by going to bed with the British Queen—Caroline, not the present incumbent. It may have been this episode that caused Buckley's friend Clare Booth Luce to call the novel "a male chauvinist piece of imagination without parallel in fiction."

Did Buckley agree?

"I'd find it very dangerous to disagree with Clare," he smiled. "No, I don't think it's male chauvinistic at all, because the queen is such an independent person. It's a succubus, not an incubus relation. *She* was the seducer."

There are other sex scenes in the novel, including some rather perfunctory rites with Sally, Oakes's girl (he refers in one instance to their "copulation,"
surely a cold word to choose). More eyebrow-raising is a scene in a deluxe Pari-
sian *maison de joie*, where Oakes and a buddy are entertained in the same upstairs
room by two *cocottes*. There is an "obligatory" feeling about the writing of these
passages, *Bookviews* suggested.

"It is interesting that you used the word obligatory," Buckley said, "because
when I was discussing the novel with Nabokov he said I would have to put in the
OSS—the Obligatory Sex Scenes."

Asked if he had read spy novels of the old school by writers like E. Phillips
Oppenheim and John Buchan, Buckley said, "When I was a boy, I read a lot of
that stuff, but I grew tired of it about as suddenly as I was turned off comics."

How political should thrillers be? Could they be set as well in a mythical
kingdom?

"As a rule of thumb, readers desire one or the other of the contesting figures
in a thriller to ride to a fall, to catch or get away. If you cause the reader not to
care who fails, the book can become too attenuated. Le Carré with his anti-hero
is tending to move in that direction totally."

Among contemporary novelists outside the spy genre, Buckley particularly es-
teems Walker Percy. "To this admirer, Percy's *Love in the Ruins* seems the absolute
American counterpart of Orwell's *1984*. If we go down, that's the way we're going
to go. Percy is a terrifically funny man, deeply educated, a superb writer. I think
he did there what Randall Jarrell did in *Pictures from an Institution*—show the fa-
natical extremes of liberal thought."

Buckley's years as an interviewer on his television show *Firing Line* stood him
in good stead when *Bookviews* groped toward a question about his general literary
preferences. "You should ask me, 'Is there anyone among those whom you admire
who is not generally admired?'" he prompted crisply, and then answered himself:
"Chesterton, now out of favor; and I have a great admiration for Kipling. The success of *The Godfather* robbed Mario Puzo of the kind of critical acclaim he deserves. If you sell a million copies, you can't be thought of as a serious writer."

Were there any in the liberal camp he thought were good writers? *Bookviews*
next had the temerity to inquire. "Philip Roth and Norman Mailer. And Gore
Vidal—in his essays—has great style. I don't think there is anyone, as Mailer used
to say, who has been elected president. I declined to participate in a *New York
Times* symposium on the greatest living writer. I think the greatest living critic is
Hugh Kenner, author of *The Pound Era*, and he says Samuel Beckett is the greatest
living writer. If I gave anyone my proxy, Kenner would have it.

"The only people I don't like are people who write badly. I think they should be doing something else. I read very slowly. If I read something badly written it troubles me. I can't, for example, read a book of Agatha Christie's—I keep gagging. It probably lies in my experience as an editor. Whatever the reason, I can read John McPhee on anything and enjoy it, but I couldn't read a biography of *me* by Agatha Christie."

The afternoon wasn't all talk. Buckley played Mozart variations on a spindly-legged 1976 Eric Herz harpischord. Dogs were admired, particularly a King Charles Spaniel named Beep because of his honking bark, and a sulky Peke in the hall was carefully avoided as Mrs. Buckley showed the house, which she had decorated in colors more Casbah than Connecticut.

Beep was held so he wouldn't chase the car in which *Bookviews* and an attractive English woman photographer finally departed. "He certainly knows the Queen's English," she remarked judiciously as they drove away. He does—but *350,000 words a year!*

William F. Buckley Jr.: Off the Firing Line

Douglas Anderson / 1983

From *ElectriCity*, November 1983. Copyright © Douglas Anderson. Reprinted with permission of the author.

Barely inside his suite (after the October evening's speech-plus-question-and-answer-period), Buckley is already removing his coat and tie, hanging up my coat, and picking up the hotel phone to order drinks for us. The photographer, Rod Brink—a young, quiet, conscientious guy who's moonlighting—shoots perhaps thirty more frames than he really *really* needs, just to hang out. Buckley is more than courteous to him. That quick, omnivorous mind lives in horror of only this: not to be able to notice things.

He eagerly hauls from his suitcase the newest practical toys: a Brother mini-typewriter approaching pocket-calculator compactness and a Walkman-style Dictaphone. I ask, "You haven't got any Bach, have you?" He hands me the earphones: A Bach aria sends me into instant recall of the first time I noticed the human being inside everyone else's opinions about WFB the political cliché. (Nearly anybody who's publicly visible lives in a similar cartoon of only-what's-newsworthy flatness.)

He brings to the qualities that attract close friends (as distinct from any other motive) a religious loyalty to music and particularly to Bach ("the greatest genius who ever lived")—though his interest also reaches out to, for instance, Cole Porter. He plugs me in, takes care that I can hear, that it's not too loud.

A kindness.

Ah, yes, *those* qualities. Example number two: He wants to know what publication I'm representing. I describe *ElectriCity*, and he immediately recounts an experience with Pat, his wife, in the Philippines. They visited President Marcos:

". . . Every time he (Marcos) asked, he asked a question which showed he had a certain knowledge of my life . . . I found out he'd been reading an issue of *W* featuring my wife, Pat. The whole research, you see, on me, was an issue of *W*. Then he took a shine to us, so he decided to have a state party for us that night. He rounded up all the troops, the ambassadors and so on, and eighty entertainers, and they all did their acrobatics and their country dances and so forth and so on. Then all of a sudden at the end they all formed a semi-circle like a half moon around me and started to sing 'Deep in the Heart of Texas.'

"So I nudged Pat: 'What's *that* all about?'

" 'Shut up, I'll tell you later.'

"In that article in *W*, they'd gotten me mixed up with my father, and they said, 'Mr. Buckley (meaning me) was born and raised in Texas.' So President Marcos said, 'Now, at the end, we'll surprise him and do 'Deep in the Heart of Texas.' I originally didn't make the connection at all. Terrific!

"So you see, they (publications like *W* and *ElectriCity*) get around. They get around."

Example number three: I've asked him if there's anywhere he particularly wants to go, anything he particularly wants to do, during the remainder of his life.

"I wrote a piece for *Esquire* on that. It said, 'I haven't been to heaven'... I have no particular curiosity to see any particular part of the world. If I'm near the Great Barrier Reef, I'd like to dive there, because they say it's terrific. I intend to sail in 1985 from Hawaii to Auckland. And write another book, on that trip ...'"

He pauses, and is suddenly *lit up*—inspired in mid-sentence, beaming a nearly naive exuberance: "I suppose I *could* have the ambition of doing a lobotomy on Andropov, and winning the Lenin Peace Prize! I hadn't thought of that. See, that's a *hell* of an idea! I will say that that catalyzed in your presence ... wouldn't that be fascinating! Sneak him off and do a lobotomy, and then he goes back and starts acting ... all ... like the flower child in the Kremlin. You could do a better short story on that than I could. That's more up your alley.

"More up your alley," he laughs aloud. Whether or not William Buckley was a merry quipster in another life, he is in this one—even unto gleefully tossing up my hippie past one more time. He refers to my departing New York City after our first meeting: "I remember your going off to hitchhike back to Denver. You were so stoical about it."

I remark that there's little profit in being anything *else* about those things and immediately turn "the road" back to why William Buckley's on it.

Tonight, for instance, it's been a ballroom in the young, upper-class Mandalay Four Seasons Hotel in Dallas. Mostly older people—eight each at six round tables. The theme of their all-day seminar—sponsored by the Shavano Institute, headquartered in Englewood, Colorado—has been, "How Business Can Fight Back in the War of Ideas."

Two wines, with salad, baked tomatoes, snow peas, deep-fried white potatoes, and average roast beef. The guy who owns the hotel was at my table. Also in the room were high-level people in aerospace, real estate, medicine, hardware, life insurance, and precision machinery—some with international markets.

So far, that's not fair: Complete the picture with people in higher education (teachers as well as deans), a local public agency director, and a few "untitled" younger people who somehow sneaked in, mostly to hear Buckley. The group is not easily pegged "right-wing crazies." Right or wrong, they, like many other minorities, feel disenfranchised from the political machinery of their own country. Vanity is no more the motive behind their paying for and attending the full-day seminar than it would be in, say, people attending a union convention or a grassroots organizing session in Five Points. Vanity, no more than elsewhere: money, lots more.

"Bill" (as they all seem to call him) presents the crowning event of their day. He speaks for about forty minutes (in a stylistic marriage between canned and extempore), then takes questions for another twenty-five minutes (ditto).

Why is William Buckley in Dallas, Texas? To give of his time to further the cause? Prepare to run for office again? Engage in lively exchanges from which he learns and grows?

Not by his account. He's on that dreary circuit again, like a treadmill. By comparison to the super rich, he is modestly wealthy. But the needs of William Buckley's enterprises far outstrip his income. And *National Review*, his baby, still isn't breaking even. So he does it for the . . .

"Money . . . If *National Review* didn't lose its five- or six-hundred-thousand dollars a year, I would then choose to lecture ten times a year . . . I certainly wouldn't lecture forty-five times a year . . . I've been lecturing for the support of *National Review* for twenty-five years.

"I lectured eight times week before last . . . If I were playing Bach instead . . . assuming I had the stamina to play eight times the Goldberg Variations, I probably wouldn't hesitate . . .

"Nor do I deny that there are politicians who eat it up. These people give seven or eight speeches a day . . . they get tired, sure; but they enjoy it. It's never been a temptation I've ever had in my entire life. To me it's a sheer drudgery . . .

"It doesn't matter what you charge for the magazine. Twenty-five years ago, if somebody'd said to me, 'You'll be able to charge $25 (a year) for *National Review*' (we were selling it for $8 then), I would have thought, 'My god! We'll be rich!' But we continue to lose money. It's just something about general opinion: You just never quite hack it in terms of advertising. Paper's gone up 600 percent. And paying out postage, we paid $60,000 seven years ago. We paid $265,000 last year. For postage."

So he's had to become his own best fundraiser. Over and over. And, like most people with highly creative minds, William Buckley is not fond of grooves. Schedules, yes: Schedules let you get things done. Grooves, no: Repeatedly addressing groups of people who already agree with you does not add appreciably to what you know.

This also means he's not home all the time. Then how does Pat feel about that? What does she do while he's on the road?

"Well, she has a very active life in New York on all those benefit businesses she's involved with. But I was talking to Nancy Kissinger about it the other day. She said, 'Oh my god, Henry's going off to the Far East next week.' And Henry had said to me a few days before, 'I'm going off for purely commercial reasons. Because the amount of time I'm giving the Central American business, at a dollar a year, is simply taking up a lot of my productive time.' So she says, 'I just hate it when Henry goes off.' But it also gives him the capacity to be as independent as he wants . . .

"My father was missing from my own home four or five days a week . . . I simply grew up with the culture that the probabilities are very high that the husband is going to be away from the hearth a certain percentage of the time. If you actually counted the number of nights that I am at home with my wife, they're probably much higher than the number of nights that my father was home with my mother. We have two straight months of Switzerland and most of the summer. So I'm really away only when I sail and when I lecture."

How does he do it? Year in and year out: (1) *National Review*; (2) *Firing Line*, 3) a nationally syndicated newspaper column. In addition: (4) he spends two months a year in Switzerland; (5) he finds time to sail; (6) he writes books about sailing; (7) he writes novels; (8) he lectures, hopping across the country for days at a stretch like a hyperactive frog; (9) he has time to spend with people like me.

How does William F. Buckley Jr. realize the output of four or five less effective people? How does he manage time?

"It's just scheduling . . . deadlines are tremendously liberating . . . I had three deadlines this weekend. And because they simply had to be done, they were done. And if you know that you've got to phone in six columns, they get phoned in. The people I pity are not the people who have deadlines, they're the people who don't have deadlines.

"If someone says, 'Well, when you finish that book send me the manuscript and I'll look at it,' those are the people I feel sorry for. There's no pressure to finish it."

The key to time management for William F. Buckley is *deadlines*? That's all?

"Now, it's also true that there is no deadline that can't be made up to a certain level at my own convenience. For instance, I was asked weeks ago whether I would accept a proposition to do a television show in New York that would film every Tuesday afternoon at six. I said, 'You must be *crazy*; you're absolutely *nuts*; the answer is *no*.'

"As long as I produce forty-six (*Firing Line*) shows a year, I can produce with some reference to my own schedule. You can do four in two days, or six in three days, which is rough but you can. Then you have five weeks in which you don't have to do them. Or you can write your column ahead for a week . . .

"The only deadline that requires me to be at a certain place is *National Review*, and you know I meet 75 percent of those, and those that I don't meet I can make altered provisions for, which Walter Cronkite could not. Walter Cronkite had to be there every afternoon for twenty-five years of his life at 2:30 in the afternoon. So in that sense . . . I feel almost overwhelmingly self-indulgent."

One experience he has *not* indulged (much) during the past few years is in Denver, Colorado. Several years ago at his home in Stamford, Connecticut, he remarked to me, "Denver. Ah, yes. Denver's kind of like Houston, isn't it?"

Does he still think that? And what does "Denver's like Houston" mean?

"All I can tell you is the perspective from New York, which is uninformed but superficially interesting. We tend to think of Denver and Houston as the two principal 'go-go' cities, which have increased hugely in every direction, including unpleasant directions. Crime . . .

"When I was in the broadcasting business, I was told that Denver was the toughest market to crack because they had more broadcasting stations per capita than any other city in America, including New York. And the rate of building in Denver . . . the second highest in the country, or third highest or whatever . . . you get the same statistic about Houston. You read about smog developing in Denver, and you read about smog developing in Houston. So there are those similarities."

And what does "go-go" mean?

"Dynamic."

And if William F. Buckley Jr. could play God, and wish on Denver some intelligent thing it might do, or be developing or thinking about, what might that be?

"Well, Number One, control its crime rate, and Number Two, cultivate its sense of community, which is very hard for a dynamic city to do.

"A sense of identity comes last to dynamic cities, because it's such a swirl;

New York is, of course, the famous case in point. It is often said by sociologists about New York City that it has yet to acquire a sense of identity, because the people come and go so fast . . .

"Ideally, a generation from now, you would see similarities between Houston and Denver and, say, Zurich and Frankfurt. Dynamic cities, but with a sense of the past."

Then what identifies a sense of the past? Or an identity?

"Well, probably a sense that there are people who want to continue to live there irrespective of inducements which might change day after tomorrow. One of these days there are going to be X number of people who say, 'I am a Denverite,' or 'I am a Houstonian'—not because they have a salary of 37.5 thousand dollars per year, but because Denver is *their home*. Yet my impression is, that hasn't yet happened, nor has it happened yet in a lot of California. It certainly is beginning to happen in San Francisco and in parts of Los Angeles."

Okay. Then why? What for? What is the advantage to having such an identity?

"Well, that you feel a stake in your community, and under the circumstances you are willing to sacrifice for it—which you tend less to be willing to do for a city with which your habitational flirtation is entirely adventitious.

"If tomorrow you may go somewhere else, (then you have) the kind of attachment that Army people feel for the city to which they are assigned. They know it's a three-year civil duty, and it may be San Antonio. And the next year it's Kansas City. And the next year somewhere else."

Though William Buckley is one of ten children, he himself has only one—his son Christopher. The opportunity to ask him how Christopher's life is going arose from a question I'd asked earlier.

I had wanted to know, first, how Buckley himself assesses his genuine public influence. After all, he does not realize power as the head of a real estate empire or a corporate cartel; he's not in international banking or shipping or weapons. How would he define his influence on Americans?

This was the only question all evening which he mostly skirted. Perhaps he doesn't know the answer. He responded primarily with a list of eliminations: what he isn't, or, more precisely, what he "is" only by virtue of public outlets. For example:

"I'm a publicist. And I've got a lot of forums—television, the magazine, newspapers, and books. Other than also being a rock star, I've got all the traditional forums by which people communicate, but it's true that none of them is ex officio . . . You're correct: There is nothing that issues from the foothold I have in any of those offices that makes you automatically influential . . . if you (are published in) three hundred newspapers . . . that doesn't necessarily make you influential."

If given to address this question myself, I suppose I'd begin by observing that which Robert Wagner/Stephanie Powers, for instance, and a lot of politicians have in common is that their media images are almost entirely created, written, produced, and directed by others, and that their do-or-die priority is to entertain. Whereas, Buckley writes his own not-notably-entertaining script, then carries the part on the sheer force of his own character and charm. Then we could talk about what those are.

Speaking for himself, the closest he came to a direct answer was this, and self-reductive to an aristocratic fault (Buckley? Self-reductive? Yes! And he's not coy about it. His almost tiny handwriting is only one gesture of the flip side of the coin of bolder character we see nearly anytime he gets a pen in his hand or steps in front of a television camera.):

"I think probably (my influence) arose primarily from the heterodoxy involved in somebody defending a series of positions which had been for a generation or even more associated with a kind of chamber-of-commerce type defense. And I was not of that mold, and therefore was more theatrically interesting than I would have been if I had been of that mold."

He then returned to his earlier method of elimination. The balance of his response led neatly to my later question about Christopher:

"Now, for instance, the son of Nelson Rockefeller is interesting because he's the son of Nelson Rockefeller. For a while. And the son of poor John Lindsay is interesting for a while. And the son of Robert Kennedy, for a while. Although my father was in his own way distinguished, he wasn't publicly prominent. So being his son is not going to catapult you anywhere."

Well, then how's the son of William F. Buckley Jr. doing? And further, "Is there anything you want to see him do, or which would particularly please you?" (Lord help me! I once mused: What if I'd grown up with William Buckley as my father?! My dread eased once I met them, sensed how close they are, and understood that the father would be mortified to learn that he had professionally cloned himself, either within his own family or anywhere else.) How's Christopher doing?

"Well, he's terrific; he's just out of this world.

"He's not married. I told him when he was twenty-one that his grandfather, my father, married at age thirty-six, had ten children, and lived a splendid, active life . . . He's thirty-one . . . he still has five years to go . . . He's always in love with somebody, but there's no scheduled marriage.

"He's a very good writer, and I would be catastrophically disappointed if he lost that skill. I think it's unlikely that he will; given that he has it, I hope he will develop it . . . He has a certain Puritan, I've-got-to-work-ten-hours-a-day sort of stuff. His personal habits are kind of slouchy, 'cause he likes to go to bed at 3 o'clock in the morning and get up at noon . . . actually it doesn't mean that you work less in the course of a week, but it does mean that you have eccentric schedules.

"I'd want to see him keep his religious faith, which is very important to me. He's very devout, actually. So that pleases me hugely. And obviously, I want him to be happy.

"Nobody's really happy, in the Pollyanna sense."

It comes to being human: Find a good wife, continue the line, work hard, develop your gift, keep the faith, and be happy. William Buckley's dreams for his son are not hardly so sacerdotal, so severe, so loaded with expectation, as many folks would deduce from only his *Firing Line* presentation. Politics does not a family make.

Politically, I've occasionally stood on the same ground with William Buckley—often as not, on some other. (My "position" re politics—an occasional amusement to him—is roughly analogous to correspondent Michael Herr's, whose "position" on the Vietnam war is that he was *in* it.) I've also spent as much time defending William Buckley-the-human-being to others as I have for any other two among my friends. I'm not alone.

You can't say "He's just like the rest of us." No one is who's worth much. You *can* say he's altogether human, and that the lives of a great many authentically influential people might well be a little easier if we let them be human more often. (Those who don't *want* to be human are not often authentically influential, at least not in America; i.e., no amount of money—or impoverishment, for that matter—makes you somebody for very long.)

At fifty-seven, he's in remarkably good shape. (Sailing the high seas, in a relatively small boat with a handful of companions, is emphatically not recommended to the soft or the weak.) He has also been up since 5 a.m., and he has given me more than two hours. When you're tired and landlocked, it doesn't particularly matter where you are, how fancy or funky the hotel room, how pleasant the ambiance. Fatigue is no respecter of class.

"Look: I don't want to wear you out, and I'm getting a little sleepy. I don't want to say anything dumb. I mean anything dumber . . . I want you to know this is the longest interview I've given since I was twenty-three . . .

"How many hours did you spend on the road today?"

Buckley's Delicate Dilemma

John Reagan "Tex" McCrary / 1985

From *United*, March 1985. Reprinted with permission of United Airlines.

At a time when terrorism and assassination haunt every chief of state, including the Pope, and at a time when U.S. Secretary of State George Schultz calls America "the Hamlet of nations," Prime Minister Margaret Thatcher should send for James Bond, Agent 007, and President Reagan should call William Casey at CIA headquarters and bark out a command decision:

Reagan: *"Bill, forget Delta Force. You better bring in Blackford Oakes. Jack Kennedy did. So should we. Pronto."*

Casey: *"Blackford who?"*

Reagan: *"Oakes. 'Blacky' Oakes. You still don't know him, after five books and a new one on the launch pad? I keep them all up at Camp David. Just read the pitch on the cover of his first book,* Saving the Queen: *'America's vital secrets are slipping through the Queen's private chambers. The CIA needs an agent, suave, audacious, and dashing enough to infiltrate Windsor Castle, slip into the Queenly quarters, and plug the leak. They need Blackford 'Blacky' Oakes.*

" 'Movie-star handsome, rich, self-assured, and an ex-combat pilot, fresh out of Yale, Oakes is a man the young Queen Caroline might take into her confidence. Indeed, he's the man Her Royal Personage might take into her bed!' "

She did, and only William F. Buckley Jr. would dare pump out such a plot to launch his cold-warrior spy hero. Ian Fleming's James Bond might have a go at forbidden flesh now and then. But the *queen?* Outrageous, but it worked for Buckley and Blackford. And it still works. The latest book, *See You Later Alligator*, is a certain best-seller for Buckley, as each of his five previous Oakes books has been.

Once you've built the better mousetrap, you're in the cheese business. Buckley has baited his suspense serial brilliantly by placing his fictional Blackford in the midst of actual major east/west confrontations during the Cold War. In *Saving the Queen*, Blacky is saving the formula for the hydrogen bomb; in *Stained Glass*, he's outwitting sinister schemers who want to unite postwar Germany; the plot of *Who's on First* involves the satellite race during Sputnik's heyday; in *Marco Polo*,

If You Can, Buckley tackles the shooting down of the American U2 spy plane over Russia; and *The Story of Henri Tod* revolves around the building of the Berlin Wall. *See You Later Alligator* finds Blackford smack in the middle of the Cuban missile crisis. The reader, of course, knows the outcome of each real incident, but Buckley masterfully weaves Blackford into the fabric of history.

Buckley believes that *Alligator* is his best book yet. It centers on a fast-paced, carefully woven plot in which Blackford goes to Castro's Cuba to negotiate a trade and noninvasion agreement initiated by the infamous revolutionary Che Guevara.

Buckley's plot takes off when everyone—the Cuban leaders, the Russians, the readers—everyone, that is, except Blackford, discovers that our hero is being used as a pawn in an attempt by the Russians to deploy the missiles in Cuba.

In some respects, it's difficult to draw the distinction between Blackford and his creator, the two being at once soul mates and opposites. Buckley also came from a moneyed family. He served in World War II, although not as a combat pilot. So many of the Oakes adjectives—suave, audacious, dashing, self-assured—all also happen to apply to Buckley. Furthermore, he did a stint in the CIA after graduation from Yale, while the sharp-tongued conservative maverick (he dared to go head to head with Reagan in a televised debate on the Panama Canal Treaty in 1974) has been outwitting the Russians in one way or another ever since.

While Blackford may choose the darkened alleyways of Moscow or Budapest to confront the communists, Buckley takes them on regularly in the pages of his fortnightly magazine, *National Review,* as well as in his thrice-weekly editorial column syndicated in 275 newspapers nationwide and on his weekly public-television program, *Firing Line.* Buckley and Blackford share a distrust of Eisenhower, although they split on their opinions of Kennedy.

Today Buckley remains close friends with Reagan. At the same time he's a darling of the conservatives, thanks to his tireless championing of them even during the liberal heyday of the sixties. He's also a darling of corporate America and the New York and Washington society sets, all of which has made him fair game for those detractors who accuse him of elitism.

Meanwhile, Oakes is impeccable. ("You are disgustingly handsome," one female character tells him; he reads *Antigone* and Jane Austen for fun.) He may itch, in Cuba, but he never scratches.

Book critic John Leonard wrote recently, "If Blackford is [Buckley's] alter ego, Buckley ought to be a trifle embarrassed. Because Blackford is almost perfect. To be sure, his French is a 'disability,' although not his Latin or his German."

Buckley licks his lips with more than his signature glee when he responds. "I made Blackford Oakes such a shining perfection to irritate, infuriate the critics," he says. "And I *scored!*"

How would Buckley cast Oakes for a film—Burt Reynolds, maybe a young Clint Eastwood, a Robert De Niro, or an early David Niven?

"David Niven was one of my closest friends," he answers. "We painted together in Switzerland, where I write. But, no, Oakes is not a Niven—David was too English. Oakes is completely American—maybe a Robert Redford."

Has he ever written a screenplay for Oakes?

"No, *I* haven't," he says. "But a couple of awful scripts were written on *Saving the Queen*. Nothing since. However, there is a group talking about packaging all the novels and making films. They hope to raise about $50 million."

But right now Buckley is faced with a problem that affects his and Blackford's future, as well as the value of their entire spy book *oeuvre.*

Throughout his adventures and misadventures, Blackford has remained spiritually devoted to his stateside sweetheart, Professor Sally Partridge, PhD, Yale, English literature—a bit like Miss Moneypenny in Ian Fleming's *007.*

Even as many books ago as *Marco Polo, If You Can,* Blackford wrote to her, "Dear Sally: . . . Don't we belong to each other? Even if we haven't made it formal? But besides that, we should talk. Talk and talk and talk endlessly."

Sally wrote back: "My precious, beautiful, brainy, arrogant, reckless, bloody cold warrior! Oh, dear Blacky, how I long to see you!"

As of *Alligator,* Blackford and Buckley finally make it formal: Blackford Oakes proposes marriage and Sally Partridge accepts. Therein lies the tender trap for the three of them, but especially for Buckley.

"I'm in a real bind for my next book," he says. "You see, I'm nothing if not square. I can't have Oakes fooling around after he marries Sally, can I?"

The Oakes books follow one another chronologically from the early days of the Eisenhower administration through Kennedy and the Bay of Pigs. But if Buckley hooks Blackford up next with the Johnson White House, our once dashing and debonaire Blackford—now older and, yes, hitched—is sure to be less promiscuous.

Aficionados of spy novels expect their heroes, even those dreamed up by Bill Buckley, to be promiscuous. This considerable problem has been weighing heavily on Buckley's considerable mind of late. A quote of Blackford's comes to mind: "Sometimes," he says, "an encore becomes too much to ask." But then what's true for Blackford is not always true for Buckley, and the latter thinks he has found the solution.

"It came to me in the middle of the night," he says. "I called my editors. I asked them, 'Can I go backwards? Can I reverse the sequence, chronological so far?' They said, 'Why not?' "

So he turned to *Facts on File* to find a peg. He reached back to 1954, a year, he explains, when British intelligence was heavily infiltrated. The next Blackford Oakes book may very well place the spy back in England, where Buckley's first spy thriller took place, and thus back in Britain's finest boudoirs.

As a result, more controversy is certain to follow, but then, Buckley seems to invite the confrontation. On a more personal level, in 1983 he deliberately took aim at his critics by publishing his week-in-the-life-of-Bill-Buckley book, entitled, accurately, *Overdrive.*

It was a direct hit. "So who is this preposterous snob?" Gene Lyons asked in his *Newsweek* review. In the *Washington Post,* Curt Suplee wrote, "Buckley maunders along like Macaulay on Quaaludes about his house, limo, kids, and friends, gloating and quoting his snappiest ripostes."

Recalling the outcry now, he borrows a bit from Robert Frost and answers his critics with the same artillery. Of his stretch Cadillac, he says, "My limousine has miles to go before I sleep . . ."

But Buckley is a master of making light of himself, especially of his image as an elitist, high-brow intellectual. On the television comedy show *Laugh-In,* when asked why he is always seated during *Firing Line,* he replied, "I could not possibly stand . . . underneath the weight . . . of all that I know." He also doesn't seem to mind playing the role of antisnob. He once confessed to his host, Nelson Rockefeller, that he was late for dinner because he was watching *All in the Family.*

I needle him now, temporarily standing in for his absent critics. "Your favorite enemy, John Kenneth Galbraith, PhD, has nineteen quotes and eighty-seven lines in *Bartlett's Familiar Quotations,*" I say. "But like the president you admire so much, Reagan, you have none. Of all that you have said and written, what would you nominate for *Bartlett's?*"

"A wisecrack," he says. "I said that if elected mayor of New York"—he ran and lost in 1965—"I would demand a recount."

Thinking it over, he changes his mind. "Seriously," he says, "I once wrote that I would sooner be governed by the first two thousand names in the Boston telephone directory than by the two thousand members of Harvard's faculty."

Stained Glass: An Interview with the Playwright

Thomas Augst / 1989

From *Actors*, March 1989. © Tom Augst. Reprinted with permission of the author.

Thomas Augst: Why did you accept a commission from Actors Theatre to write a play?

William F. Buckley: Well, I hadn't done one before, and I thought it would be interesting to try it.

TA: Had you thought about writing one before?

WFB: No, I hadn't . . . though my son had produced a play the summer before, at Williamstown, and he thought it was an exhilarating experience. So I thought, well, I'll try it.

TA: And how did you find it, writing a play?

WFB: Writing a play was very difficult, very novel, in the sense that after a day's work I had no idea if I had done anything particularly good. Obviously, if you are a professional playwright, you develop enough experience to coach you on whether you are moving in a right direction or in a bad direction. I can do that in a novel or in nonfiction, but not yet in a play. It was very illuminating to me to have the thing read professionally. Then I got some idea of what it was that I had performed. It made a tremendous difference.

TA: From your various novels why did you choose to adapt *Stained Glass*?

WFB: It seemed to me to have a high dramatic potential, and also one that didn't require visas to six planets in two acts; most of the action is concentrated right there. To the extent that it isn't, you can *make* it happen there. Now, I had a wildly permissive letter from Jon Jory which said in effect that anything you write we can produce, but my son warned me against excesses of that kind.

TA: The Blackford Oakes character and the series of novels he appears in certainly make for some dramatic material. I'm surprised that we haven't seen

93

any movies. Has Hollywood ever been interested in making films of your novels?

WFB: Yes, they dart in and out, they're doing that right now. There was a big hiatus as a result of the financial failure of Robert Redford's CIA film, *The Day of the Condor*, some years ago. They lost their shirt on that, so no one would touch a spy film. Anyway, this will be the first venture in non-book form. Several screenplays have been written, not by me, but by others of various of the novels, but none of them have been produced.

TA: You're known as a very prolific writer, and you seem to move quite easily from political essays to books on sailing and novels. At the end of the process of writing *Stained Glass*, did you find yourself more comfortable with playwriting?

WFB: Yes, by the time I sat down with the script a couple of months later to look at it again and rewrite it, I found I had achieved a perspective that I didn't have the very first night I started in. That may have been simply the passage of time, also comments on draft one from one or two people, especially my son, who had had some dramatic experiences. So it's fair to say the missing perspective began to crystalize—the idea of communicating with an audience exclusively through spoken words, without the reliance on nonspoken words which all novelists rely on very heavily.

TA: Do you find that it's easier to make a political point, in writing a play instead of an editorial or novel?

WFB: The availability of another voice, so to speak, a Greek chorus sting in your pocket to be trotted out anytime you wanted, can't be discounted. It's obviously advantageous. On the other hand, the stage has the overwhelming advantage of the utterly direct experience with a listener who is engrossed, or who is supposed to be engrossed—he is a captive audience for a couple hours—so *that* obviously gives you a dramatic purchase on the stage that you don't have in the passive material. What I'm trying to say is the advantage of the novelist is the one I've exploited, having written eight novels and only one play.

TA: In the play we get a sense that the U.S. is buckling under, giving into pressure from Stalin. Do you feel that the U.S. allowed itself to be intimidated and could have more strongly opposed the Soviet occupation of Eastern Europe?

WFB: Absolutely. In that respect a lot of renowned strategists agree that from Yalta on, until we started to wake up, we did really nothing. The Marshall Plan was an important economic step, and NATO was an important economic step, but we in effect sat around while the Soviet Union developed hydrogen bombs and crystallized its hold on Eastern Europe. It's of course wildly ironic when you consider the reason we went to war was to save Poland's freedom in 1939.

TA: In the play we get the sense that the reasons for the Americans' intimidation is fear. Why did we sit around letting the Soviets develop hydrogen bombs?
WFB: The big example is 1956 when the Soviets moved into Hungary and Eisenhower had an opportunity to do something or not do something. He opted to do nothing. In doing that he more or less documented the fact that as long as they stayed behind their own frontiers they were absolutely safe. *Stained Glass* foresees the fear felt by Western leaders every time an ultimatum was handed down by Stalin.

TA: East-West relations have changed since 1952 and since 1978, when you wrote *Stained Glass*. In the age of Gorbachev and glasnost, what point does *Stained Glass* make about East-West relations?
WFB: In *Stained Glass*, set in 1953, Stalin was still head of the Soviet Union. He was succeeded by a troika, which became Khrushchev; the violence of Khrushchev was documented in his oppression of running tanks over students in Czechoslovakia. Khrushchev denounced Stalin and then Brezhnev came in. He denounced Khrushchev. And now Gorbachev just denounced Brezhnev. But none of them denounced Lenin, and we're still dealing with a country whose huge, huge overhead is inexplicable except in terms of wanting to dominate the politics of the world. We've had all these ups and downs of détente and friendship and summit conferences, but the substantive causes of antagonism have not dissipated and won't dissipate until they renounce that part of Lenin that says, "Go out and make the world a huge socialist state, which you will serve as a motherland." They've got a lot of problems that distract them from doing that right now, of course, but none of the elements of the drama of *Stained Glass* is in any way affected by what's happened since.

TA: What about the reunification of the two Germanies? Is that a dead issue?
WFB: It's pretty dead, and it's not really an issue concerning which there's even German solidarity. The East Germans are afraid of the West Germans, and the West Germans are not absolutely sure that East Germany can be assimilated, and all the surrounding countries who twice in this century have been mauled by united Germany are in no particular hurry to patch them up. Clemenceau made a great line at Versailles; he said, "I love Germany so much I think there should be more of them."

TA: In the play Rufus makes a point that the end can at times be justified by the means. That reminded me of *Darkness at Noon,* in which the excesses under Stalinist oppression could be justified by referring to its historical goals. What's the difference, with Rufus talking about U.S. covert action—

WFB: Rufus was saying, don't use the cliché "The end does not justify the means" because the end *very often* justifies the means. The correct statement is, "The end does not justify *any* means." We had a first strike potential against the Soviet Union in 1953—we didn't use it, we didn't think of using it, quite correctly. If there is a single lesson to be learned from the novels I've written, it is that there is a world of difference between *their* doing something and *our* doing something because the motives in both cases are entirely different. They want to maintain their slave state, we want to defend free people from being enslaved by them.

TA: So when the U.S. plays dirty in terms of manipulating a nation's elections (as in *Stained Glass*) and that sort of thing, it's because the Russians play dirty—?

WFB: No, it's to save them from the Russians. Italy would have gone communist in 1948 if we hadn't gone in there and spent millions of dollars and, as you put it, manipulated the vote. I wish to hell we'd manipulated the vote in Germany before Hitler got in, but the answer is what are we trying to accomplish? We're not trying to enslave somebody. We're trying to keep them free. We haven't dominated Italian politics since then. We left them on their own, but meanwhile they were free to act on their own rather than free to act as their communist boss would have told them to do—as Stalin would've told them to do.

TA: So it's a matter of the superiority of our goals?

WFB: Sure. The way I put it is if a man knocks an old lady out of the way of an oncoming bus, and another man knocks an old lady into the way of an oncoming bus, it shouldn't be talked about as people who knock old ladies around.

TA: This is a central point in your play; what place does personal morality have in government service?

WFB: We were reminded at Nuremberg that personal morality *at some point* transcends any loyalty to the state so that if the state were to say, you, I give you instructions to kill all Jews, or all Catholics or all blacks, you just say I'm not going to do it. So there is always a surviving role for the conscience in any state, notwithstanding a presumptive obligation to obey orders.

TA: Is that the case in *Stained Glass?*

WFB: Yes, Blackford Oakes reserves for himself a tiny little area of independent action, and he says, "Okay, I work for the CIA, I acknowledge that the commander-in-chief thinks there's a danger of a world war, and under the circumstances I don't consider this a Nuremberg type of event, but let someone else do the actual pulling of the trigger." Now I don't necessarily defend that . . .

TA: What is the significance of the chapel to you in the play?
WFB: It was a metaphor in the novel as it is in the play: the desire by Count Wintergrin to reconstitute the chapel fused in his spirit and his imagination with his desire to reintegrate Germany. They were part of the same dream.

TA: I read somewhere that you were briefly in the CIA yourself. Is that correct?
WFB: Yes, I was nine months in the CIA, 1951–1952.

TA: So you were recruited right out of Yale, then. What interested you in joining up?
WFB: Well it was during the Korean War. I had just been married and I had served in the infantry in the World War, and I thought, well, if I had to go one more time I'd rather do something more interesting than serve in the infantry. A particular professor who was an undercover recruiter for the CIA approached me, and I went along . . .

TA: So why did you decide to leave the CIA?
WFB: I was a deep cover agent. Deep cover agents are called in for special deals. The principal responsibility of the deep cover agent is to be utterly inconspicuous, i.e. no one would think he was other than a missionary, or a teacher, or an engineer, or whatever. His cover has to be absolutely convincing. Then he's called in for assignments. The stuff I was doing, which remains secret, while I could see why it was done, and could see its importance, bored me so I wanted to get back to the journalistic scene. I quit and went to work for the *American Mercury* for a couple months, and then I quit that and wrote book number two. And then I founded the *National Review*.

TA: People have suggested similarities between you, or your public persona, and Blackford Oakes. Where do you see those similarities—?
WFB: For reasons of sheer sloth, I had gone to Yale, so I could describe a campus I knew in the first book. He's a scientist, I'm a liberal arts type; he's a Protestant, I'm a Catholic; he's a technician, I'm not; he's a flyer, I'm not. He stayed in the CIA, I didn't. So the only similarities are that he and I both believe that there is such a thing as a struggle for the world, and that the Soviet Union are the bad guys and we're—whatever our faults—the good guys.

TA: So you never wanted to grow up to be Blackford Oakes?

WFB: No, no. Blackford Oakes is an activist. He's engaged in every one of these books in hard action. I am by profession a critic. My adventures in the CIA were utterly sedate and clerical and brief.

William F. Buckley Jr.:
Happy Days Were Here Again
Brian Lamb / 1993

From *Booknotes*, C-SPAN, October 24, 1993. Copyright © National Cable Satellite Corporation. Reprinted with permission of the producer.

Brian Lamb: William F. Buckley Jr., on the cover of your new book it says "Reflections of a Libertarian Journalist." Have you always called yourself a libertarian?

William F. Buckley Jr.: Off and on. Of course, you know, something called the fusion movement was encouraged by me and by *National Review* during the late fifties. The idea was to point out to the straight libertarians and to the conservatives how much they had in common and how effective the symbiosis would be between them. So from time to time I stress the fact that I'm conservative and, every now and then, that I'm a libertarian. And there's a certain amount of libertarian—well, in most of what I write there's a certain amount that is oriented to, "Does this augment or diminish human liberty?"

Lamb: Do I remember you saying, maybe when you ran for mayor of New York,—this may not be you—that as far as you're concerned, you would just as soon . . . you would throw the garbage out the window and let people pick it up and deal with it rather than having the government deal with it?

Buckley: No, your memory is of an exchange I had with James Baldwin, in which he was defending the littering of the streets, on the grounds that it was a form of protest against the city for not paying close enough attention. And I said, "Look, it isn't very helpful to use that as a means of protesting. Should I throw my garbage out into the street when John Lindsay walks down, since I don't think he'd make a good mayor?" So it was really just sort of a rhetorical joust-about.

Lamb: If somebody buys this book, what do they get?

Buckley: Well, they get the best I can give them, in various modes. Over the past eight years I have—those were very eventful years because they covered the collapse of the Soviet Union; they covered the death of some very important people, plus a certain number of personal episodes. What I do, assisted by my sister, who serves as the editor, was to attempt to divide into appropriate sections the moods in which I write.

The first she calls Assailing, where I'm rough on Carl Sagan and Jesse Jackson, Mario Cuomo, Teddy Kennedy, Lowell Weicker, Elizabeth Taylor, and so on; then Analyzing specific problems, I hope shrewdly. And then a section on Commenting, a section on Reflecting, and then ending up Celebrating and Appreciating various people and a sports activity or two. So it's a wide-ranging collection. It's my ninth. And the rest have been well received, so I hope this one will be.

Lamb: Do people ordinarily buy former columns and former articles and stuff like that when you put them in a kind of a compendium like this?
Buckley: The operative word in your question is ordinarily, and the answer is that ordinarily people don't buy anything unless they are a part of the hard constituency. Robert Ludlum can count, the day after tomorrow, on selling 400,000, 500,000 copies of his new book. But if a publisher brings out your ninth collection, that usually means that people bought the first eight.

Lamb: What's this, in numbers of books, that you've written?
Buckley: Thirty-fifth.

Lamb: Of all those books, which sold the best?
Buckley: The book that sold the best was the second of my four sailing books called, *Atlantic High.* And then the mystery books all came in somewhere, you know, between seventy-five and a hundred, except the very last one, which came out shortly after the end of the Cold War and suffered—I was a casualty of the end of the Cold War. And then the others—well, most of the books I've written have been on the best-seller list.

Lamb: Which ones did you enjoy the writing part of it the most?
Buckley: This is going to annoy you, but I really don't like to write. It's terribly hard work. That may be one reason why I have managed to develop the facility to write quickly. If I had the same kind of languorous pleasure in writing that my younger brother has or that, say, Eudora Welty has, who just gets up with a light in the eye, thinking, "My God, this is a day in which I write," then I could answer your question with a greater sense of hedonism. You know, George Will once said to me, "I write three times a week, and when I wake up in the morning, the first question I subconsciously ask myself is: Is this a day in which I have to write a column? And if the answer is affirmative, I wake up bright and happy." It happens exactly the reverse with me.

Lamb: Do you then write for an end instead of . . .
Buckley: Yes.

Lamb: I mean, what are you trying to do?
Buckley: Also, you know, a lot of us do things for the after-pleasure of it, even weeding your garden—the after-pleasure of seeing the roses and the grass come up; or practice your scales for the after-pleasure of helping to develop your technique. As Whittaker Chambers once put it to me, "I like to have written." And that's a nice feeling, to have written, in part because it is so onerous.

Lamb: Other than the big names, the ones that would be obvious—the Ronald Reagans and the Richard Nixons—do you know—I went through and counted, so I think I know this, but do you know which person you quoted the most or talked about the most in this book?
Buckley: No, I don't.

Lamb: Would it surprise you if I said Whittaker Chambers?
Buckley: Well, you obviously surprise me. On the other hand, I'm weighing what you said. Whittaker Chambers, during the period where we were very close friends, which is about seven years, wrote me—in fact, he wrote me such beautiful letters that they were published as a book. And he kept saying things that were very arresting both in what he said and in the way that he said it.

As a matter of fact, the novel I have coming out next January, one of the high points in it has to do with the discovery by young veterans of the Afghan war in Moscow of the description by Whittaker Chambers, in one of his letters to me, of the Narodniki. They were the group of young people who met silently in the czarist days and swore to give their lives over to the assassination of a tyrant.

So Lenin celebrated the Narodniki, as Whittaker Chambers pointed out, but then discovered that they were pretty dangerous because people could get the same idea as being applicable to Lenin and therefore all trace of them was removed from Soviet literature, so that you had to turn to Whittaker Chambers to find out about this enormously important and romantic development in Russian history.

Lamb: What kind of an impact did he have on you, and when did you know him? Let me just throw in this one, for somebody that's never heard of him . . .
Buckley: Sure.

Lamb: Who is he? Who was he?
Buckley: Well, Whittaker Chambers was the *Time* magazine senior editor who, in

sworn testimony, named people he had known while working as a secret intelligence agent for the Soviet Union, and one of those was Alger Hiss. There ensued the greatest ongoing division, I guess, in American cultural history on the question of who was lying. The evidence is pretty overwhelming that the person who was lying is Alger Hiss, who is still alive, by the way. But we became friends in 1954, and he became, actually, formally a senior editor of *National Review*, though he came up very infrequently. And he died at a very young age, sixty-one, of a heart attack.

But he had an enormous impact when his book, *Witness*, was written. They ran the first chapter, which was a letter to his children—the famous letter in which he said, "When I left the Soviet Union, left the Communist cause to join the cause of the West, I couldn't help but feeling that perhaps I was leaving the winning side to join the losing side." So there was that great sense of melancholy in much of his writings.

I was about to point out that they serialized the first chapter of his book, "Letters to His Children," in the *Saturday Evening Post* and sold 500,000 more copies than normal. So it had a huge impact on everybody who read it. And from that moment on, he became something of an American legend and probably still is. So I don't think any quotation of him is likely to bring on tedium in the reader.

Lamb: I saw a reference a couple of months ago to the fact that in August of 1948, in that hearing, that it was the first ever televised hearing.
Buckley: I didn't know that.

Lamb: The Alger Hiss, the HUAC—the House Un-American Activities Committee. I want to go back to that, to ask you what impact—Richard Nixon was on that committee? Was he on that one?
Buckley: Yes, he was. As a matter of fact, that was the first episode in Nixon's career that gave him an enormous launch because the committee was a little bit dazzled by the firepower of the pro-Hiss forces. And they were about to pull away and say, "Hiss was right and Chambers is a liar," when Nixon moved in, mobilized the evidence, and persuaded the congressional committee that, in fact, Hiss was probably lying, not Chambers.

So he became very conspicuous during that period, and it was that that gave him the reputation that awarded him a seat in the Senate two years later; and two years after that the vice presidency of the United States.

Lamb: Where were you then?
Buckley: Well, he was elected vice president in 1952 and I graduated from college

in 1950, so I was sort of around. But the Hiss-Chambers drama was a very significant episode when I was in school. Liberals tended to assume that Hiss was correct because of his pedigree. It was so formidable. He had gone to Johns Hopkins,
then he had gone to the Harvard Law School, then he had clerked with—who was
it?—in the Supreme Court, the famous Jewish liberal . . .

Lamb: Frankfurter.
Buckley: Frankfurter—yeah, Frankfurter. And then Dean Acheson had sort of
testified to the nobility of his character. And all this time he was piping out secrets to the Soviet Union with his wife, Priscilla Hiss. So he was a tremendous
blow to the liberal establishment. This shining legacy of the New Deal was, in
fact, a traitor. Now most people who are identified with the New Deal years ago
conceded that that's what he was—Arthur Schlesinger, for instance. But some
people are still hypnotized with the subject . . . sort of like the grassy knollers on
JFK. It's more fun to believe that there was a conspiracy beneath the conspiracy.

Lamb: Do you remember, back in those years, who was influencing you the most,
back—you went to Yale?
Buckley: I went to Yale. Well, you know, I had a few professors who you probably
wouldn't have heard of, who were influential. I've always found it hard to answer
the question, "Who influenced you the most?," because it seems to me that in ret-
rospect, it is a kind of a collage of people and it's very hard to sort out what it was
that influenced you in respect to this particular thing.

My colleague for twenty-five years in *National Review* is James Burnham, who
is probably the best-known American geophysical strategist, by training a philosopher, first in his class in Princeton, so on. And he influenced me enormously.
But I didn't meet him until the magazine began.

Lamb: What year did the magazine begin?
Buckley: '55.

Lamb: In the back of your book is the section called Appreciating. A number of
people that you write about are no longer alive. Let me pick a couple of these—
some of them are alive—and ask you about them.
Buckley: Sure.

Lamb: Malcolm Muggeridge. Who was he?
Buckley: Well, Malcolm Muggeridge was, I think it's probably safe to say, the
best-known British journalist, up until, say, ten or fifteen years ago. He was married to the niece of Beatrice Webb, and he went to the Soviet Union as sort of

a committed young socialist, pro-Communist. And he was there for about one winter and wrote a devastating critique of life under Stalin. This was in the early thirties.

He still stayed over, pretty much, on the socialist side of the world, and he wrote industriously for the *Manchester Guardian* and others. There's several books. Then during the war he was very active, and then after the war he was the editor of *Punch* magazine. One had to be sort of a humorist to do that, plus a very skillful journalist. Meanwhile, he was simultaneously editing the book section for *Esquire* magazine.

But little by little he began a march that would turn out to be ineluctably directional towards Damascus. He became a Christian and his perspective changed, but not his idiomatic powers, so that when he was talking about Christ or about the commandments or about our duty to one another, he would manage to do so as a humorist. And it, under the circumstances, gave a kind of a lift to his evangelism that was quite distinctive.

I saw him, believe it or not, speak to the ASNE—the American Society of Newspaper Editors—in Washington, the editor of every principal newspaper in the United States. He was just the after-dinner speaker, and he ended up with a paragraph that embellished the idea of the meaning of the star over Bethlehem and had these pagans absolutely stupefied by the sheer beauty of it. So, anyway, he became probably the most influential English-speaking intellectual evangelist.

Lamb: How well did you know him?
Buckley: He was on *Firing Line* actually quite a lot of times, seven or eight times, and we became very close personal friends. As a matter of fact, he and I once did a program in the Vatican on the Sistine Chapel. And he called me up, he said, "You know, I hate famous people. I've known them all and they're always a disappointment, but I want to meet this pope." So I said, "Well, you crank up your muscle, I'll crank up mine." So he and I and David Niven and my wife had a private audience with the pope, which was very amusing because the pope hadn't been briefed on who we were. So when he came to Malcolm Muggeridge, he looked at him with that sort of benign face . . .

Lamb: This is the current pope?
Buckley: The current pope, yes. He said, "You are radio?" Now, however often do you ask yourself the question: What is the appropriate answer to "You are radio"?, so it's hard to come up with one. So Malcolm Muggeridge just said, "Yes, Your Holiness, I do a certain amount of work on radio." Then he turned to David

Niven, and he said, "Ah, you were the great friend of my predecessor." Now dear David had probably never even heard of Pope Paul VI, but, you know, it quickly became plain that the pope thought we were visiting basketball managers or something. At any rate, Muggeridge was vastly amused by that episode.

Lamb: Did he know who you were?

Buckley: No, but I thought I'd tip him off because here we had access to the Sistine Chapel, the first time in history, as a result of an intermediary who had gotten permission for us to use it for forty-eight hours to make a documentary. So I thought I'd tip him off. So I said, "Your Holiness, it's going to be very hard for me to get used to my private chapel when I get home after having had access to yours," thinking, "You get it?"—thinking that would flash back.

Well, he was so alarmed by what I said that he sort of snapped his fingers and the monsignor showed up, pictures were taken and we said goodbye. But, anyway, after that Muggeridge said to me, "I want to do a show with you called 'Why I Am Not a Catholic.'" I said fine. So we did it, and he gave all the reasons why he wasn't a Catholic. And two years later he called me up and said, "I want to do another show with you." I said "What?" He said, "Why I Am a Catholic." He had "poped," as they say in England, in the interval. He was a wonderful, wonderful, wonderful man, a great wit and a brilliant, brilliant analyst.

Lamb: I want to ask you about a quote that you put in your column, by the way, when you—how often do you write, about—with an R . . .

Buckley: Three times a week.

Lamb: No, I'm sorry, with an RIP after it—a Rest In Peace? Do you often do that?

Buckley: I do a fair amount. I've been doing it for *National Review* for years and years and years. I mean, I don't know how many I've done. Maybe five hundred. I don't know.

Lamb: In other words . . .

Buckley: I'm not an obituary writer. I mean, that's not my profession.

Lamb: But is there some way to describe what it takes to get you to write somebody's obituary? I mean, do you have to like them?

Buckley: Or dislike them, one or the other, or they have to have been a friend of the *National Review* or of mine or have had some historical importance. When I was editor of my own journal, I wrote about them when I assigned them. Now that John O'Sullivan is the editor, I write them when he asks me to and when I agree to do so. And occasionally I send one out as a regular column, as I did in the case of Muggeridge, and I don't know whether—maybe he's the only one here that I sent out as a column.

Lamb: Let me just read you this quote and ask you whether you agree with it. "As an old man"—this is Malcolm Muggeridge—"As an old man, Bill, looking back on one's life, it's one of the things that strikes you most forcibly, that the only thing that's taught one anything is suffering—not success, not happiness, not anything like that. The only thing that really teaches one what life's about—the joy of understanding, the joy of coming in contact with what life really signifies, is suffering."

Buckley: Well, let me comment on that by saying two things: number one, I understand the historical discipline that caused him to write that way. It is, you know, the lesson of Job, that Job taught us that suffering can be ennobling. And in the case of Malcolm Muggeridge, he seemed to feel that impulse very sharply.

But it may have been part of his weltschmerz—there was a certain sense in which his sort of gloom about the materialism of man and man's failure to be inspired by that particular part of our patrimony that should inspire us, caused him to feel that an expiation, of sorts, was in order. For instance, he became a vegetarian and he didn't drink any booze, any wine or anything. He didn't used to be that way, but one had a sense that he was taking some sort of a pleasure from the mortification of the flesh, but that pleasure never affected his mood.

John Leonard, in his introduction, in thinking back on his days at the *National Review*, was listing the various things he did. He said, "I had lunch with Whittaker Chambers, which was like lunching with 'The Brothers Karamazov.'" And although it's incorrect to say of Whittaker Chambers that he emanated melancholia when you were with him, it's not incorrect to say about him that you felt the palpability of his melancholy. With Muggeridge, you didn't. Muggeridge was a consistent entertainer, without in any way getting in the way of his own message.

Lamb: Do you feel that people expect you to entertain them all the time?

Buckley: Well, I think it's a terrible sin to bore people, and I'm easily bored myself. I mean, I'm perfectly prepared to admit that if I attended a lecture by Immanuel Kant, I might very well go to sleep. But that's my fault, not his. So under the circumstances, when I write, I do make an effort to please the reader in the same way that, oh, a pianist at a dive, a boite, wants to use chords that please the listener. If you sit down to play a musical repertoire and limit yourself to a dominant or subdominant and a tonic, you're never going to give music the kind of variety that makes it so special.

By the same token, it seems to me that if you deny yourself the hard work and at the same time the pleasure of using the language exploitatively, you shouldn't really be writing professionally.

Lamb: You've got a bunch of letters also in here, letters that have been sent to you—"Dear Mr. Buckley"—this is from Hamilton Morgan of Harrison, New York—"regarding your *Firing Line* interview with Henry Kissinger, from a qualified TV professional objectively concerned American:"—colon, number one— "The manner in which you sit is rude." Do you remember this?
Buckley: No, but . . .

Lamb: "Can't you sit upright in an adult fashion? In single shots you appear tilted; in two shots, you sit as if your guest has BO. Two, even in questioning, you appear rude. You don't ask questions of a guest, even one whose opinions you favor, but your questions come in a long form of interrogation. Three, you always come up with the personal insecurity of a long preface, attempting to show what you know."

You answer him. The first thing you say is, "No, I can't think straight— congenital"—but when you get a letter like this, first of all . . .
Buckley: What was my comment?

Lamb: What is your comment? "Most people don't talk about it out loud. If you think my questions are long, try Socrates. Three, of course I want to share what I know about the subject—after all, I spend three hours reading up on it at night before. Have you ever jumped out of an airplane at midnight with a parachute"— question mark—"with the mission of eliminating the guard at the end of the bridge? Well, I haven't either, but if I did, I would certainly want detailed introductory instructions," and on and on.
Buckley: Oh, well, I took it more seriously than I remember having done so. Having brought the subject up, which you just did, I don't usually appear on television dressed this way, but I've just finished a two-thousand-mile hike, so I asked your permission not to have to go and change and you kindly gave it to me.

The answer is we all have our idiosyncrasies, but he's actually wrong on point five and point six because my program has been going on for twenty-nine years. It's the longest-running program with the same host in America. I have one complaint in those twenty-nine years from my guests that I didn't give them all the time they wanted to say, in the way that they wanted, what they wanted to say. So that's not bad.

Number two, on the matter of introducing the guests, since I often have people who are not widely known—you know, philosophers or poets or whatever—I feel an obligation to acquaint the listener with them. And if you take a couple of minutes to do that, I don't think that's inordinate, especially back when the program was one hour rather than the half-hour it is now.

Lamb: When you get a letter like this, what's your first reaction? Do you smile or do you . . .

Buckley: Well, when I get a letter, the first thing I ask myself is: Is this a letter I should publish in *National Review*, where I have a column called Notes and Asides, which is a column of letters directed to me, are they instructive or bellicose or interesting in whatever way.

In respect to the one you just read me, obviously my reaction was I ought to tell this guy a couple of things. Plus, also, I shouldn't shield from my readers the fact that some people react this way, with that kind of hostility to everything from my comportment to my behavior on my own program.

Lamb: Here's another one. You wrote this letter, and this is to the editor of the *Baltimore Sun*. By the way, on these letters, did your sister pick all these herself?

Buckley: She nominated them and I OK'd or didn't OK.

Lamb: You say, and you're commenting on what the *Baltimore Sun* said in an editorial about you, and then you write—you're talking to the *Baltimore Sun*, "William F. Buckley Jr., whose elegant arrogance"—first of all, do you think you have elegant arrogance?

Buckley: Is this a quote from them?

Lamb: From them—"and affectations of a British accent has won him fame and fortune."

Buckley: Well, that's kind of dumb because people with a fake British accent don't necessarily have fame and fortune, do they?

Lamb: You go on to say at the end here, "Arrogance and affections being separate modifiers, they require the use of a plural verb," so you were shooting back at the editor.

Buckley: Oh, yeah. Well, is that all I said?

Lamb: Yes. Well, you have a list of stuff earlier than that, but it was that—I just wanted to ask you, when people write you and talk about the tilt and your presence on the set or your so-called affectation of a British accent, do you know that that's the way you look to people on the outside?

Buckley: Well, somewhere—and maybe in this book or somewhere, I say, "Look, up until age six I spoke only Spanish. That was the only language I spoke. Then I went to my first school in Paris, where, of course, they spoke French. Then at age seven I went to London, and that's where I learned English for the first time. Now what ought I to sound like? You tell me." So, incidentally, nobody who's British thinks I have a British accent, so it's just, you know, occasionally people would say to me, in Minnesota, "Where are you from?" I say, "I'm from Connecticut." And they say—well, they say, "Well, maybe that's how they speak in Connecticut." But there's nothing cultivated in my accent, as my family and friends would tell you.

Lamb: What were you doing in all those places?
Buckley: Well, my father was in the oil business, and he had a very large family, so he had a Mexican—he was bilingual himself, and he had a family staff who spoke French or Spanish.

Lamb: How many brothers and sisters did you have?
Buckley: Ten.

Lamb: How many of them are alive?
Buckley: Seven—I was the sixth.

Lamb: And you have a brother that's a federal judge, Homer.
Buckley: Yes, he was a senator from New York. He was beaten by Moynihan in '76.

Lamb: You ran for mayor once and lost. Do you wish that you had won?
Buckley: No, I didn't run thinking that I would win. I ran under the conservative label, which up until then, the most they had gotten was 1½ percent, so I got 13 percent. But my joke, made for the benefit of the people who teased me about having done so poorly, is that I think if you ran for mayor of New York and you get 13 percent, it's dangerously close to winning, so that if I were to run again, my campaign slogan would be "Voting by invitation only."

Lamb: What's your life like today? You're no longer running the *National Review*.
Buckley: No. I am no longer the editor of *National Review*, but I'm the president of the board and the owner, and I rejoice every day that John O'Sullivan is such a brilliant editor. I have a book about—which you were discussing—a novel coming out in January, and I'll write another one in Switzerland. I have a piece coming

out in the fortieth anniversary of *Playboy* and one in the sixtieth anniversary of *Esquire*, I'm reviewing a 1,600-page travel book by Henry James for the *New York Times*. And I lecture a lot, so I keep busy.

Lamb: Where do you live?
Buckley: I live in Stamford, Connecticut.

Lamb: Where do you spend most of your time?
Buckley: Well, there and on boats, and then traveling around. But my wife and I go to Switzerland, and that's where I do my book-writing in February and March.

Lamb: And how long do you plan to do *Firing Line*?
Buckley: Well, put it this way: I don't plan not to do it, so presumably it will continue to go on as long as it serves a purpose.

Lamb: Has the fact that *Firing Line* is on a public television network, tax-supported, ever bothered you in relationship to your politics?
Buckley: No, because I came to terms very early with the proposition that a minority in a democracy lives by the rules of the majority, and even if I wanted to see the post office privatized, I'm not going to protest it by not using the facilities of the post office.

On this I agree 100 percent with Milton Friedman, and as recently as a few months ago he wrote a letter to *National Review*, agreeing with a position I took against a former editor of *National Review* who hadn't wanted to take Social Security because he was opposed to the Social Security law. And his answer was though Social Security was voted in, continue to criticize that aspect of it that you think is wrong or how it's run, but to fail to participate in it is a failure to live by the verdict of a majority which dominates—which runs a republic in which you are a participant and whose rules you agreed to abide by unless they become tyrannical.

Lamb: Has *National Review* ever made any money?
Buckley: No, no, no. I don't know of any journal of opinions that ever made money, with—perhaps with the exception of the *New Republic*, when it was the house organ of the Progressive Citizens of America, which was then a fellow traveling outfit designed to make Henry Wallace president of the United States. Journals of opinion tend not to make money. But we're doing better than ever before.

Lamb: How do you keep it going then?
Buckley: Through an annual fund appeal, plus directing a certain amount of my own income in its direction.

Lamb: Back to the back of the book again. William Shawn . . .
Buckley: Gee.

Lamb: . . . this is a column, January 18, 1993—or it was, I assume published in *National Review*. Who was William Shawn?
Buckley: Well, William Shawn became the editor of the *New Yorker* in 1953, right after Mr. Ross died, and he was its editor for about thirty-five years, up until three or four years ago. He was a man of spectacular talent and of very idiosyncratic personal manners. He was terrifyingly shy and very reclusive, enormously well-organized. And when I sent a manuscript of a book in which I simply recounted what I had done during a week of that year and he accepted it for publication, I couldn't believe it because, see, I'm a conservative and the *New Yorker* was pretty liberal.

Lamb: What year is this?
Buckley: This was in 1970. So then I sent him a second book and he accepted it, and then a third book and he accepted it and then a fourth book and then a fifth book, so that I had this extraordinary hospitality by this extraordinary man. Now about once a year he assigned himself the job of editing, line by line, a book that had been accepted by the *New Yorker*. And it fell to me to fall under his personal direction for the first of these books, which meant having a lunch with him. Having a lunch with William Shawn was—well, the next thing to a defloration.

Lamb: Why?
Buckley: Because you felt that you were getting in the way of his privacy. And he was very formal and very genial, always, "Mr. Buckley"—I mean, he wouldn't think of calling me by my first name. But it was an enormous experience because of the care and love that he devoted to every single sentence. He once said to me, "Mr. Buckley, I really don't think that you know the proper use of a comma." Enormously amused me, and it's true that I take sort of liberties in the use of the comma, intending certain effects which every now and then dismayed him. But he would never publish anything except after your approval of exactly the way it appeared. He was very fastidious on that point.

So my association with him was wonderful. And then when he retired, as I recount in this obituary, I thought, "Gee whiz, now he's no longer a man who's sort of in charge of my literary fortune. Should I ask him to lunch?" I would never have asked him to lunch while he was still editor. So I did and he accepted. So we had a lunch. Then another year goes by, I thought, "Now should I ask him for lunch again?" The arguments against doing it are—you know, respect his privacy; the arguments for doing it are that I might, by having had lunch with him just one time, have given him the impression that I was discharging an obligation and now, thank God, having discharged it, I could let him go ahead and rusticate.

So I did and he accepted, but didn't make a date. And then I received the day that he died a letter that he'd written me the day before, making pleasant references to a couple of books that I'd sent him. So he was an unusual man who had an enormous influence on American letters and a great patron of people like John Updike, whom he discovered.

Lamb: Did you also say that he would call up months in advance and, with your secretary, make sure that when you're trying to get a date set, he's—"Well, we'd better do that off a couple months from now"—at the end?

Buckley: Yes, he loved to talk to your secretary, as distinguished from speaking with you, and he would almost be—by his standards, informal with a secretary. But he would say, "Oh, yes, I would like very much to have lunch with Mr. Buckley, and I will call back and suggest a date, and see if it's all right with him"— that kind of stuff. And he wasn't at all shy about talking with a secretary, but was much more reluctant to call you.

Lamb: You have a tribute in the back here, under the Appreciating section, to Nancy and Ronald Reagan. And at some point I think I remember you writing about their dancing together. Do you remember that?

Buckley: Well, that was a piece I did for *Vanity Fair* and they ran it on the cover—a picture. They got an interview with the Reagans, Tina Brown, and the interviewer—this was in the private quarters of the White House—they'd only been there a couple of years—and said, "Would you consent to dance for us?"— meaning for the photographer.

And instantly he said, "Well, of course." So the music went on and they started to dance. The photographer took his pictures, thinking he'd have fifteen seconds to do it, but they just kept on dancing. And, you know, *Vanity Fair* isn't used to situations like that, where the president of the United States and his wife dance as though they had just exchanged a commitment to marry each other.

But that's the way they are, and nobody who has seen it close thinks it's phony. It isn't phony. It's a case of perpetual, abiding devotion.

Lamb: And another . . . and I'm just looking . . . I underlined it. As I mentioned earlier, the name that I saw the most often was Whittaker Chambers. It's in that piece where you say, "The last time I heard the legend of Philemon and . . ."—is it Baucis?
Buckley: Baucis, yes.

Lamb: ". . . educed seriously was in the final paragraphs of Whittaker Chambers's book, *Witness*. Chambers was given to melodrama, but those who knew him and his wife, Esther, never doubted that it was so between them." It . . .
Buckley: That's such a beautiful story, isn't it? You want to read it or you want me to say it?

Lamb: No, go ahead.
Buckley: Well, a god—well, I feel it would be a Greek god, dressed like a beggar, appears in this humble little shed where this old couple are looking with some longing at the little porridge that they have saved to eat that night, and he says—can he have something to eat. Without hesitation they take half of it and give it to him, whereupon, having tested their capacity for charity, he transfigures himself. And they see that he is a resplendent god. And in Whittaker Chambers's face he raises his caduceus, which is the great imperial staff, and he says, "Tell me what one wish you desire."

And they stammer out the wish that they wish to die at the same time. No one wants to outlive the other. So with his caduceus he touches them on the head, and suddenly they are transformed into two trees, which nestle together in the breeze and leave the impression of a continuing perpetual symbolism, of a tender and beautiful love.

It's a beautiful story.

Lamb: Theodore White—Teddy White?
Buckley: Well, Teddy White once said to me, "You know, I'm probably the most expensive journalist in America." And I said, "Well, Teddy, that's terrific." He said, "Well, as you know, I don't like to boast, but it's probably true." This was about ten, fifteen years ago, and I think he was probably correct. He was the most sought-after journalist and for several reasons. One, he was a terrific writer; second, he was a terribly industrious reporter; three, he knew everybody. He also had a capacity to make you talk to him and say things that probably you weren't really predisposed to tell him. He had that extraordinary quality—Bob Woodward has the same gift. But anyway, Teddy White was sent by *Life* magazine to

do a piece on John Lindsay when he was running for mayor, which required him to do a piece also on me at the same time because I was running for mayor.

And so he came to see me, and I said something pleasant to him. He said, "First, business; we'll become friends later." And we became very good friends. In fact, we both followed Nixon to China. We were two of the journalists who went to China in 1972 and spent a lot of time together. And he and I and three or four other friends met always, six or seven times a year, for lunch. So he was a dear, wonderful, talented human being.

He came from a very poor Jewish ghetto in Boston, which he liked to write about; sort of worked his way through Harvard; became a Sinologist, was entranced by Mao Tse-tung for a while—a little bit of a fellow traveler on the Chinese question; saw the light of day a few years later; was very, very high up in the Luce organization, a very close friend of Henry Luce. But then they had an ideological parting of the ways. So he had a very vivid, wonderful productive life.

Lamb: What do you mean by fellow traveler?
Buckley: Well, he tended to think that everything that Mao Tse-tung came up with was probably correct. I'm talking about the late thirties and early forties, during the period when Chiang Kai-shek was sort of withering on the vine and there was a lot of corruption. But his hospitality to the Maoist movement alienated Henry Luce, who was very fervently on the other side, and caused that resignation.

Lamb: We're used to seeing you play Bach at the Phoenix Symphony or write about Bach, but in this Appreciating section you have a column "Is Beethoven a Monument?" What's that all about?
Buckley: Well, that's a very interesting point. Adam Smith said that the state can legitimately do certain things. And those are a very short list. It can look after the common defense, and it can be the custodian of monuments. So I asked myself the question: Does the authority of Adam Smith attach to a state enterprise that takes dead musicians and makes their music available? I had specifically in mind something that happens in Switzerland. In Switzerland, for about, like, a buck a month or whatever it is, you can plug your telephone line into six channels, and one of those channels, if you push button number three, has nothing but classical music day and night.

It is simply a marvelous amenity. So I was trying to manipulate conservative orthodoxy in such a way as to suggest that a monument need not only be something chiseled in marble, sitting in the middle of a park, but might also be keeping alive a musician and providing the wonderful amenity of access to him cheaply.

Lamb: Of all the things you do in the public—speak, interview on television, being interviewed, writing books, writing columns, what brings the most fun and joy to you, and what's the most difficult?

Buckley: Well put. What brings, I suppose, the most and the easiest pleasure is sailing. I sail a lot and I've done it since I was thirteen years old. And it's, to me, a marvelous, marvelous form of recreation, but it is a recreation. I used to ride a lot when I was a boy, but I don't do that anymore. In terms of what's most difficult, there is nothing for me as difficult as trying to master a piece of music on the harpsichord, in part because I have very bad fingers, so they don't behave well and they are insufficiently disciplined.

Lamb: What about in the more public policy area, like . . .

Buckley: Oh.

Lamb: . . . the things like—would you rather be interviewed or would you rather do the interviewing?

Buckley: I think it probably depends on the person. Sometimes one has a guest whom one feels one ought to have on because he is on to something important that we want to talk about, but he might be an awfully boring human being. And after one hour you're sweatily glad that it's over.

By contrast, now with some people—I think, for instance, of Harold Mac-Millan. At the end of forty-two minutes he said, "I say, aren't we through yet?" And I said, "No. We have seventeen more minutes to go." He said, "Very well." Whereupon he told some more marvelous stories about what he said to Churchill, what Churchill said to Hitler and so on and so forth. So that was a sheer joy.

So I think it depends completely on the person. An interview by somebody who really doesn't follow what you're saying is hell because you feel that you have explained something, and the next question absolutely establishes that they haven't the remotest idea what you said or if they heard it, they didn't understand it. And that hurts.

Sometimes they're people who have—"OK, there are thirty questions I want to ask Mr. Buckley." So they ask question number one; you give a reply to it, but it's a reply that obviously takes you through Act 2, not Act 3 of the exchange, but they don't know enough to lead you into Act 3; they go right to the next question. And that shows that it is a discontinuity there that makes the whole thing terribly abrupt and unsatisfying.

Lamb: Did you ever have anybody get up and walk off a set on *Firing Line?*
Buckley: No, no. I think it's very bad manners to do that, you know, unless someone engages in a profanity or I could—as a novelist, I could write a situation in which my guy would walk off the set and people would applaud him for doing so. But I've never walked into such a situation.

Lamb: What year was it that you and John Kenneth Galbraith slugged it out on— was it the *Today* show?
Buckley: Yeah. Well, we did it in 1972 and in 1976.

Lamb: As I remember, and it's a little bit—a few years have passed—that you really got at each other.
Buckley: Well, let me tell you something. It was a very interesting debate. In 1972 we were in Miami. We were there for both conventions. We had twenty-five minutes, and in twenty-five minutes you can get a certain amount done. By 1976 all the format in the morning news shows had changed, and to have more than seven minutes, you had to have a meeting of the board of directors. So in seven minutes neither of us could unwind. And, you know, our specialty is not the Johnny Carson jab, but something which, to the extent that it has a point, might require a minute of analytical overture. And both of us agreed that we simply didn't work attempting to exchange views in seven minutes, so we never asked to do it again.

Lamb: Was that ever personal, though? I mean, for people who haven't seen it, they can't remember, but you were, as I remember, you were saying some pretty strong things at one another.
Buckley: Oh, yeah. He and I almost arrived at a mutual covenant that because we were close personal friends, we would under no circumstances going to permit that friendship to mitigate the harshness that we feel for the other person's position.

   I mean, I remember saying to him, "Ken, if you'd been president of the United States, by now we'd have been a Soviet republic," which is absolutely correct. And he says complimentary things about my . . . (unintelligible)."

Lamb: Some conservatives have criticized you for living in two different worlds. I mean, I've seen, various times—and, matter of fact, I think I interviewed Bob Tyrrell in his book, where he talks about a dinner or something he had up here in New York with you, when they criticize you, they criticize you for being a pal of the liberals.
Buckley: They what?

Lamb: A pal of the liberals.
Buckley: A-ha.

Lamb: You go to dinner with them and you have lunch with them and you have friends at the *New York Times* and things like that. You've undoubtedly observed these criticisms.
Buckley: Yes.

Lamb: What do you say to somebody that criticizes you for being friends with the other side?
Buckley: Well, I say, frankly it's odd, because you can disagree very pointedly with somebody and still have an enormous bond of friendship. Curiously, this is absolutely routine in England. The editor of the *New Statesman* and *Nation* might be the godfather of the new child of the editor of the *Tablet*. Nothing there's considered unusual about a member of the Labour Party and a member of the Conservative Party being very close friends.

And so I don't think that's unusual to have somebody with whom you disagree—in the first place, I don't spend my time talking politics. I go to London tomorrow. I have to talk politics three days from now because it's a political seminar, but I doubt very much between now and then I'll talk about politics to anybody—not to my wife, not to my hosts over there— because it's not the kind of thing that interests me that much. You see, there are other things to talk about that—so that in—I could spend time with Ken Galbraith, as I have, hours after hours after hours, in which political discourse never come up.

Lamb: Well, what do . . .
Buckley: When they do come up, we just do this sort of form of calisthenics.

Lamb: What do you talk about?
Buckley: Trollope—skiing, what he did when he left Canada and came over here as a scholar . . . there's nothing we don't talk about. There's no problem at all. In the first place, when you talk with Kenny Galbraith, mostly he talks, but he's so entertaining that one doesn't mind.

Lamb: On the cover of your book and inside the flap it's an introduction by John Leonard—the same John Leonard that we see on CBS on Sunday morning?
Buckley: Yes.

Lamb: Isn't he a liberal?
Buckley: Oh, yeah, very much a liberal, and once in a while, when he confesses, but when I started *National Review* I saw a magazine called *Ivy*, in which I had an

essay—which was 1955—and there was an essay by John Leonard. So I called him up because it was beautifully written, and said to him—would he like to take a summer job with *National Review*. He said, "I'll take a job anytime with anybody, since I've just been kicked out of Harvard."

So he worked for us for a year and a half, did marvelous work. Then he went off to Berkeley to be radicalized, which was very completely done. But he's a brilliant, brilliant writer.

Lamb: In the acknowledgments in the beginning—we're just about out of time—you say, "I'm indebted primarily to Mrs. Bozell, senior editor of Regnery Gateway." Who is Mrs. Bozell?
Buckley: She's my sister and she's a full-time editor for Regnery Gateway.

Lamb: How did she . . .
Buckley: Regnery published my first book.

Lamb: Oh, I see, and this is Random House.
Buckley: Yes.

Lamb: She was doing it just as a friend, or just as a brother—sister?
Buckley: Yes.

Lamb: Well, you say in here, "I would not give out the date of the Declaration of Independence without first checking with her."
Buckley: No, it was with Dorothy McCartney . . .

Lamb: Oh, I'm sorry.
Buckley: . . . who is chief researcher at *National Review*, so I was paying her a compliment that she's owed.

Lamb: Other than the novel that's coming out in January, what's next in nonfiction?
Buckley: In nonfiction. Well, I'm about one-third of the way through a book on the Catholic religion, which I suspended because I didn't have enough time to do the reading I felt I had to do. Whether I will crank that up or not, I don't know. There are a couple of other ideas floating about which I haven't yet decided. But I will write a book, though.

William F. Buckley Jr.:
The Art of Fiction CXLVI

Sam Vaughan / 1996

Interviewer: What sort of things had you been writing before the novels? You tend to group your previous books into categories, yes?

William F. Buckley: The most obvious category, I suppose, is the collections of columns, articles, and essays, four or five of those before my first novel. There were two or three offbeat books: a book on the United Nations and the term I served there, a book on running for mayor of New York, a book on crossing the Atlantic, which has the ocean as mise-en-scène, and then a sort of autobiographical book on a week in my life, *Cruising Speed*. So when you suggested that I write a novel, I had at that point published twelve or fifteen nonfiction books.

Interviewer: I remember saying you might like to try a novel one day. The name *Forsythe* came up, and I thought your reference was to the *Forsyte Saga* which was then on television . . . as well as in the literature. You said, no, like *Frederick Forsyth*.

Buckley: Well, my memory of it was that I had just read Forsyth's *The Day of the Jackal* and admired it hugely. That the reader should know exactly how it ended and nevertheless still pant his way with excitement through three hundred pages—I thought that was really a splendid accomplishment. I remember saying something along the lines of, "If I were to write a book of fiction, I'd like to have a whack at something of that nature."

Interviewer: So you liked the challenge of writing about an occurrence in contemporary history where the reader knew the outcome and . . .

Buckley: Yes, although I proceeded not to do so. That is, *Saving the Queen* did not have a predictable and well-known outcome, though some of the succeeding novels did. However, I have this problem—perhaps some people would think my problem is greater than this—which is that I have never succeeded in prestructuring a book. I've never started a novel knowing what the end is going to be. When I get about halfway through—and I go into this only because I assume it's of some technical interest to other writers—then need to stop and force myself to figure out how the Gordian knot is going to be severed, because at this point there are a lot of characters and dramatic questions that need to be consummated. Some people feel that a book comes out better written that way—if the author himself doesn't know what's going to be in Chapter Two when he writes Chapter One, Chapter Two might then be more freshly minted and read that way. I'm skeptical. It seems to me that a thoroughly competent operator would sit down and think of what's going to be in Chapter One through Chapter Forty, and simply move ahead. What I do at the end of an afternoon's work is write two or three lines on what I think is the direction of the narrative, and where we might logically go the next day.

Interviewer: If you stop yourself halfway through—almost as Ellery Queen used to stop three quarters of the way through and say, "Now that you have all the clues necessary for a solution, what is the solution?"—is there a tendency then to load too much resolution into the end of a book?

Buckley: I think that's a danger. It's what I hope I've avoided, in part because I'm very easily bored, and therefore if I can keep myself awake from chapter to chapter, I assume I can keep other people awake. That is why I don't reserve all the dynamite for the end. This may be the moment to say that in all of my novels—to the extent that I have a rule—my rule is to devote a very long chapter, close to the beginning, to the development of a single character. In book one it's Blackford Oakes, which is natural. In book two, *Stained Glass*, it was Erika, a Soviet agent. I lifted her as though Vladimir Nabokov had a daughter, not his son, Dimitri. I confided my invention to Nabokov, which perhaps precipitated his death. He didn't live to read the book, but he was very enthusiastic, as you remember, about the first book, and his widow liked *Stained Glass*. In any event, I've always felt that the extensive development of one character gives the book a kind of beef that it doesn't otherwise have. That's the only regimen to which I willingly subscribe and towards which I naturally drift.

Interviewer: One of the questions about your novels is: how much is true, and how much is invented?

Buckley: Well, I poach on history to the extent that I can. For instance, when I was in the CIA, it was reported to me that the evidence was overwhelming that the destruction of Constantin Oumansky's airplane—he was the Soviet ambassador to Mexico—was an act of terrorism, executed by Stalin. Stalin was killing people capriciously anyway in those days, so it was inherently believable. On the other hand, as I remember, Oumansky lived for a few hours after the plane came down, so the explosion wasn't very efficient. Thus there's a school of thought that sees it as a genuine accident. But for a novel I don't trouble myself about matters of that kind. That is to say, if something was in fact a coincidence, but might have been an act of treachery, I don't hesitate to decide which is more convenient for the purpose of the narrative. The books are, after all, introduced as works of fiction. Everybody knows that Charles de Gaulle is going to survive the OAS, and everybody knows that Kennedy is not going to survive the twenty-second of November 1963, and everybody knows that the Berlin Wall is going to rise. Even so, I attempt to create suspense around such episodes. And manifestly succeed. The books get heavy criticism, positive and negative, but no one says, "Why read a book in which you know what's going to happen?"

Interviewer: Still, it's a nice challenge of art to put yourself up against history.
Buckley: Sure. And I owe that idea to Forsyth.

Interviewer: In the patterns you've developed, one of them is the unspoken premise: this is the way it *might* have been behind that great event that we all know about.
Buckley: That's right. I found myself attracted to this idea of exploring historical data and visiting my own imagination on them. The very successful book on the death of Kennedy written by Don DeLillo, *Libra*, does, of course, that. In a sense overcomplicated and ineffectively ambitious in some of its sections, it's a magnificent piece of work, in my judgment. As long as the reader isn't persuaded that you are trying, via fiction, an act of historical revisionism, I don't think you meet any hard resistance.

Interviewer: So the reader will go with you in a combination of invention and known history, but won't accept so cheerfully an editorial.
Buckley: Yes. Of course, I think it probably depends also on how contentious the theme is. For about twenty-five years, dozens of books were published to the effect that Roosevelt was responsible for Pearl Harbor. Never mind whether he *was*, in a sense, or was not, I think that if during that period a novel pressing his guilt had been written, there would have been a certain amount of polemical resentment. If one were to write today a novel about a senator from Massachusetts and a young woman in Chappaquiddick, and how he drowned her or deserted her or whatever, readers would tend, under those circumstances, to think of it as more an effort to make the case against Teddy Kennedy, rather than as a work of fiction.

Interviewer: There seems to be a period that has to elapse before you can safely . . .
Buckley: I think so. At this point I think you can speculate about the death of JFK and not get into trouble. Like Sacco and Vanzetti.

Interviewer: You consciously stayed away from that event for a long time.
Buckley: Until novel number eight. *Mongoose, R.I.P.* flatly says that although Oswald took the initiative in suggesting that he intended to try to assassinate the president, Castro, without acting specifically as an accomplice, urged him to proceed.

Interviewer: To go back for a moment to the one character you choose to develop at length: do you decide, as you're writing your way into the novel, which character you will give a full history, or do you decide that before you write?
Buckley: I sometimes don't know who the character is going to be until I've launched the book, but I'm consciously looking for a target of opportunity. For instance, in *Stained Glass*, I decided that the Soviet woman spy—who is acting as a translator and interpreter for Count Wintergrin, the protagonist—was the logical person to have a complex background. So I made up the daughter of Nabokov and went through her whole childhood and love life and her apostasy from the West.

Interviewer: The Cold War is an essential handicap?
Buckley: I hate to use the word in this context, but I must—these are novels that *celebrate* the Cold War. I don't think that's a paradox that affronts, any more than, say, a novelist who celebrates a world war. But my novels celebrate the Cold War, and therefore the passions awakened by this titanic struggle are really a narrative obligation. The fact of the matter is that in our time—in my adult lifetime—somewhere between fifty and sixty million people were killed *other* than as a result of war or pestilence, and in most cases—the great exception being the victims of Hitler—were the victims of the Communists. Now that struggle is sometimes made to look like a microcosmic difference, say some slight difference of opinion between Alger Hiss and Whittaker Chambers. In fact, it was a typhoon that roared across the land—across bureaucracies, academia, laboratories, chancelleries. One week after Gorbachev was here in New York, I found myself using the past tense about the Cold War, which shows you how easily co-opted I am. But the Cold War is the great political drama of the twentieth century, and there is extraordinarily little literature about it written in the novel form. There are great

exposés—*The God That Failed, The Gulag Archipelago.* But if you think about the American scene, there isn't really an abundant literature, is there?

Interviewer: Why do you think this is so?

Buckley: I think that there's a sort of feeling that much of the conflict has been an *alien* experience. Of course, there are those New York intellectuals who are exceptions. I remember one middle-aged man who came to *National Review* a couple of weeks ago and said that when he was growing up he thought the two political parties in the United States were the Communist Party and the Trotskyist! That was all his mother and father ever talked about. Irving Kristol will tell you that the fights at the City College of New York were always on this or that modality of communism. But on the whole it has not been a national experience. When you think of Updike or Bellow or Walker Percy, and the tangentiality of their involvement in the Cold War, there isn't really a hot concern for it. It must be because our novelists disdain such arguments as grubby, or because they think that it's an ideological quarrel with no genuine intellectual interest for the mature person. But of course it has been the great struggle of our time. For that reason I think of my novels as entertainment but also as designed to illustrate important problems in that setting. It means a lot to me to say this: when I set out to explore the scene, I was determined to avoid one thing, and that was the kind of ambiguity for which Graham Greene and to a certain extent Le Carré became famous. There you will find that the agent of the West is, in the first place, almost necessarily unappealing physically. He drinks too much, he screws too much, and he's always being cuckolded. Then, at some dramatic moment there is the conversation or the moment of reflection in which the reader is asked to contemplate the difficulty in asserting that there *is* a qualitative difference between Them and Us. This I wanted to avoid. So I was searching, really, for a little bit of the purity of Herman Melville's Billy Budd in Blackford Oakes. Billy Budd has no sense of humor, and without a sense of humor you can't be genuinely American. Therefore, Blackford Oakes couldn't be Billy Budd. Furthermore, I made him almost spectacularly good-looking in defiant reaction to these semidisfigured characters that Greene and Le Carré and Len Deighton specialize in. I got a little tired of that after novel three or four, so I don't belabor the point as much.

Interviewer: Your reference to Graham Greene. Does he matter to you?

Buckley: Graham Greene always struck me as being at war with himself. He had impulses that he sometimes examined with a compulsive sense to dissect them, as though only an autopsy would do to dissect their nature. He was a Christian more or less *malgré soi*. He was a Christian because he couldn't quite prevent it. And therefore he spent most of his time belittling Christianity and Christians. He *hated* the United States, and his hatred was in part, I suppose, a reaction similar to that of some finely calibrated people to American vulgarity. But with him it was so compulsive it drove him almost to like people who were professional enemies of the United States. And since the most conspicuous critic of the United States in this part of the world during the last twenty-five years has been Fidel Castro, he ended up being, God help us, pro-Castro. He once gave the answer—it might have been in the *Paris Review*, I forget—to the question, "What is the word you least like in English?" *America*. And he set out to prove it. Given the refinement of his mind, it's always been a mystery to me that he should have been so besotted in his opposition to that towards which he naturally inclined—Christianity and all that Christianity bespeaks—in order to identify himself with those he saw as the little men. Okay, but when the little men were such people as Fidel Castro or Daniel Ortega? It all defies analysis.

Interviewer: Who else among the people practicing this kind of fiction do you pay attention to?

Buckley: Well, I'm not a systematic reader. I read a little bit of everything. I've never studied the achievement of any particular author seeking to inform myself comprehensively of his technique or of his point. I occasionally run into stuff that deeply impresses me. For instance, Updike's *The Coup*, which I reviewed for *New York* magazine. It astonishes me that it is so little recognized. It's *the* brilliant put-down of Marxist Third World nativism. It truly is. And hilarious. It's a successor to *Black Mischief* but done in that distinctively Gothic style of Updike's—very different from the opéra bouffe with which Evelyn Waugh went at that subject fifty years ago. And then I think that Walker Percy's *Love in the Ruins* is another *1984*. An exquisite extrapolation of what life might be like if we didn't dominate technology, and yielded to totalitarian imperatives. He combined in it humor with a deep and often conscious explanation of human psychology via this vinous character—the doctor—who dominates the novel so convincingly.

Interviewer: Somehow, for some unannounced reason, we are talking about Christian novelists. I'm struck by this only because the much remarked phenomenon of the 1950s, 1960s, and 1970s has been—certainly in America—the Jewish novel, or the novelist who writes from a background in Jewry.

Buckley: That reminds me that along about 1951 or 1952—whenever it was that Graham Greene wrote *The End of the Affair*—one critic said, if Mr. Greene continues . . . if he writes one more book like this, he must thereafter be evaluated as

a *Catholic* novelist. He didn't say Christian novelist. And indeed Greene's succeeding book was a rather sharp departure. It occurs to me that the point you really
make is more nearly about Christians who write novels, not Christian novelists.
G. K. Chesterton, Hilaire Belloc, and Wright Morris *were* Christian novelists. But
Updike is a Christian who writes novels. A reading of his work wouldn't permit
you to decoct from it, with any sense of certainty, that the author was a professing Christian. I don't think from *Love in the Ruins* you could guess Walker Percy
was a Catholic.

Interviewer: I was thinking about your own deep religious faith.
Buckley: Well, yes. I'm a professing Christian, and every now and then I take
pains to let the reader in on the fact that so is Blackford Oakes. On the other
hand, it would be hard, I think, to pronounce my books as Christian novels unless you were to go so far as to say that any novel that acknowledges epistemological self-assurance to the point of permitting us to say, "They're wrong and
you're right," has got to be traced to that sense of certitude that is distinctively
Christian.

Interviewer: Yes, you're certainly not *preaching* in the novels. Blackford Oakes occasionally prays, which is just as natural to him as breathing, but his Christianity
doesn't color everything. I was just wondering whether the Christians who write
novels have become an underground sect, as Christians were at the outset.
Buckley: I think to a significant extent they have. Raymond Williams—the late
British novelist—was the last novelist I can think of off hand who was a flat-out
Christian novelist. Am I wrong?

Interviewer: Frederick Buechner has been plying his trade as a Christian novelist. George Garrett. His big novels are set in the Elizabethan era, but they're written with Christianity very much alive and at issue. And, at times, include spies. I
wonder if spying and religion are in some way natural literary bedmates?
Buckley: Well, isn't it safe to say that people who pursued the Communist
objective—certainly early on—were motivated by ideological convictions that
were almost religious in nature? Religious in the sense that they called for sacrifice and for the acceptance of historicism. That became less and less so as fewer
and fewer people of moral intelligence actually believed in Leninism and communism. What they then believed in was Russian expansionism, and they became
mere agents of the Soviet Union.

Interviewer: So it began with religious fervor, which supplanted what traditional
religion might have been for some.

Buckley: I think so. These days it would be hard to find somebody in his twenties comparable to Whittaker Chambers in his twenties. This doesn't mean that there aren't still communists—Angela Davis is a very noisy communist, but she's shallow. There isn't really a sense of life in the catacombs, the kind of thing you had in the twenties and thirties, when people like Malcolm Muggeridge (until his early epiphany) were, temporarily, in thrall to the idea of the collectivist state.

Interviewer: Do you think that in a time when the visible attachment of many people to formal religious institutions has been waning there has been a corresponding attraction to other causes?
Buckley: Yes, I do. And for that reason it is not easy to command a large public. Most writers want a large public, and tend for that reason not to write religious novels. And explicitly religious—God, it's been so long since I've read one—an explicitly religious novel would be looked on merely as a period piece.

Interviewer: How do you handle the technical stuff in the novel? Do you do your own research?
Buckley: I am very unmechanical. I remember once, halfway through writing *Stained Glass*, I had to fly back to New York from Switzerland to do two or three episodes of *Firing Line* to catch up. I called my electrician in Stamford and I didn't have a lot of time; so I just said, "Could you please tell me how to execute somebody with electricity?" Well, he was sort of dumbfounded.

Interviewer: He doesn't make house calls of that kind?
Buckley: That's right. And he hadn't really given it much thought, he sort of muttered a couple of utterly unusable things like, "Put him in a bathtub and have him fix electricity." So I mentioned this in a letter to a historian at the University of San Jose. He wrote back and said, "I must introduce you to my friend, Alfred Aya." Aya turned out to be a bachelor, aged then about fifty-five, who worked for the telephone company. As my friend described him, at heart a physicist—and more. When he was six years old and traveled with his parents, he would inevitably disappear for four or five minutes in the hotel, and from that moment on anybody who pushed UP on the elevator went down, and anybody who pushed DOWN went up. Aya loves challenges. So I wrote him a letter and said, "Look, I've got this problem." He gave me the idea of executing him via this device, what I call a Chromoscope, which was entirely plausible. Later, he gave me all the information I needed to write satellite scenes in the later novel that dealt with the U-2, including how to make the thing appear to be coming down, and how to destroy

it, et cetera. I remember when I came to the nuclear missile question—at this point we communicate with each other via E-mail because he's an E-mail nut, as am I—so I shot him a message via computer. Here's the problem: there's one nuclear weapon left in Cuba, and I have to know what it looks like. I must know what is needed to fire it, what is needed to redirect it to a target other than the one prescribed for it. And twenty-four hours later, I had a 29,000-word reply from him. Absolutely astonishing. Which made me, temporarily, one of the world's foremost authorities on how to handle a single nuclear bomb.

Interviewer: Does he give you any credit for helping him work off aggressions?
Buckley: He's absolutely delighted to help.

Interviewer: What else is your system of research, since there is so much fact?
Buckley: Wherever there is something concerning which I have a factual doubt, I put in a double parenthesis, which is a code to the librarian at *National Review*, who moonlights on my books, to check that, so she often will find five or six or seven hundred of those in the course of a novel. And she then copes.

Interviewer: Are you aware of the category they now call the techno-thriller, like the novels of Tom Clancy and so on?
Buckley: Well, I know Tom Clancy.

Interviewer: I wonder whether these writers who make a fetish out of hardware have influenced you?
Buckley: No, except that I admire it when it's done skillfully. For instance, Frederick Forsyth, in the book mentioned earlier, describes the assembly of the rifle with which he's going to attempt the assassination; I like the neatness with which he names the various parts. I have a book called *What's What*, in which you can look up *shoe* and find out exactly what you call this part of one, or that, et cetera.

Interviewer: Now, famously, you write *everywhere*. You write in New York at *National Review*; you write in New York in your home; you write in Connecticut in your home; you write in the car; you write in planes; you write presumably in hotels. Is it only writing novels that is done in Switzerland?
Buckley: In order not to break the rhythm, I almost always write a chapter on the airplane from Switzerland to here when I come back for my television work. Working on a novel, I like to write every day so as not to break it up. There are two nights when I cannot do it. Those are the nights when I am preparing for the television the following day. But I try not to miss more than two nights.

Interviewer: Do you think when a novelist begins a novel, he has to live the novel, that you have to begin to become one or more of the characters, and you don't want to be interrupted playing those roles any more than an actor wants to be interrupted?

Buckley: Oh, I am *feverishly* opposed to that idea. I've seen people wreck their lives trying to do it. I know the MacDowell Colony and Bread Loaf and such are pretty successful, but I also know that some people seclude themselves to write and become alcoholics precisely because they have nothing else to do. I have a close friend who has that problem, because when he sets out to write a novel, he wants to clear the decks. Nothing would drive me battier than to do *just* a novel over the course of an entire month. I have only *x* ergs of purely creative energy, and when I'm out of those, what in the hell do I do then?

When one sets out to write a book, I do believe one should attack it two or three hours a day, every day, without fail. You mustn't interrupt it to do a week's lecture tour or whatever. On the other hand, don't ever devote the entire day to doing just that, or the chances are you'll get bored with it, or simply run out of energy. But I'm glad you asked me that question, because I feel so strongly about it. I'd like to see more novels *not* written by people who have all the time in the world to write them.

Interviewer: As an editor I spend half of my life trying to persuade people who think they should write books that they don't have to give up careers and certainly not family in order to write a book. They do have to find time—they have to make time—but they don't necessarily have to jump ship.

Buckley: It seems so marvelous when you realize that and can say, "Look, fifteen hundred words a day," and you've got a book in six weeks.

Interviewer: Now, when you wrote your first novel, I found it a surprise—an agreeable surprise—because I somehow thought it would be in homage to writers you liked.

Buckley: Imitative? I don't have the skill to imitate. For instance, I admire people who can come up with a touch of a foreign accent. I just don't know how. There may be a school somewhere—Cornell?—that teaches you how to do that. And if I thought I could go somewhere for a half-day and learn how to make a character sound like a Spaniard, I would. My son has that skill, marvelously developed. I can't do it. I can't in speaking either. I sometimes call somebody and don't want to be recognized. But I don't know how to do it. And I don't know how to write like anybody else.

Interviewer: At the start, I didn't think you'd write a page-turner. I thought, as I've said, that you would write a clever novel, an intelligent novel, maybe ideologically weighted. What I didn't see coming was the novel that moves ahead. I wonder if that comes at least in part from the fact that you write quickly?

Buckley: Well, perhaps in part. But mostly it's my terribly overdeveloped faculty against boredom. I was introduced into the White House Fellows annual lunch affair by a man who had done some research on my books, and he picked up a line I had forgotten. "Mr. Buckley," he said, "has written that he gets bored winding his watch." True, I was greatly relieved when they developed the quartz. I never *just* brush my teeth, I'm reading and brushing my teeth at the same time. So, if something bores me, then it's certainly going to bore somebody else.

I live a hectic life. Someone once asked me if I ever could lay aside my Christian scruples so as to have a mistress, and I said, "I really don't have the time."

Interviewer: You once said to me that you are not particularly reflective or thoughtful. How can you write a novel with as many parts and qualities, as many components, as many subplots and themes as you do, and still say that you're not thoughtful, not reflective?

Buckley: Well, what that takes is hard concentration. I don't think that people who are very busy are for that reason diluting the attention that they give to what they are doing when they are doing it. For instance, Churchill in his wonderful essay on painting said when he's painting that's *all* he's thinking about. When I'm painting, that's all I'm thinking about. I happen to be a lousy painter, I should admit instantly, but I enjoy it and I concentrate on it. Sometimes, going up in the lift with, say, Doris Brynner, a ski-mate, who's a wonderful listener, I'll say, "Now I've got to the point where I've got this problem, and this girl has to come out alive. On the other hand, she's going to be in the Lubyanka," that kind of thing—and just saying it helps. I only really think when I'm writing or talking. I suppose it's a gift of extemporaneity. But also, added to that method, I think is the usual one. When you reach a knotty problem in your novel, you sometimes have to sit back in your chair and think, "What am I going to do next?" I don't want to give the impression that I simply keep using my fingers.

Interviewer: Reviewers have noticed, and it has always intrigued me, that you write your enemies so well that it sometimes seems as if you characterize them better than *our* guys—the good guys. Your portraits of Castro, of Che Guevara, of Khrushchev, Beria, and so on, are all close, pores and all. . . .

Buckley: Nobody can possibly like the Beria that I depicted.

Interviewer: No, I don't mean it's necessary to *like* them, but you give them so much color. Blackford sometimes pales—and I suspect this is your intention—by comparison to the roster of heavies.

Buckley: Well, exposure to these historical characters is almost always limited. In the first book in which Khrushchev appears, he makes, I think, two appearances. Therefore you take the essence of Khrushchev and give it to the reader, and the reader is grateful, because it *is* the essence of what we know or can imagine about him. If you had to write 450 pages about Khrushchev, you'd run the danger of etiolation. I think I've read enough about these characters to have some idea of what they're like. I depended heavily on Carlos Franke when I wrote about Castro and Che Guevara. Guevara was a very magnetic human being. Cruel, and entirely obsessed, but nevertheless attractive. Fidel Castro is more attractive to ten thousand people than he is to ten people, whereas Che Guevara was the other way around. I think I captured Castro well, but I'm equally pleased with the portraits I've drawn of Americans, the Dulles brothers and Dean Acheson.

Interviewer: Let's speak for a moment of the amount you write and the presumed speed at which you write, novels and everything else. Do you have any models or inspirations who helped you to this sustained burst of intellectual and creative activity?

Buckley: I'm not sure I'm all that fast or all that productive. Take for example, Trollope. He'd rise at five-thirty, do his toilette and have his breakfast, all by six. He would then begin writing, and he had a note pad that had been indexed to indicate intervals of 250 words. He would force himself to write 250 words per fifteen minutes. Now, if at the end of fifteen minutes he hadn't reached one of those little marks on his page, he would write faster. And if he passed the goal in fifteen minutes he would write more slowly! And he wrote that way for three hours— 3,000 words a day.

Interviewer: Do you approve?

Buckley: If you were told to write a cantata every Sunday, and you got what Bach got out of it, how could you disapprove of it?

Interviewer: Do you keep to a particular standard with your work?

Buckley: It's true about everybody, that some stuff is better than other stuff. But I don't release anything that isn't, roughly speaking—I say *roughly* speaking—as good as it can be. If I reread, say, my column, a third time, I probably would make a couple of changes. I'm aware of people who create both, so to speak, the "quality stuff" and the "non-quality stuff," who think nothing of writing two or three pulp novels per year. Bernard DeVoto was that way. I can't do that, and I don't do that. I'm not sure I could. What I write—especially the books—needs a lot of work. So I always resent critics who find themselves saying, "Mr. Buckley's novels look as though they were written with one eye on the in-flight movie."

Interviewer: Nobody's been clever enough to say that.

Buckley: R. Z. Sheppard in *Time* magazine did. Who, by the way, has often praised my books. So it would be odd, I think, for someone who has reached age seventy, which I have, to write as much as I do without being able to discipline himself.

Interviewer: Although you don't measure it out like Trollope, nevertheless you know you have so many days and weeks in February and March in which to write a novel.

Buckley: Well, I'm much slower than Trollope . . . and never mind the differences in quality. If Trollope had given himself, say, six hours instead of three, would his novels have been that much better? I don't know that anybody could reach that conclusion. But then he took three hours to write three thousand words, which is very fast writing when using a pencil, but not fast at all when you're using a word processor.

Interviewer: It should change the statistics.

Buckley: When I sit down to start writing every day in Switzerland, which is usually about a quarter to five to about seven fifteen—two and a half hours—it's inconceivable to me that I would write less than fifteen hundred words during that time. That's much slower than Trollope, even though I have faster tools. So, although I write fast, I'm not a phenomenally fast writer.

Speechwriters get told by the president that he's going to declare war the next day and to please draft an appropriate speech. And they do it. Or, Tom Wicker. I've seen him write ten thousand words following one day's trial proceedings, and all that stuff will appear in the *New York Times*. Now it's not belletrism, but it's good journalistic craftsmanship.

Interviewer: There's no automatic merit in being fast or slow. Whatever works, works. Georges Simenon, who was a phenomenon of production, always got himself in shape to write each novel. I hate to mention this in your presence, but he usually wrote his novels in seven or eight days. He had a physical beforehand, I think perhaps particularly for blood pressure, and then went into a kind of trance and wrote the novel, and then was ordered by his doctor to go off and take a vacation.

Buckley: I'll go you one better. Rotzan Isogner, who does not go to sleep until he has finished the book.

Interviewer: Your workroom in Switzerland. What is that like?
Buckley: Well, it's a converted children's playroom. I have my desk and my reference library at one end; there's the harpsichord and gramophone, and there's a Ping-Pong table on which all the paints are . . .

Interviewer: Do you play music while you're writing? Do you write to Scarlatti, or to Bach, or . . .
Buckley: Do I play? . . . Oh, my goodness! Heavens, yes! I thought you meant, did I play myself? Occasionally, I get up and—you know, in a moment of boredom or whatever—hit a few notes. But the answer is, yes, I have the record player on most of the time. Also, in Switzerland one of the better socialized institutions—but I love it—is that you can, for a few francs per month, attach to your telephone a little music-box device which gives you six channels, one of them a good music channel.

Interviewer: Is there any link between what you're writing and what you're listening to?
Buckley: No, none whatever.

Interviewer: So you could play Fats Waller one time and Beethoven another?
Buckley: I don't play jazz when I write. I don't know why but I just plain don't. But I do when I paint.

Interviewer: What about revising?
Buckley: Of all the work I do, it's the work I look forward to most—rewriting. I genuinely, *genuinely* enjoy that, especially with the invention of the word processor, which makes it mechanically so neat.

Interviewer: So partly it's the technological joy of working with these instruments?
Buckley: Yes.

Interviewer: You've said more than once that you find writing is hard work.
Buckley: But how would the reader know? Writing, if it's done at all, has got to yield net satisfaction. But that satisfaction is long after the foreplay. I'm not saying that I wish I were otherwise engaged professionally. I'm simply saying that writing is terribly hard work. But it doesn't follow at all that because it's hard work, it's odd that it's done so quickly. I think that's quite natural. If writing is pain, which it is to me, it should follow that the more painful the exercise is, the more quickly you want to get on with it. The obvious analogy, I suppose, would be an

execution. For years they've been trying to figure out how to execute a person more quickly, so that he feels less protracted pain. That's a *reductio ad absurdum*. In any event, if your living depends on writing a piece of journalism every day, and you find writing painful work, you're obviously much better off developing the facility to execute it in an hour rather than ten hours.

Interviewer: You're a computer maven, you've been through all the known stages of man with regard to writing and its instruments. You presumably started writing by hand or, as some people would insist, with a quill pen, yes?

Buckley: Well, I did in this sense: until I was writing every day for the *Yale Daily News*, as its editor, I would write by hand and then type, so the typewritten copy would be draft number two. It happens that my handwriting is sort of mal-formed. In fact, my father, when I was fifteen years old, sent me a typewriter with the instructions: learn to use it, and never write to him in longhand again. So I learned the touch-type system, and by the time I was twenty-three it wouldn't occur to me to write anything by hand. In fact, I was so unhappy doing so that I would ask my professors' permission, on the honor system, to type an exam in-stead of writing it. And with one exception, they all said sure. I'd take one of those blue books into the next room and type away.

Interviewer: About vocabulary: you get criticized, or satirized, for your use of ar-cane words. Are you conscious of reining in your vocabulary when you're writing a novel?

Buckley: No, I don't think I am. In the novels, there's less obvious analysis than in nonfiction work. I'm attached to the conviction that sometimes the word that you want has an in-built rhythm that's useful. And there are some words that are onomatopoeic, and when they are, they too can be very useful. Let me give you a concrete example. This morning, I wrote about Arafat's speech, and the coverage of the speech, which consumed most of the television news last night. This had to do with the question: did he or did he not live up to the demands of the State Department that he denounce violence absolutely, agree to abide by the relevant resolutions of the United Nations Security Council, and acknowledge the exis-tence of Israel? Now, all the commentators said he skirted the subject, that his language was sometimes ambiguous. I concluded that he had more nearly con-summated his inherent pledge—"however *anfractuous* the language." Now the word came to me not only as a useful word but also as a necessary word. I first ran into that word in a review by Dwight MacDonald of Norman Mailer's book on the Pentagon, *The Armies of the Night,* and I didn't know what it meant; I couldn't figure it out by internal inspection, so I looked it up. And that's *exactly* the word to describe Arafat's discussion of Israel's existence. There is an example of where one could use *ambiguous,* but that extra syllable makes it sound just a little bit more "windy."

I remember once in a debate with Gore Vidal at which David Susskind was deriding me in San Francisco, 1964, I used the word *irenic,* which didn't disturb Vidal, of course. So after it was over, Susskind said, "What's *irenic?*" I said, "Well, you know, sort of serene, sort of peaceful." "Well, why didn't you say serene or peaceful?" And I said, "Because the other word is a better fit." At this point believe it or not, Vidal, who was on Susskind's side a hundred percent during the exchange, said, "You know the trouble with you, David, is that you don't learn anything, ever."

Interviewer: *Irenic* is a nice word.

Buckley: And again onomatopoeic. So, in defending the use of these words, I begin by asking the question: why were they invented? They must have been invented because there was, as the economist put it, "a felt need" for them. That is to say, there came a moment at which a writer felt that the existing inventory didn't quite do what he wanted it to do. These words were originally used because somebody with a sensitive ear felt the need for them. Do you therefore, because it's very seldom that one hears an A-flat diminished tenth, say to yourself, I won't use that chord, notwithstanding the pleasure it gives to people whose ears are educated enough to hear that little difference? People don't say to a musician, please don't use any unusual chords.

Interviewer: *Anfractuous* is a more vigorous, almost violent word.

Buckley: Yes, it suggests a little hint of the serpentine, a little bit of the impenetrable going around and around. So therefore why not use it? Years ago, the review of *God & Man at Yale,* again by *Time* magazine, referred to my "apopemptic" book on leaving Yale. So, of course I looked it up, because I didn't know what it meant, and it's different from *valedictorian,* because an apopemptic speech, if memory serves, is usually what the ruler gives to the pilgrims en route somewhere. His sort of final message and advice. So the writer on *Time,* whoever he was in 1951, was making a very shrewd difference between *valedictory*—I'm leaving Yale—and giving Yale my parting advice; in effect, *Time* set me up as if I were the ruler of Yale, giving my subjects my advice. Very nice. So occasionally I use *apopemptic,* and when I use it, it's strictly when I want that tiny little difference in inflection, which is worth making.

Interviewer: You once said you use the words you know.

Buckley: A good point. Everybody knows words that other people don't know. Reading *The Coup,* I found twenty-six words in it I didn't know. I listed them in a column, and there were great hoots in my office because everybody knew quite a lot of them. So we went around the table—there were, you know, eight or ten editors, including James Burnham—and by the time we got all the way around, all twenty-six, there was, as I say, much jollity over that.

Interviewer: So words are put into your vocabulary by other writers?
Buckley: Yes. I'm offended by people who suggest—and some have—that I spend my evenings with dictionaries. I'm reminded that in his wonderful review of *Webster's Third*, Dwight MacDonald referred to "words that belong in the zoo-pages of the dictionary." There are certain words that I couldn't bring myself to use, not because they aren't instrumentally useful, but because they just look too inventionistic. How they got there, one never quite knows. A lot of them are sort of medical.

Interviewer: So, for those who might have thought your use of language elitist, you have quite the reverse view. You trust your reader to either know it, or look it up, or go over it like a smooth ski jump.
Buckley: The reader can say, "I don't care, it's not worth my time." But there's no reason why he should deprive other people grateful for that tenth augmented chord, which gives them pleasure. Did you know that 40 percent of the words used by Shakespeare were used by him only once? I've never read a satisfactory explanation of the seventeenth-century capacity to understand the stuff we hear with some sense of strain. Shakespeare used a total of twenty-eight thousand words, most of them were within reach of the audience. And when you consider that books by Cardinal Newman were serialized as recently as a hundred years ago. *The Apologia* was serialized and upped the circulation of a London daily. Imagine serializing *The Apologia* today. Or take the difference between a Lincoln-Douglas debate and a Kennedy-Nixon debate . . . Lincoln, in that rich, biblical vocabulary of his, was not at all self-conscious about using a wide vocabulary.

I've never seen a test, though I'd like to see it done, that would scan say three or four pages of the current issue of the *New York Times* and three or four pages of a hundred years ago of, say, the *Tribune*, and find out what the so-called Fog Index reveals.

Interviewer: The Fog Index?
Buckley: The Fog Index is the average number of syllables per word and the average number of words per sentence.

Interviewer: In writing fiction, your vocabulary is nevertheless somewhat constrained by the fact that you are limited to the words that your characters would use?

Buckley: Absolutely. Except that one of my characters is a Ph.D., and I remember on one occasion she used the word *syllepsis*. Christopher Lehmann-Haupt wrote, "Mr. Buckley's character doesn't even know how correctly to use the word *syllepsis*; she really meant . . ." Anyway, he gave me a wonderful opportunity, since a second printing was coming out right away, to go back and rewrite the dialogue to have her say, "*Syllepsis*—a word the correct meaning of which is not even acknowledged by the *New York Times* critics."

Interviewer: To shift a bit, in a conversation with Louis Auchincloss, you asked why people take less satisfaction from novels than they used to.
Buckley: Well, I mentioned television as the principal time-consumer, and it just plain is. It's been established statistically that the average American has the television set turned on between thirty-five and thirty-nine hours per week.

Interviewer: If people derive fewer rewards from novels than they used to, does this reflect something about the novels themselves, rather than the competition for time?
Buckley: Well, it certainly can. It can also suggest that the passive intelligence is less resourceful than it used to be. My favorite book at age nine was called *The Magic of Oz*. If you could correctly pronounce a string of consonants, you could turn yourself into a giraffe. I can't imagine a nine-year-old today being engrossed—being *diverted*, let alone being engrossed—by that because he would want to see it happening on the screen.

Interviewer: He'd want to see dancing consonants.
Buckley: That's right.

Interviewer: People have traditionally turned to novels, at least some, for a way to get a grip on the world, a way to see the order in the chaos. Have we gone past that period? Is it that many novels are not so avidly consumed because they provide small delights, rather than provide epiphanies, or grand epiphanies?
Buckley: I think reading the many contemporary novels you get some of that feeling of, "Where in the hell have I been that it was worthwhile going to?"

Interviewer: People often think you are writing about yourself in the Blackford Oakes novels.
Buckley: Of course, it becomes very easy if one takes the obvious profile. You begin with the fact that we were both born the same year and went to Yale at approximately the same time. Now, I made him a Yale graduate—I think it was the class of 1951—for sheer reasons of personal sloth. I was in the class of 1950, so

I knew that I could coast on my knowledge of the scene without having to go and visit a fresh college and see how things happened there. Then, for the same reason, i.e., sloth, I made him an undercover agent of the CIA, so that I could give him the identical training I had received and know that it was absolutely legitimate. So that much was, if you like, autobiographical . . . if you can say it's autobiographical that two different people went to Yale and to the CIA, and spend time describing Yale and the CIA. But beyond that, people who want to sustain the parallel have a tough time. In the first place he's an engineer, a Protestant. He has a sweetheart whom he has yet to marry—I married when I was twenty-four years old. He's a pilot, which I was not. He signed up in the CIA as a *profession,* which I didn't. I knew I was only going to be temporary and I'd quit after nine months. He's not a writer. There's a little touch of James Bond in his experiences, which there never was in mine, which were very sedentary. To be sure, it is quite true that he's conservative. In fact, for the fun of it I have him read *National Review* and occasionally read stuff of mine and Whittaker Chambers and so on. And he's also pro-American. And we're both bright, sure.

Interviewer: And you're both admirers of Bill Buckley.

Buckley: Exactly! Though sometimes he kind of lags behind a little bit. Should I tell my favorite story about the reviewer in Kansas City? He reviewed *Saving the Queen* for the *Kansas City Star,* and he had obviously spent much of his adult life abominating everything I had ever done, said, or written. But he didn't quite dislike the novel, and this terribly disturbed him. He got over it with his final line. He said, "The protagonist of *Saving the Queen* is tall, handsome, endearing, engaging, compassionate, amusing—from which at least we have the satisfaction of knowing that the book was not autobiographical." Nice line.

Interviewer: About Blackford Oakes again: there are some disagreements about your style. Just running barefoot through some of these critical notices, I see: "Oakes is as bloodless as well-done English roast beef,"—that's a reviewer in Florida—vs. Anatole Broyard in the *New York Times*: "In every respect he is a welcome relief from the unromantic superiority and disengagement of a James Bond. Beneath this Cold War there beats a warm heart." Then we get from another reviewer: "Blackie has a distinctive personality"—and from another lines like: "A flat character and an annoying name-dropper." You attract lines like: "A Rambo with a Yale degree," and all sorts of things. This character of yours seems to be capable of stirring up a lot of confusing and conflicting opinions. Maybe that's biographical.

Buckley: Well, yes, I have a feeling—I hate to say it—but I have a feeling this is mostly a confusion of things about me. I simply decline to believe that two or three of those things said about Blackford Oakes would have been said if the books had been written by Mary Gordon, say. They just wouldn't have said it, and they wouldn't have *thought* it. Now, whether they convinced themselves that this was so, or whether they feel the stereotypical compulsion to say it must be so because I wrote it, I don't know. I've never asked anybody. I'd like to think that Anatole Broyard is not easily seduced—at least not by me—and I like to think that Blackford Oakes is an interesting human being. True, in certain of the novels he plays a relatively minor and flat role. But never quite as minor as people have sometimes charged.

Interviewer: You seem to attract reviews that don't have much to do with the book at hand.

Buckley: My son Christopher thinks I suffer from overexposure, and I'm sure he's right. I'd like to think some of my books would have done better if they had been published under an assumed name, so that people wouldn't feel they had to do the Buckley bit before talking about the book. It's especially true in England, by the way, although I'm underexposed in England in the sense that I'm not all over the place. Some aspects of my situation as a novelist are probably unique. Gore Vidal is very public in his experiences, but he's episodic. He goes away for a year and a half—thank God—and then he writes his book and then he comes back and publicizes it. Norman Mailer, during his *Village Voice* period, and right after, was almost always in the news, not for something he had said or for a position he had taken, about which people ceased caring, but for something he had done. You know, urinated in the Pentagon, or married his seventh wife or got drunk at his fiftieth birthday, that kind of thing. But I assault the public three times a week in the column and once a week on television, and every fortnight if they elect to read the *National Review*. So that's kind of a hard battering ram for people disposed to be impatient, either as critics or as consumers, with a novel written by me.

Interviewer: That puts your critics to a particular test, that is, to detach themselves.

Buckley: Anatole Broyard was very attentive and receptive, and so was Lehmann-Haupt. Between them they've reviewed almost everything I've written.

Interviewer: Did you say once that when you decided to write a novel John Braine sent you a book on how to write one?

Buckley: We were friends. John Braine was born again, politically. This was along around 1957 or 1958, when he ceased to be an angry young man and became an early deplorer of the excesses with which we became familiar in the 1960s and 1970s. So he used to write me regularly, and I had lunch with him once or twice in London; he was on my television program, along with Kingsley Amis. But then he . . . he was a little bit moody and he sort of stopped writing his letters. There wasn't any implicit act of hostility, I just had the feeling he wasn't writing his twenty-five people per week, that kind of thing. But when I sent him a letter saying that I was going to write a novel, he said, "Well, I wrote a book on how to write a novel, and here it is." So I read it.

Interviewer: Was it helpful?
Buckley: I remember only one thing—which doesn't mean that I wasn't influenced by a hundred things in it—but he said that the reading public expects one coincidence and is cheated if it isn't given one, but scorns two.

Interviewer: Have you written a lot about other authors?
Buckley: Not a lot, some. A lot of authors have been on *Firing Line.*

Interviewer: I remember Borges especially.
Buckley: He was stupendous. He was living in Buenos Aires. I had lunched with him a few years earlier, in Boston, while he was visiting professor at Harvard. A friend—Herbert Kenny, then the literary editor of the *Boston Globe*—had brought us together. Borges was already blind. He did not mind it, he said, because now he could "live his dreams with less distraction."

Then we met in Buenos Aires, in 1977, during the military junta days. He seemed astonishingly frail, but he spoke without a pause. I remember thinking of Nabokov, who told me he couldn't come on *Firing Line* because he would need to memorize everything he would then say. I said, come on, your extemporaneous talk is absolutely lapidary. He said no, he had never spoken in public in his entire life, including lectures to students, without first memorizing what he would say.

Anyway, Borges was like that. I didn't interrupt him. I remember beginning by asking whether he thought of himself as in the company of other blind poets, Homer and Milton. Here is what he says, I'll give it to you from my book *On the Firing Line.* He said . . . "Of course, when you are blind, time flows in a different way. It flows, let's say, on an easy slope. I have sometimes spent sleepless nights—night before last, for example—but I didn't really feel especially unhappy about it, because time was sliding down that—was flowing down."

I asked him how he refreshed himself, as a blind man. "I'm reading all the time. I'm having books reread to me. I do very little contemporary reading. But

I'm only going back to certain writers, and among those writers I would like to mention an American writer. I would like to mention Emerson. I think of Emerson not only as a great prose writer—everybody knows that—but as a very fine intellectual poet, as the only intellectual poet who had any *ideas*. Emerson was brimming over with ideas." We talked about Emerson a bit and then I said, "Who else?" He mentioned Hawthorne but came in with a qualification right away. "What I dislike about Hawthorne is, he was always writing fables. In the case of Poe, well, you get tales; but there is no moral tagged on to them." He didn't linger but went to Melville. "But I think of Melville, one of the great writers of the world, no?"

I agreed. I asked him then—I'm looking at my book, since my memory, on its own, couldn't re-track this way, though Borges's certainly could—why he chose to be unfamiliar with new writers.

"I am afraid that I'd find the new writers more or less like myself." I'm glad I had the wit to comment, "You won't."

But what really got me was his handling of language. Listen: "I have no Greek, but I had Latin. Of course, my Latin is very rusty. But still, as I once wrote, to have forgotten Latin is already, in itself, a gift. To have known Latin and to have forgotten it is something that sticks to you somehow. I have done most of my reading in English. I read very little in Spanish. I was educated practically in my father's library, and that was compounded of English books. So that when I think of the bible, I think of the King James Bible. When I think of the *Arabian Nights*, I think of Lane's translation, or of Captain Burton's translation. When I think of Persian literature, I think in terms of Browne's *Literary History of Persia*, and of course of Fitzgerald's. And, frankly, I remember the first book I read on the history of South America was Prescott's *The History of the Conquest of Peru*."

We contrasted English and Spanish, and why he considered English a far finer language than Spanish—during which, I might add, he did a little cadenza in German, which he taught himself so he could read Schopenhauer in the original. Then I asked him if the fact that the Spanish language is less resourceful than the English language necessarily makes it less complete as poetry. He replied, "No. I think that when poetry is achieved, it can be achieved in *any* language. It's more that a fine Spanish verse that could hardly be translated to another language would turn to something else. But when *beauty* happens, well, there it is. No?

"What Whistler said—people were discussing art in Paris, about the influence of *heredity, tradition, environment*, and so on—was in his lazy way, 'Art happens.' 'Art *happens*,' he said. And I think that's true. I should say that *beauty* happens.

"Sometimes I think that beauty is not something rare. I think beauty is happening *all* the time. *Art* is happening all the time. At some conversation a man may say a very fine thing, not being aware of it. I am hearing fine sentences all the time from the man in the street, for example. From anybody."

I asked him if he considered himself a transcriber, to a certain extent. He said, "Yes, in a sense I do, and I think that I have written some fine lines, of course. *Everybody* has written some fine lines. That's not *my* privilege. If you're a writer you're bound to write something fine, at least now and then, off and on."

I brought up Longfellow. "Longfellow has some very beautiful lines. I'm very old-fashioned, but I like, 'This is the forest primeval. The murmuring pines and the hemlocks.' That's a very fine line. I don't know why people look down on Longfellow."

I asked him if in his experience it was possible to stimulate a love of literature. Was it possible to take twenty people and make them love literature more? He replied, "I'd been a professor of English and American literature during some twenty years, at the University of Buenos Aires. And I tried to teach my students not literature—that can't be taught—but the love of literature. If the course has to be done in four months, I can do very little. But still I know there are many young men in Buenos Aires—maybe they're not so young now—young men and young women, who have their memories full of English verse. And I have been studying Old English and Old Norse for the last twenty years. And I have also taught many people the love of Old English. I find something very stirring about Old English poetry."

I asked, "It has to stand on its own two feet, you mean?" Borges replied, "It has to. Or maybe because I like the sound of it. 'Maeg ic be my sylfum sothgied wrecan, / Sithas secgan'—now, those sounds have a *ring* to them. They mean, 'I can utter a true song about myself. I can tell of my travels.' That sounds like Walt Whitman, no? That was written in the ninth century in Northumberland. 'Maeg ic be me sylfum sothgied wrecan, / Sithas secgan'—and Ezra translated it as this (I think it's a rather uncouth translation): 'May I for my own self song's truth reckon, / Journey's jargon.' Well, that's too much of a jargon to *me*, no? Of course, he's translating the sounds. 'Maeg ic be me sylfum sothgied wrecan, / Sithas secgan / —'May I for my sake song's truth reckon,'—'sothgied wrecan.' He's translating the sounds more than the sense. And then 'sithas secgan'—'tell of my travels'—he translates 'journey's jargon,' which is rather uncouth, at least to me."

I asked him—after all, he'd said Pound's was uncouth—how he would have translated it. He replied, "I would translate it literally. 'I can utter, I can say a true song about myself. I can tell my travels.' I think that should be enough."

Interviewer: You obviously enjoyed him.
Buckley: I wrote in my book that his was the outstanding show. But I'd better stop here, though he went on, in his magic way.

Interviewer: Is there anyone or anything you would never write about?
Buckley: I wouldn't write anything that I was simply not at home with. I wouldn't write a western novel, for instance. I'm not sure I'd want to write *Advise and Consent*—the inside-the-Senate type of novel.

Interviewer: Why don't you think about writing a novel like Tom Wolfe's—the novel of manners, of certain strata of society, of the mixture of social and political and business life. You have the keen observer's eye, and maybe not quite the same rapier instinct that Tom has for the false note, and . . .
Buckley: And certainly not his descriptive powers, nor his talent for caricature. Because those are indispensable weapons. For the first few chapters of *Bonfire of the Vanities*, I underlined just his descriptions of people's clothes, and in a million years I couldn't achieve that.

Interviewer: It's true, there are no caricatures in your novels that I can think of, tempting as it must have been to do so with some of the darker figures.
Buckley: Well, some people thought the queen was. I didn't think so. I thought she was a somewhat Dickensian, original creation. I'm really quite serious. The fact that she's terribly sharp-tongued and terribly sarcastic, terribly aware of the fact that she's nominally sovereign and actually powerless, I think adds to the credibility of her character. I would love to see her on the stage. As done by Bette Davis.

Interviewer: It's amusing to think back on how difficult it was for your agents to find publication in England for *Saving the Queen* because of your sacrilege in having Blackford Oakes bed down with her, even though a fictional queen.
Buckley: And I have no doubt that not only killed that book in England, but probably inhibited its successors also.

Interviewer: Have the novels been any kind of turning point? What have they meant to you? I have a feeling you took on the first one as a challenge—you wanted to test yourself against the form and have some fun, which you certainly did—and then?

Buckley: I did find that there were reserves of creative energy that I was simply unaware of. Obviously, as a nonfiction analyst, one has to think resourcefully, but if, let's say in the novel I'm depicting a Soviet prison train going from Moscow to Siberia. I've got to create something that can hold the reader's attention during that journey. The answer became: you can do that. And it's kind of nice to figure out that you *can* do that . . . create a story that carries you from there.

A Novel Individual: An Interview
with William F. Buckley on His
Fiction

William F. Meehan III / 1996

From *The University Bookman* 36.2 (Summer 1996). Copyright © Educational Reviewer Inc. Reprinted with permission of the publisher.

WFM: What is the function of the novelist in society?

WFB: The function of the novelist is to depict reality and excite the imagination.

WFM: Will you write another Blackford Oakes novel?

WFB: No. The Cold War's over.

WFM: Did the Blackford Oakes novels require the approval of the CIA since you were an employee?

WFB: No. It's amusing you ask that because when I lectured at the CIA seven or eight years ago, maybe a bit more than that, the director of the CIA teased me that theoretically I should have had approval.

WFM: What is Blackford's most distinguishing feature or characteristic?

WFB: I didn't intend for any particular one to stand out except his actual loyalty to the United States and the Western cause.

WFM: Blackford reads *National Review,* and he has *Up from Liberalism* in one of the early books, even mentions your name in several others . . .

WFB: That's my little cameo.

WFM: . . . so in what ways does Blackford exhibit libertarian or conservative values?

WFB: Libertarian only in the sense that he's generally antistatist; he reads *National Review.* He is conservative in the sense that he thinks that values of the West are worth a nuclear deterrent, and devotes his life to corollary propositions. So, that's pretty conservative. But it is interesting, he was very attached to Kennedy, personally attached in a couple of those books, and he was absolutely dumbfounded when he couldn't rescue him from the assassin. So he had a personal attachment to Kennedy. But I can't remember that in any of the books I had him simply expatiate in general on any political policies. These aren't political books in the sense that *National Review* is a political magazine. He has no pine on socialized Medicare or anything.

WFM: Is that because spies are supposed to be apolitical?
WFB: Spies traditionally work for whichever government is in power, so in that sense they are apolitical. But you're not required to be apolitical. They can be very fervent socialists or very fervent antistatists, and it wouldn't theoretically affect their power to exercise their calling.

WFM: How did you prepare to write a Blackford Oakes novel?
WFB: What happens is that two or three weeks before going on my annual retreat to Switzerland I would decide on what the mise-en-scéne would be. I might decide, for instance, it's going to be [a] Castro novel, and it's going to feature the Bay of Pigs or whatever. Then I'd get my people here to line me up with two or three books on the subject and take them with me to Switzerland, and then start in.

WFM: What are the advantages to writing in Switzerland?
WFB: The advantages are that people don't call you up every five minutes, which happens here. And there's some allocation of time. I do my administrative work in the morning, and my column. Then have lunch and go skiing. Then I start writing around 4:15 or 4:30 and write till about 7:15 or 7:30, and do that every single day until the book is finished.

WFM: Do you set a time frame to finish the novel?
WFB: Yeah. It's taken as few as four and as many as six and a half weeks.

WFM: Which months of the year do you go there to write a novel?
WFB: February and March.

WFM: What about your immediate environment in which you do your writing? What's around you? Do you look out over a lake, a ski slope?
WFB: For twenty-seven years we rented a chateau that belongs to a friend. It's an enormous twelfth-century place that started out as a monastery. It had a very large room, which had been a children's playroom with a ping-pong table at one end. And it looks out into the base of a mountain in Gstaad, Switzerland. That's where I wrote most of my books. There was a fire at one point, in 1973. So for two years we had to rent individual chalets. The owners sold part of the chateau, so we now have a chalet, up high, that looks over the same mountain, next to which I used to be.

WFM: When you're writing your fiction, are there any rituals you follow? Do you listen to music, drink coffee?

WFB: My rituals are that I start around 4:30 after I take my bath and my shower. I work pretty regularly. Sometimes I hear the fax machine working and say, "Should I get up and see if it's urgent?" Always at exactly 7:00 o'clock our cook brings me a Kier, which is white wine with a little touch of créme de cassis. I take out one of my little cigars, and I have the most *glorious* feeling of satisfaction. Sometimes I might just finish a few paragraphs. But three years ago I gave up booze at Lent, and Lent, of course, always happens halfway through my novels. And so therefore I had to satisfy myself with grapefruit juice and my cigar. Last year I gave up cigars. So I had to satisfy myself, for Lent I mean, just with my Kier. I might make a deal with God to let my own private Lent begin after the novel. It's really a wonderful combination. A little Dutch cigar and Kier. I recommend it.

WFM: So, regardless of how many words you've written or how many pages you stop around 7:00 o'clock.

WFB: 7:00 or 7:15. But I also see how many words I've done. It's got to be 1,500 average.

WFM: What do you enjoy most about being a novelist?

WFB: It's fun to spin a bit of yarn. My books are very meticulously plotted. There's no sloppiness in the plot. I think I wrote somewhere that when I accepted the commission to write a novel I bought a book called *How to Write a Novel.* The only thing I remember about the book is the reader expects only one coincidence, resents more than one. I've sort of been guided by that. So there's always a coincidence in the book, but no more than one coincidence. Anyway, if you bring back a manuscript and people write, "Gee, that was neat," then that gives you a nice feeling.

WFM: How do you decide on a character's name?

WFB: It's completely improvised, except the Russian names. I'm not good at making up Russian names. So what I got was the index to the *Gulag Archipelago,* which has fifteen hundred Russian names. I tend to look for names that are slightly euphonious.

WFM: How about the title of a novel? How do you decide on that, and when do you normally decide on a title?

WFB: Well, sometimes I know right away. I remember deciding before writing it that I would call a particular book *See You Later Alligator,* which made a lot of sense to me especially in the Spanish version of it, *Hasta Luego Caimán.* This story is amusing. I went to a little party that Andy Warhol gave for about twenty people. I didn't catch the name of the woman on my left, so she turned to me and she said, "What are you working on?" Maybe I've written this, I forget. People who ask me that question I interpret, by the look on their face, whether they want the thirty-second answer, the one-minute answer, or the two-minute answer. This was a two-minute lady, so I gave her the whole works. She said, "That's fascinating. What are you calling it?" I said, "That's a real problem, because the publisher said if I don't give it a name by noon tomorrow, they're going to call it whatever they feel like." She said, "Why don't you call it *Stained Glass?*" Weeks later I found out she was Ruth Ford, the actress. So she named that book. *Stained Glass.* And *Stained Glass* is a great title for it. It's a play on words. *Stained Glass* has two meanings. The word *macula* is the Latin for sin and stain. It's nice to have a title with double entendre. And most of mine do.

WFM: Do you have a philosophy of language and if you do how does that affect your fiction?
WFB: The only philosophy of language that I have is that I won't, except in very exceptional circumstances, suppress an unusual word if the word flashes to my mind as exactly appropriate. [James Jackson] Kilpatrick will suppress them. If he feels 80 percent of the people who read this don't know what that word means, he won't put it in. I *will* put it in.

WFM: Why, because you think we should go look it up?
WFB: Well, the way I rationalize it is *that* word exists because there was what the economists would call a "felt need" for it, i.e., no other word around did what this particular word does. Therefore, the eventuation of that word enriched the choices you have. So, why do you want to be a party to diminishing the choices that you have, when you're dealing with a language which you worship for its beauty? Ronald Knox noted that the translator of the King James Bible subsumed seven different Greek words defining different shades of an ethical perception into the word "righteous" in the King James version. As a result, he said ethical exploration was set back by generations because those words had to be rediscovered. I thought it was a fascinating point. So, if you suppress a particular word, let's say, "velleity,"—something you desire, but not ardently—if you suppress that word, you diminish the choices by which people can express and distinguish between something they absolutely want and something they would like in the sense they would like an extra sweater. I don't want to be a party to that.

WFM: In your essay "In Defense of Unusual Words and Foreign Phrases," you mentioned that you have about a thousand of these kinds of words and phrases as part of your working vocabulary.

WFB: I hadn't counted them, but subsequently I did. You know why, because my nephew came up with the idea of publishing a calendar of unusual words. The very bright idea he had was to quote my actual use of it. The question was, "How many years could I go?" The answer is three. After three there weren't enough unusual words, so they started reprinting them in different formats. Therefore, you're talking about a thousand words that I routinely use, or have used, which would be unusual enough to engage the attention of people who want to learn. The average buyer of one of these calendars would probably know two-thirds of them, and a third he wouldn't know. I once, having read the latest Updike book, underlined the words I didn't know. And at our next editorial meeting I went around my company of learned associates. Of the twenty-six words I underlined, twenty-four of them were known to somebody. But probably if they had read it they would have found twenty-six words of which I knew two-thirds. Everybody has a private stock of words, which for some reason stay to the memory, and it's a different stock of words. The person who uses more unusual words than any human being, alive or dead, is Patrick O'Brian—the guy who writes the sailing books. He has the world's most extensive vocabulary.

WFM: What do you think your strengths as a novelist are?

WFB: A clean plot, fast movement, and an eye for humor. There is a leanness in my novels, which some people say is characteristic of my writing when I write novels, i.e. there's not a lot of time spent describing exteriorities, which some people do beautifully.

WFM: How do you place yourself in the tradition in espionage literature or spy novels? Where do you see yourself fitting in there? And how do your novels differ from the others?

WFB: They are not like anybody else's. Having said that, I'm not quite sure how I would actually distinguish them. They're much better written than 89 percent. I'm not as good a writer, in my judgment, as Le Carré. I have certain strengths he doesn't have, among them brevity. And then of course there's the fact that I'm unambiguous when the time comes to show who the good guys are and who the bad guys are, and he's very ambiguous. But beyond that I don't know, I don't read many of those others. I probably haven't read more than ten in my life.

WFM: Ten spy novels?

WFB: Yeah. I've read four or five Bond ones, up until he got surrealistic. Mainly the early Bond, which I enjoyed, but the later Bond got out of this world, sort of Supermanish.

WFM: What role does your Catholicism play in your fiction?

WFB: I feel that Catholicism affects human character and that human character affects fiction. In my case—well in *Brothers No More*—I put up front a situation in which Caroline asks a priest what she ought to do under certain circumstances. So there's a little bit of Catholic theology built into that. I think that's beyond a sort of an implicit recognition that some things are right and some things are wrong to do.

WFM: Some people might object to the philandering of Blackford. Why do you incorporate that element into your novels?

WFB: Well, in my judgment when you write a novel post about 1955 there's got to be a sexual element. I remember one time having dinner with Nabokov in Switzerland, which was a yearly event. I said, "You look very pleased with yourself today, Vadim." He said, "I am, I have finished my OSS." "What's OSS?" "Obligatory Sex Scene." The people expect it because sex surrounds us more vividly than would have been the case fifty years ago. You don't go to a movie as a rule without having some sexual element. Most books have a sexual element. There are sex cases in all the newspapers, so it becomes a conventional daily event in the imaginary life. A book that doesn't have it is a book about which people, not even knowing what it is, tend to feel something's missing. I recognized this even starting in, and have those two scenes in *Saving the Queen*, one involving the brothel and the other the Queen herself.

WFM: Do you have a favorite among the ten novels?

WFB: I think probably *Saving the Queen* is the most fun. Maybe because it's my first, maybe because the idea of seducing the Queen is kind of fun—actually he was seduced. She did the seducing. I guess I'm the proudest of that book. Somebody did a screenplay on *Saving the Queen* and had this rather novel change, which was OK by me. They made her unmarried, so that nobody was committing adultery. And I thought it loses a couple of nice scenes with her stuffy husband, but you can do away with that and have a fairyqueen as in Elizabeth I.

WFM: What's become of the screenplay for *Saving the Queen*?

WFB: At one point, CBS was interested in the possibility of running a Blackford Oakes movie once a month. All the books, and maybe more plots. They got close enough to get me to Hollywood to talk with them, but then they turned it down. So it stalled. My son said, "Well, they didn't discover Vietnam in the movies for about ten years." Then he said to me, "You own the Cold War. When the Cold War is rediscovered, Blackford Oakes will be all over the place." I hope he's right.

WFM: My experience is that when I mention you as a novelist to my liberal English professors they automatically dismiss you because of who you are. They know you as the *National Review* guy.
WFB: That's right, and they would not read my books.

WFM: Right. Is there anything you could say to those kinds of professors who dismiss your novels so readily?
WFB: I could say, "Nabokov thinks they're good." Nabokov died just before *Stained Glass* came out (which won an American Book Award). So he only read *Saving the Queen.* But he was laudatory about it. And he was a fussy man.

Buckley on Belief

Michael Cromartie / 1997

From *Books & Culture*, November/December 1997. Copyright © Michael Cromartie. Reprinted with permission of the author.

MC: Many years ago Garry Wills said this of you: "Being Catholic always mattered more to him than being conservative." Is he right?

WFB: If he meant he has a higher loyalty to God than to civil society, then the answer is obvious: God has to be preeminent.

MC: Why did you write this book [*Nearer, My God: An Autobiography of Faith*]?

WFB: It was the idea of a publisher. I undertook it, and after a year or so despaired of doing the reading I thought necessary to consummate it, so I gave it up. Then two years later, I got that little itchy feeling that one ought not give up the occasional challenge to do service to one's Maker, so I undertook to return to it. Three or four years later, that is what materialized.

MC: You say in your book, "I grew up in a large family of Catholics without even a decent ration of tentativeness among the lot of us about our religious faith." Were you really never tentative about your faith? Never?

WFB: No, I never was. I know one brother who was, but he lay down and got over it.

MC: How do you explain your own steadfastness?

WFB: Grace. I understand the nature of temptation, and I understand that the reach of temptation gets to almost everybody. But to the extent that one anticipates that possibility, in my case one has to reaffirm the postulates. And I never found any problem or conflict with these postulates and Christian doctrine. Which is a subject that I touch in this book. Therefore, I was never won over to skepticism, though skepticism can be very alluring. The Devil can be very alluring.

MC: So the skeptical questions never got the best of you.

WFB: No, no. I wonder about them abstractly. Arnold Lunn, for instance, once asked, "How can an all-forgiving God be so adamantine on the subject of sin, ordaining perpetual torture and misery?" Now, abstractly, I have wondered about that. But my sense of question or bewilderment takes the form of "How can it be so?" not "Is it so?"

MC: You describe in your book a debate between Monsignor Knox and Arnold Lunn, where they discuss who deserves eternal damnation.
WFB: Lunn's question was: "You had a sexual night out and you wake up the next morning with a heart attack, and you don't have an opportunity to be contrite, does that mean you go to hell?" To which Knox said, "God's not going to send anybody to hell who doesn't belong there." And that answer had a miraculous effect on Lunn's skepticism.

MC: You have some very moving pages about your mother and the naturalness of her relationship with God. You say, "Her worship of Him was as intense as that of a saint transfixed. And His companionship was as that of an old and very dear friend." And then you say about her that she had the "habit of seeing the best in everyone" and "a humorous spark in her eye." And she never broke her rule of "never, ever to complain, because, she explained, she could never repay God the favors He had done her, no matter what tribulations she might be made to suffer." She had a great influence on you, too.
WFB: Well, she did. She had a great influence on all her children. She was a devoted mother and a superb human being. There is a sense in which one has to resist the temptation to assign a uniqueness to her. Which we nevertheless thought was hers.

MC: So both your parents had a great influence on your own faith, both your father's devotion and your mother's godly example?
WFB: Yes, they did. My father was never in any sense ostentatious about his faith. But, as I think I explain somewhere in the book, if I stumbled into his bedroom just before he left in the morning for wherever he was going, one would find him on his knees praying.

MC: You say in your book, "There is something about the modern disposition that compels even those who believe in Him to keep all such matters tidily secluded in one's own tent. I am one of many millions who attend church on Sundays, receive the sacrament, say every day a prayer, particularly when a friend is ailing or gone; and yet I shrink from any religious communication that could possibly be thought intrusive." Now why is this? Is this temperamental, or does it say something about the modern disposition?
WFB: I think it's the culture. I think I mention in the book that all of Ephe-

sus rejoiced when word came in after a church council that they affirmed the Homoousian view of Christ. That kind of thing doesn't happen anymore. But then I am, by nature, indisposed to bring up religious matters uninvited. I just don't do it. For that reason, I won't turn to someone, as Bishop Fulton Sheen did to the skeptical journalist Heywood Broun. Sheen phoned Broun and Broun said, "What are you calling me about?" And Sheen said, "Your immortal soul." It was very providential, because years later Broun became a Christian. But I don't have that kind of evangelistic skill or inclination.

MC: Yet you admire it in others. You talk about going to a prison with Charles Colson and hearing him preach.
WFB: That's different, because Charles Colson is a missionary, and he accepts the mandate of public instruction.

MC: But there is something about the effect of secularization that creates in the modern disposition a difficulty about discussing things that are theological and transcendent in nature.
WFB: Yes, it does. It's sort of like asking about your sex life. People consider it rude. You almost have to have a rubric that is specifically inviting: "Let's talk about God." That rubric isn't all that hard to arrange, and yet it is not done very much. I've never been invited in my life to give a college speech or a seminar about which the subject of religion was discussed. It's like a subtle sequestration that religion is something that you do on your own, and it's disruptive to bring it up.

MC: Now if someone came to you in a broken and contrite state and said to you, "My life is a mess and I've just read your new book *Nearer, My God,* and I want to meet God," it wouldn't be difficult for you to respond to that plea?
WFB: No, but what I would do is find somebody more skillful than I to send them to. If someone came to me and said, "I am a sinner," I would say, "I'll help you in any way I can." But I could think of many more people who'd be more skillful and have had more experience in doing this sort of thing than I have.

MC: What thinkers have most influenced you theologically?
WFB: I'm asked that question every now and then; I can never answer it to the interviewer's satisfaction or even my own, because it's like asking for favorite books. I don't know what my favorite books are. They sort of melt into a deposit. And that deposit is not easy to pull apart and say, "Here's Saint Thomas, or Saint Augustine, or G. K. Chesterton." Chesterton fascinates me stylistically, and of course he is enormously profound. Although I've read a lot of Chesterton, I

would be wrong to say that he was in any sense a Holy Grail in terms of my itinerary. You have to remember that I began as a believer. So that it isn't as though in my youth I was in search of something that I suddenly discovered, like finding the woman you marry. I'm a theological novice, but I simply assume that the Christian prism tends to inform Christians, whatever they are reading. In that sense, I feel the ubiquity of the Christian ideal. I like to think that Christianity is universally informative. Whatever you do, there is always something there that consoles, guides, or inhibits.

MC: Broadly speaking, there are two views of the state of the church at the end of the twentieth century. Some observers see the church in decline and retreat under the onslaught of secularization: Others see a robust presence of the church in the great moral debates of the day and perhaps even something of a religious renewal going on. How do you see the state of things?

WFB: To the extent that the lessons of Christianity are needed, their need is accentuated by the extent to which they are not heeded. So when you have a rise in crime, illegitimacy, a lack of concern for others, despair or suicide, that is in a sense a tropism that reminds you that Christianity can help in understanding a phenomenon of that kind. Now, I think the figure is that roughly 90 percent of Americans believe in God, while in England only 5 percent of the people know why Easter's a holiday. Both of those reports may be misleading. But whatever the current measures of belief or disbelief, we know the world has gone through these things before, and one has to assume that when Christ promised that the Gates of Hell will not prevail against us, he didn't mean that just three people would still believe. He must have meant something more general than that. There are young people, eighteen, nineteen, twenty years old, who are deciding every day to give their lives to spread the Word. Their willingness to do that suggests the inherent vibrancy of the Christian faith, and in that vibrancy I profoundly believe. To what extent it will reach people and help thwart the intentions of the modern academy, which is explicitly opposed to Christianity, it's hard to say.

MC: This is interesting, because you once described yourself as a philosophical pessimist who remained a temperamental optimist. Let me put it this way and see if you agree: Your philosophical pessimism is rooted in your belief in the fallenness of our human nature. And your temperamental optimism is rooted in God's sovereignty and God's ability to take chaos and bring renewal and revival in the world.

WFB: I think that's fair, but I would add to that a sort of personal ebulliency that sustains me. I'm likelier to say that the bottle is half full than half empty.

MC: Do you think that is rooted in a religious confidence?

WFB: No, I don't think so. For example, Malcolm Muggeridge always talked about how Christendom was something that had ended—that we are now in effect back in the subterranean channels, having to do it all over again. And yet he was also, by nature, very happy and amusing. I should like to think that the inherent vibrancy of Christianity is waiting to be understood and appreciated. Mind you, I move among a set of people who are the intelligentsia. They are among the most deprived. If one were moving among most other sets of people, one would feel less loneliness in this matter. It is one thing to consult only with the faculty of Yale but quite another to consult the Civic Council of Columbus, Ohio. Christianity is more likely to be a staple part of their lives.

MC: You discuss in your book George Marsden's *The Soul of the American University: From Protestant Establishment to Established Nonbelief.* When you wrote *God and Man at Yale,* did you ever believe that it could get this bad?

WFB: Yes, because it seemed to me that it was so bad in 1949 and 1950 that the vector was pretty plain. Really, there is not such an enormous difference between how it was in the 1950s and in 1997. What has changed is that any attempt to deny the imperial reach of secularist skepticism is increasingly implausible.

MC: You have sympathy for libertarian views. Are you at all concerned that libertarianism sometimes encourages moral relativism and sometimes spills over to loosen moral restraint?

WFB: Oh, absolutely; very much so. The libertarian hubris—Ayn Rand took it to its extreme—really suggests the only thing that matters is your own satisfaction. Now, they will subtly acknowledge that your satisfaction might be affected by philanthropic enterprises, but that does strike me as cynical. What they are saying is that what matters is not that you have helped the poor; what matters is that you feel better, and if you feel better, then you are simply exercising your rights under a libertarian order. What they refuse to accept, what is denounced under Randism, is altruism. It is the notion that you might help the poor because you feel it is the right thing to do.

I am a presumptive libertarian, which is to say I believe a very hard case has to be made before the intervention of the state, but the presumption is rebuttable. In many ways, a libertarian would say it's not rebuttable, it's absolute.

MC: In the book, you have some disagreements with the Catholic church concerning birth control and you have some ambivalence about annulments. Is *Humanae Vitae* binding on all Catholics?

WFB: *Humanae Vitae* is a papal teaching; it's never been enunciated as ex cathedra. So the question, *Does one need to go to confession if one uses birth control?* is differently interpreted by different Catholic theologians. Some say yes; some say no, if there is no sense of sin. I discuss that at some length in the book. I tend to feel that it's not only safe but correct to be guided by the presumptive correctness of the papal teaching in the matter. But there is something discomfiting in the knowledge that while birth control is exercised approximately in the same ratio among Protestants and among Catholics, there is no sense of reticence by Catholic women when they go to the Communion rail. So manifestly, they don't feel this as a disqualifying moral weight. They may be making a theological mistake or a mistake in docility. But I don't think they are consciously flouting Christian doctrine; otherwise, they wouldn't be in the church in the first place.

MC: So encyclicals are not binding; they are teaching instruments?
WFB: Encyclicals are a form of exercising the magisterium. The magisterium is the teaching authority of the church. The pope uses his encyclicals to make occasional pronouncements. The current pope feels very strongly, as did Pope Paul, on this particular subject, but I guess what I am saying is that if ten or fifteen years from now, if there is a modification of *Humanae Vitae*, I don't think it will be deeply troubling to most Catholic theologians. It will be to some. One of the things that attracted Malcolm Muggeridge to the church was *Humanae Vitae*.

MC: You write that we need to "nurture an ethos and to revive an ethos." Tell us what you mean by that.
WFB: It is very difficult to effect an ethos, but that doesn't mean that an ethos oughtn't to be addressed as something that is remediable. I gave as an example anti-Semitism. Anti-Semitism was endemic when I was a boy. But what happened was that the Holocaust compelled people to confront that delinquency. It happened with blacks also. And the ethos did change. There is some anti-Semitism now, sure, but nothing like what there used to be. When I was at Yale, the first Jewish professor to achieve tenure arrived about the same time I did. So the difference between then and now is simply enormous. By the same token, if one wants to beat back the idea that sex ought to always be an entirely permissive exercise—just when you feel like it—one mustn't be resigned to the opposition that it is an unmodifiable part of the ethos. Assaults on it and criticism of it can be offered. And therefore an ethos can be changed and revived.

MC: Once when defining conservatism you said it is the "tacit acknowledgment that all that is finally important in human experience is behind us." What did you mean?

WFB: I wrote that in 1957. What I meant was that it is inconceivable to me as a Christian that God forgot to say critical things, or if there was anything terrifically important, it's hard to think that Jesus would have forgotten to pass it along. Obviously, there are lots of refinements on the Ten Commandments and the creed. But in terms of importance, what has been said is what is important. All the rest is exegesis and development.

William F. Buckley Jr. on
The Redhunter, A Novel Based on the Life of Senator Joe McCarthy

Jamie Glazov / 1999

From FrontPagemag.com, May 12, 1999. Copyright © FrontPagemag.com 1999. Reprinted with permission of the publisher.

Question: Is this book true to life?
Buckley: In every conventional way, yes.

Q. Do you mean that the routine biographical data are correct? When he was born, when he got married, when he died, that kind of thing?
B. All of that, yes. But much more is correct. Every line spoken or written by every character in the book—senators, reporters, editorialists, national figures—is exactly transcribed as recorded at the time. All those words were the words they actually spoke or wrote. The exception, of course, is so to speak, off-duty words.

Q. What do you mean by that, exactly?
B. There are conversations, remarks, thoughts, which, as the novelist, I supply. I don't know what were the exact words President Eisenhower used in discussing McCarthy with his staff, but I have a pretty good idea what they sounded like.

Q. You have two scenes in which Senator McCarthy visits with Whittaker Chambers. Did such visits take place?
B. Yes, but what was said between the two is in one part conjectural—

Q. In one part? What part is not conjectural?
B. I knew both men, and both talked to me about their visits.

Q. You quote Chambers on the subject of McCarthy. Did you invent that passage?
B. No. They were paragraphs about Joe McCarthy, written the day after he died by Whittaker Chambers to me in a personal letter. What I did was take the exact language and place it in a letter written by Chambers to a fictional character in the novel, Harry Bontecou.

Q. You were known, in your book published in 1953, to have sympathized with McCarthy. Does this novel reflect second thoughts?
B. I have thought for a long time that McCarthy did more damage to his cause than benefit—

Q. Why?
B. For a number of reasons, all of them dealt with in the novel. Senator McCarthy was disorderly, reckless, impulsive, and, toward the end, alcoholic.

Q. Why read about somebody with all those disabilities?
B. You're talking to somebody who spent two years writing this book about McCarthy. Obviously I thought it worth doing.

Q. You obviously have some sympathy with him, or has that changed too?
B. No. As a person I found him genial, kind, and good company. As a senator, he was devoted to the anti-Communist cause.

Q. If he wanted to serve the anti-Communist cause but, as you put it, did more harm than good, why do you have sympathy for him?
B. Because he was the historical vehicle, in America—in those days—for an attitude about the Soviet Union I sympathized with.

Q. Do you mean, you sympathized with charging around accusing everybody of being a Communist?
B. McCarthy did a lot of indefensible things. But he didn't, in fact, go around charging everybody with being a Communist. His biggest target, as a "Communist," was one professor. That professor figures in *The Redhunter*, figures very prominently. As usual, McCarthy exaggerated his accusations. But Owen Lattimore was, in my opinion, on the other side in the Cold War.

Q. Isn't it true that McCarthy never actually named one member of the Communist Party?
B. He gave the names of a half-dozen people who, in my judgment, any American jury surveying the facts would conclude were on the side of Moscow.

Q. Why is McCarthy so important a figure?
B. Because a majority of the American people thought he was the incarnation of the anti-Communist cause. A young senator, the youngest member of the Senate when he was elected, a farm boy who entered high school at age nineteen and worked his way through to a law degree and to municipal judge, who served in the marines—

Q. Wasn't the decoration he always boasted about, for valor in combat, wasn't it phony?

B. I think it was. I think the decoration was contrived by Joe McCarthy. But in fact he did volunteer to engage in combat duty.

Q. Isn't it true that he didn't latch on to the anti-Communist business until he gave one speech—in Wheeling, West Virginia—that set the ladies on fire and made him his reputation?

B. That is substantially true. And the novel goes with him to Wheeling, and explores what he said and what he thought and what the reactions were during the stupendous week that gave rise to his reputation as the most militant anti-Communist in town.

Q. If his charges were so disorganized and if his exaggerations were so egregious, how did he get so much support? Was it just an American mob out there thirsting for Communist targets?

B. Oh no. McCarthy had the support of most Republican senators and many Democrats. He had a great deal of support from the press, from columnists and editorial writers.

Q. How do you account for that?

B. How do I account for that, or how did McCarthy account for that?

Q. Well, both.

B. McCarthy got a taste of bureaucratic ineptitude and indifference to loyalty/security standards. J. Edgar Hoover felt the same frustration, which is why, under the table, he sided with McCarthy. He gave voice to popular frustrations.

Q. How do you account for his popularity?

B. He appeared on the horizon as the man in Washington who said: We are screwing things up and we should get rid of the people who have been running things, from the President (Truman) on down. A month before McCarthy's Wheeling speech, Alger Hiss was convicted as a spy. He had been vociferously defended in the academy, in the press, and by President Truman. Six months before, the Soviet Union exploded an atomic bomb, using methods and tools made available by American and British espionage agents. Two months before, free China fell to Communism, to Mao Tse-tung. Six months later, the North Koreans attacked the south, precipitating a war in which forty thousand Americans were killed. All of that was less than five years since we had fought a world war, at the end of which Stalin enslaved the whole of Eastern Europe.

Q. You can't be suggesting that McCarthy thought western leaders were pro-Communist?
B. No, but he thought they had been fooled, had been given bad advice, and hadn't stood up forcefully enough to Stalin.

Q. Did McCarthy think Dean Acheson was a Communist?
B. No. He thought him crazy-wrong as Secretary of State. He did think Philip Jessup had been a Communist. Joe McCarthy was a proto John Bircher. Several years after he died, the John Birch Society was founded and its governing assumption was that traitors were in charge of things.

Q. On the matter of Jessup, did he actually say that?
B. Not quite. But he told me he thought that, that Jessup had been on the other side.

Q. Does the novel reveal much stuff he told you but didn't tell the public?
B. No. But I was there at several moments that illuminated McCarthy, his idea of himself, and his idea of the struggle. I wrote a speech for him one time and went to bed in his house, dog-tired, just before midnight. He said he'd wake me at seven. I woke up when he knocked, still terribly tired. He had a cup of coffee in his hand. "Before you go to work," he told me, "I want to show you"—he got down on his knees over a huge map of Asia—"my plan for liberating China." I looked over at the grandfather clock. It was two in the morning. I was severe with him. On thinking back, maybe my fatigue aborted the liberation of China! . . . Anyway, that episode is in the book, and others I experienced myself, or learned from my late brother-in-law, and co-author of the earlier book, Brent Bozell, who worked for McCarthy for a period.

Q. Is it your intention, in *The Redhunter*, to revive Joe McCarthy?
B. No. Though that could happen. My book bares all of McCarthy's weaknesses. But in doing that, it exposes what it was that McCarthy wasn't guilty of, didn't do, was not responsible for. And that is a very big story—the lengths McCarthy's enemies went to, disfiguring not only Joe McCarthy, but American history.

Q. Is your book intended, then, as a correction?
B. It is intended to tell a story about a human being with a lot of warts who for reasons understandable, some not so, won the loyalty of a lot of people including a bright and personable aide, and won the hand of a very beautiful woman, then drank himself to death, his cause having apparently petered out.

"Live" with TAE: William F. Buckley Jr.

John Meroney / 2002

Originally published in *The American Enterprise*, January/February 2002. Reprinted with the permission of the American Enterprise Institute for Public Policy Research, Washington, D.C.

TAE: Several of the warhorse publications of the conservative movement have fallen on hard times. The *American Spectator* is virtually defunct; *Policy Review* has faded to a tiny circulation; even the *Weekly Standard* is reportedly on shaky ground. Are you optimistic about conservative journalism when each subsequent generation of Americans seems less literate and more oriented toward electronic devices?

Buckley: There's a real problem. But, look, when Franklin Roosevelt became president, the circulation of the *New Republic* was only about 35,000 and it dictated the policies of the New Deal. When Ronald Reagan stood up and said, "My policies derived from what I read in *National Review*," that was, of course, very gratifying. It's almost inevitable that some of our publications would falter when people spend more and more time watching television or on the computer.

TAE: So, do you read *National Review Online*?

Buckley: No. I read the print magazine. I don't read easily online. The challenge for the Internet is, How do we turn that into income? People have to get paid.

Incidentally, all this is as true on the Left as on the Right; the *Nation* is more robust now than it used to be, but it loses money, and so does the *New Republic*. One has to persuade people willing to make a sacrifice to help sustain these kinds of magazines, because it is publications like ours that create new crystallizations.

On certain issues, we come to hard conclusions. On the Soviets, for example, we came to a hard conclusion shortly after World War II, and we stayed there until the Soviet Union collapsed. Today, beyond the current war on terrorism, the issues are: How do we deal with China? What do we do with the World Trade Organization? Should we champion free trade? All that's in flux, especially after the terrorist attacks. As a conservative, what one has to be hopeful for is that the basic guidelines stay in place. *National Review* and the *American Enterprise* will be helpful in this regard.

TAE: Recently, Rudolph Giuliani has been crowned "The Mayor of America." Some have compared his leadership spirit after September 11 to that of Winston Churchill during the bombing of London. How do you think he has done as mayor?
Buckley: He's been very effective, and that's in large part due to his personality. He's a curmudgeon, and New York really needs a curmudgeon in that job.

TAE: What did he accomplish?
Buckley: Look at the decline in crime. Of course, that was a national phenomenon, too. And New York City still has many challenges. Though Giuliani sharply reduced the number of people who work for the city, the number is still huge, and the demands of that contingent are out of proportion to the rest of the population. Schooling remains abominable. But for ideological reasons, it becomes almost impossible to do anything about it. Another major economic problem is the municipal unions. Even when I ran for mayor in the mid sixties, they were a foreseeable problem.

TAE: Which John Lindsay's administration only made worse.
Buckley: Well, when he became mayor, he gave everyone the kind of privileges that had been restricted to people who endanger their lives for a living, such as police and firemen. New York City suddenly had tons of people who, at age forty, could retire on two-thirds of their pay for the rest of their lives, then they'd go out and get another job. That's a massive overhead for the city.

Then there are ravages like rent control. Giuliani didn't solve these things, and the only way we'll get closer to correcting them is if enough people ask, Do we really want to live in this place? New York City is so marvelous in terms of what it offers. But having access to the city is so costly that I don't think it's possible to predict that ten years from now New York will be as vibrant as it has been over the last few years.

TAE: There seems to be a debate within the Bush administration over how far the U.S. should take the war against terrorism. Some seem to argue that we should seize this as a chance to remove Saddam Hussein from power. Do you think we should?
Buckley: We must make this a war of decisive confrontation, and the theater for that is Iraq. The U.S. made a serious mistake in failing to consummate the Gulf

War. We lost the first round when we called an end to the engagement before up-
rooting the prime instigator of the aggression. The word to Saddam Hussein
ought to be: We are coming to Baghdad. From here on, enemies who are associated with terrorist activity will not cohabit the globe with America.

TAE: Before terrorism, America was threatened by communism. Yet for many
years, a cottage industry existed in journalism and the history profession to argue
that Americans who actively resisted communism were unfair and maybe crazy.
Buckley: Anti-communists were harshly undermined. The establishment just refused to believe that somebody of the elite social, intellectual, and political background of Alger Hiss, for instance, could actually be engaged in treasonous communist activity. When Whittaker Chambers asserted that Mr. Hiss had been, this
was hotly contested during two trials in which Chambers finally prevailed, yet
many liberals still refused to believe him.

Chambers didn't just blow the whistle on Hiss's perfidy, he was a prophet in
the broader sense. He wrote this masterly book, a throbbing intellectual and spiritual tonic, called *Witness*. Political columnist Robert Novak told me that he'd read
Witness one year after it was published, and it changed his life. Novak said it made
him a conservative, and years later it made him a Christian. He said the influence
of the book stays with him. That's true of many who read it.

TAE: Since the fall of the Berlin Wall, much evidence has emerged of deeply en-
trenched communist infiltrators in the United States and elsewhere. Do you think
this will reverse the stereotype of the 1940s and '50s as the "Red Scare" era?
Buckley: What we now know about the extent of Soviet penetration and intel-
ligence, here and especially in England, is extraordinary. The communist spy
Kim Philby very nearly became the head of England's main intelligence agency
MI6. He revealed to Moscow ultra-secret conversations between Truman and
Churchill. We *had* to defend ourselves against that.

Henry Kissinger once said, "The trouble with Senator Joe McCarthy is that
he didn't go far enough." He was exaggerating, of course. But I wonder. With
the Cold War over, people actively forget the intense degree of the Soviet threat.
People don't feel the kind of strategic gratitude that's appropriate for those who
helped us to survive this palpable threat.

TAE: The recently discovered spying for Russia done by former FBI agent Robert
Hanssen also seems extremely serious.
Buckley: But there's a lack of indignation about him. Yes, Hanssen will prob-
ably go to jail for a long time, maybe for life. But his case is treated as a routine

misadventure. Look, I was in the CIA. I feel intense indignation about someone who would actually betray human beings—not only Americans but Russians, too. Fury at people who betray others to their deaths has to find an apt form of public disapprobation—and it hasn't with Robert Hanssen.

TAE: What about Jonathan Pollard?

Buckley: There's a heavy Jewish lobby for letting Jonathan Pollard off. A few years ago, I was given an award by the Anti-Defamation League, and in accepting it, I gave a speech about anti-Semitism. Afterwards, someone came up to me and said, "Don't you think Pollard ought to be let go?" I said, "No. I think he ought to be executed." That didn't go over well. It's proper to feel indignation for traitors, but in the absence of a palpable threat, what they did sometimes seems to be more innocent.

TAE: You've just written a new novel—about Elvis Presley. How did William F. Buckley decide to write a whole book about the King?

Buckley: Well, I didn't set out to write a book about Elvis. My goal was to chronicle a young American who goes left. In so doing, I wandered into the late fifties—and Elvis Presley is everywhere. He was an enormous cultural presence. He intrigued me because he was iconoclastic and permissive. I read as many things about Elvis Presley as I could, and I believe he's faithfully reproduced. There's the good *and* the bad.

TAE: But couldn't you have written the same coming-of-age story using another cultural figure, such as John Wayne or Frank Sinatra? Surely their style would have been closer to your political philosophy.

Buckley: Well, there's so much drama in the Elvis scene, partly because he was so young and exuberant. There are fascinating elements of his story, such as when he goes to see President Nixon in 1970 to get deputized as an arm of the law—while he's committing suicide with prescription drugs. Elvis was a true eccentric; he didn't follow any patterns. He was religious and patriotic. He didn't smoke, drink, or swear. He had this enormous impact, but people still aren't quite sure how to distill all of it.

TAE: You reconstruct Elvis's meeting with President Nixon in your book. Nixon tells him, "I want to thank you for your support of our war on drugs," and deputizes him.

Buckley: The conversation between Elvis and the president is reproduced almost exactly as it took place. And the details about Elvis being taken on a tour around the White House are historical fact.

TAE: Conservatives were among those who criticized Elvis when he became popular in the fifties, not just because of his music, but because of how he performed physically. In 1956, there probably weren't too many *National Review* subscribers who approved of his gyrating.

Buckley: You're probably right. For Elvis, rock 'n' roll simply required that kind of physical action. He maintained, with sincerity, I think, that he didn't intend to be provocative; this was just the way he felt about the music. His hips had to sway. Eventually, people got used to it, but for a while the TV networks wouldn't allow a camera to photograph him below the waist. Today, Elvis Presley seems like such a conservative figure, especially when compared with the excesses of many contemporary musicians.

TAE: One of the great influences on your novel's protagonist is a socialist teacher who tells him that the only thing that distinguishes America from other nations in the world is its capitalist wealth and nuclear army. He argues that the Cold War is a great distraction from the pursuit of a world in which property is commonly owned. He quotes Thoreau.

Buckley: Yes, my fictional hero Orson was moved by that teacher, like so many students are moved by their teachers in real life. Partly because of that influence, Orson becomes this totally committed left-wing eighteen-year-old. That's what I set out to write about. I wanted to find out what was going on in the minds of members of that generation. I saw novelistic possibilities in the relationship between Elvis and Orson, and the book begins when Orson is fifteen and Elvis is twenty-one. Then, it's a paternal relationship. Decades later, it's the other way around: Orson is looking after Elvis—or at least trying to. Nobody ever succeeded in doing that.

TAE: Orson also comes into contact with another iconoclastic American figure— Senator Barry Goldwater, whom you actually knew.

Buckley: Orson falls in love with a girl who's seventeen, and she's a right-winger. Her parents voted for Goldwater. So Orson and she are driving to Phoenix, Arizona, and she says to him, "Let's go say hello to Senator Goldwater." Goldwater had just lost the national election three weeks earlier, and Orson tries to explain that a person doesn't just drop in unannounced on a presidential candidate. But the girl, wearing a "Goldwater for President" sports shirt, prevails. They drive up to Goldwater's house, where I've often been, so I describe what it's like there.

TAE: And Barry Goldwater takes them into his ham radio studio, where he lets them listen to broadcasts from Radio Moscow.

Buckley: Goldwater is able to hear the Soviets denouncing him. (laughs)

TAE: Did you ever visit Goldwater's radio studio?

Buckley: Oh, yes. I was there two or three times. I was even in a ham radio station with him in the South Pole once. On that particular trip, a man who had a small radio station asked Goldwater if he wanted to come in and sample it, and he did. I went with him.

TAE: During the fifties, did you listen to Elvis Presley or Frank Sinatra?

Buckley: I listened to Sinatra, of course. One can't *not* listen to Sinatra. But Elvis? No. I've heard a great deal of him over the last year and a half, and I like about 20 percent of it.

TAE: Does the kind of music a person prefers have anything to do with his political views?

Buckley: I have to assume that it does, but I'm absolutely at sea in attempting correlations that are satisfactory to me. The iconoclasm and demanding rhythm of rock 'n' roll causes people to indulge primitive impulses. It's primitive to get up and scream and yell so loud that you can't hear. I don't understand it—but obviously many people do, because that's what's on the radio. Correlations have to exist, but how to deduce them from cause and effect, I'm incapable of doing.

TAE: In researching your book you traveled to Elvis's home "Graceland," one of the great American pop landmarks.

Buckley: Jack Soden, the CEO of Elvis Presley Enterprises, took me through the house late one night because I wanted to see it as Elvis did. Going through the house, you feel as though Elvis could appear at any moment. But you also get this real sense of his self-indulgence. Every room is crammed with Elvis's impulse of the moment. There are his flashy jump suits and golden discs. There's the jungle room.

Soden told me that one year after Elvis died, people spontaneously began to accumulate on the street outside. He asked permission of Elvis's wife, Priscilla, to let these fans come in. Some 10,000 still show up every August, the month of his death, and they come with candles for a candlelight pilgrimage. There's no chewing-gum wrappers or popcorn—it's all very reverential. What's amazing is that even though Elvis became so overweight and unattractive, his impact has survived that grotesqueness.

TAE: Two Southern towns are featured in your novel: Camden, South Carolina, and Memphis, Tennessee.

Buckley: Camden is where I spent winters growing up, and in the book, it's where Orson's grandparents live. It's there, in 1956, that he turns on his grandfather's television set and sees Elvis. It moved him so much that the next day, he got on a bus to Columbia to buy Elvis's record. That kind of indenture took shape and stayed with him the rest of his life. Camden, though, isn't at all like Memphis, which was a natural conduit for Elvis's kind of music, which was almost a Pentecostal rock 'n' roll.

TAE: Many have said that *Elvis in the Morning* is one of your best books. One review called it a "small masterpiece." Critics have expressed surprise that "the cultivated Buckley could understand Presley's enormous visceral appeal," and readers have talked about how "tender," "gentle," and "sweet" the book is. Is the author of *McCarthy and His Enemies, Up from Liberalism,* and *The Redhunter* going soft on us?

Buckley: I don't know how to answer that. I really came to like Elvis Presley. He was a pain about a lot of things, but I liked him despite that. Perhaps because so much of Elvis is considered disruptive, and I wasn't more critical of him, people think I'm going soft. But this is just a story.

It's nice to think that your books can imaginatively tell a story. *Sweet?* I've always distinguished between sentimental and sentiment, and I'm all in favor of sentiment.

TAE: For several years now, Paul Weyrich and some other conservative activists have argued in favor of retreating into parallel universes as a way of escaping degraded popular culture. They say we should stop trying so strenuously to change majority culture and instead enjoy this rich life that America allows us to live as a cultural and moral minority. Do your passionate detours into sailing, and novels such as this one, represent your partial retreat from political life into private passions?

Buckley: Any conservative who's interesting has to be *interested* in many things. Music, art, stories, love—all those are important. To express those interests in books one writes strikes me as entirely normal. I've spent many hours on sailboats and I've written four books about sailing, but I don't think that has anything to do with conservatism. I suppose it would if those books reflected a complete indifference to the wonders of nature, but on the other hand, how could a conservative do that? A conservative must have concern for our nature, and marvel over it. It's incorrect to imagine that a conservative has to have interests limited exclusively to expressions of a political character.

TAE: Where's the next generation of the Buckley family headed politically?
Buckley: Well, I have forty nieces and nephews and none of them is a dissident in the sense of my protagonist Orson. There's no generational revolt in my family.

Objectivist Sex—and Politics: An Interview with William F. Buckley Jr.

Kathryn Jean Lopez / 2003

Q: Mr. Buckley, why did you write this book, *Getting It Right*?
A: Because I wanted to write a story about politics, sex, and legendary American figures.

Q: Legendary like who?
A: Like whom.

Q: Like whom.
A: Like Senator Barry Goldwater, President Lyndon Johnson, General Edwin Walker, Ayn Rand, and Robert Welch.

Q: Hey, slow down a minute. We all know who Senator Goldwater was—
A: —Yes, but you don't know some things about him that I know.

Q: That you know from personal observation? But this is a novel.
A: That doesn't matter. The novel talks about things that actually happened when the conservative movement in America was shaping up, like the big struggle inside the Goldwater camp on whether to disavow the support of the John Birch Society and Robert Welch.

Q: Robert Welch. The candy manufacturer?
A: Well yes, in the sense that one might identify Abraham Lincoln as The Railsplitter.

Q: Your Robert Welch, when he left the candy business, did what?
A: He founded one of the most powerful political organizations in the postwar world. It was called the John Birch Society. It had 100,000 members and tried to influence public affairs, beginning with a drive to impeach Earl Warren, who was then Chief Justice of the United States.

Q: Well, your Mr. Welch didn't get very far, did he? Who else did he go after?
A: President Dwight Eisenhower.

Q: What did he have against Ike?
A: Welch thought he was a secret agent of the Communist party.

Q: Holy God. (*Joking laughter.*) He didn't persuade anybody to believe that, did he? I mean, Mamie didn't believe it, did she?
A: You're making fun of it, and I don't blame you. But the business about Ike being a Communist wasn't the central organizing principle of the John Birch Society. It was an anti-Communist society. It had a senior council of big figures in American industry. It had 30,000 chapters. Welch published books and magazines and wrote letters and gave speeches and high-powered two-day seminars. He persuaded a lot of Americans that the Soviet Union was winning the Cold War and that the reason for this was that the whole government of the United States was riddled with traitors and with men and women who were reconciled to Communist victory.

Q: Well, that's hard to believe, but you said Senator Goldwater was reluctant to denounce the John Birch Society?
A: He didn't want to single it out for denunciation in San Francisco when he was nominated for president. He only went so far as to denounce "extremists." There was a ton of pressure on him to name the John Birch Society, but he said he didn't want to do that, denouncing them meant denouncing some of his best supporters. As a matter of fact, his own campaign manager was a member of the John Birch Society. So was my mother.

Q: How does that all figure in your novel?
A: The twenty-three-year-old protagonist of the novel worked full-time for the John Birch Society.

Q: A kind of a dumb guy?
A: Oh no! Woodroe Raynor was an honors graduate from Princeton. He had been on the spot when the Soviet tanks moved in on the Hungarian freedom fighters in 1956. Woodroe had been doing missionary work as a Mormon, and got shot by a Communist soldier a few days after losing his virginity to a Hungarian spy.

Q: Maybe that was just punishment! . . . But did your hero believe that business about Ike and Warren being Communists?
A: No, but he was like Goldwater, attracted to the society as a fighting anti-Communist organization—

Q: Fighting what?
A: Fighting appeasement in foreign policy, fighting Castro in Cuba, fighting the construction of the wall in Germany by Khrushchev, fighting Ho Chi Minh in Vietnam, fighting for the loyalty/security program in the federal government.

Q: You mentioned sex as an important feature in life—
A: An important feature not "in life," in the life of Ayn Rand.

Q: You're not saying sex is not an important feature in, well, just life. . . . I mean, you're not saying sex was important only for Ayn Rand, which by the way, who's she?
A: Ayn Rand is the most widely read novelist in the history of the world.

Q: You mean, more than *Gone With the Wind*, or John Grisham?
A: Oh yes. Her major novel is *Atlas Shrugged*, and last year it sold 200,000 copies. It was published in 1957. Forty-five years ago.

Q: So why does a novel play an important part in your book, and what is *Atlas Shrugged*, a sex book?
A: Oh no, though it's true that Russell Kirk said people read *Atlas Shrugged* "for the fornicating bits." It is a great big novel with good guys and bad guys and the good guys are engaged in promoting a view of life. Ayn Rand called it Objectivism.

Q: What was that?
A: The philosophical position that the way to lead the right life is to acknowledge objective features in life, and to do everything you want, to act with pure concern for what your reason tells you to do, and to augment freedom by restraining government to the barest essentials of life, like policemen and firemen, preferably volunteer firemen.

Q: How does this Objectivism figure in the novel?
A: Well, the whole movement advanced a view that political arrangements should be anarchistic in character, i.e., in favor of repealing almost all existing laws and regulations.

Q: How did Ayn Rand involve herself with Goldwater?
A: When Goldwater wrote his book, *The Conscience of a Conservative*, and headed toward the Republican nomination in San Francisco, Ayn Rand wrote him a letter volunteering to shape his political platform and his thinking.

Q: Did this have much of an effect on Goldwater?

A: Well, he listened, but turned her down on the matter of religion—he didn't go along with her atheism. But Ayn Rand had Objectivist institutes all over the country, where they studied her philosophy, and her point of view—making personal self-seeking central to Objectivist political philosophy and scorning concern for others. "Altruism," Miss Rand called that—her fear was that Goldwater would nudge the conservative movement in that direction.

Q: How did sex get into all that?

A: Well, that became a big deal—*a very big deal*, as David Halberstam might put it. Ayn Rand's philosophy claimed that Objectivist reasoning, by elevating reason into total control of everything you do, say, and think, would make for perfect dominance of yourself, etc., etc. And then—

Q: I can't stand the suspense.

A: And then along came Nathaniel Branden.

Q: From where?

A: He was a handsome, precocious Canadian who, age nineteen, read the first major Ayn Rand novel, which was called *The Fountainhead*. He was truly smitten. I mean, not since St. Paul was there anything like it. He thought he had discovered the Holy Grail. He traveled to Los Angeles where the great lady was then living, just on the off chance of having ten minutes with her. Well, that resulted in a conversation, at her ranch house where she lived with her nice, compliant husband, lasting from about five in the afternoon when young Nathaniel arrived, until about five the following morning, when they finally said good night. Rand took a great liking to the bright young man, twenty-five years her junior. A couple of years later they were all living in New York City, Nathaniel and his new wife, and Ayn Rand and her husband. Nathaniel had become her chief associate and had founded a national institute to further her work, and he lectured on Objectivism in New York. When *Atlas Shrugged* was triumphantly published, he learned that the highest honor that could be paid him had happened: The great book she had been working on for thirteen years was dedicated to two people, her mousy little husband—and Nathaniel Branden.

Q: Did that lead to you-know-what?

A: I'll say. She decided they had to sleep together to fulfill Objectivist destiny. So she rounded up Nathaniel, Nathaniel's wife, and her own husband, and told them all jointly that she would be sleeping with Nathaniel one day every week.

Q: That doesn't sound like an all-consuming romance.
A: But it was. Then things happened, and readers get a good look at the inside story because Woodroe, the young Princeton graduate working for the John Birch Society, has a girl friend, an ardent Jewish anti-Communist who works full-time for Nathaniel Branden and his Institute. She shares an apartment with Woodroe, and argues that Ayn Rand's Objectivism is the best way to forward the conservative movement, while he pursues the Birchite line.

Q: So?
A: Yes, back to sex. Well, some time after *Atlas* is published, Ayn Rand has a psychological depression. For a couple of years, she suspends the sexual union with Nathaniel. But then her passion returns. But something awful has happened: Nathaniel is on to another lady, twenty-five years younger than the goddess of Objectivism. He figures he just has to tell Ayn the truth—that there is somebody else—and a scene shapes up of the highest theatrical drama: The two couples, Mr. and Mrs. Ayn Rand, Mr. and Mrs. Nathaniel Branden, meet in Ayn Rand's sacred study with one close friend and associate of both parties. Speaking nervously from notes, to make certain he says it *just right*, Nathaniel Branden tells Ayn Rand that he has—somebody else. Well, in the history of Women Scorned, there was nobody could *touch* Ayn Rand scorned. She denounces Nathaniel, she anathematizes his male organ, she screams that he is a traitor, she announces that she will withdraw his name from *Atlas Shrugged*'s dedication page, she says that she will abolish the Nathaniel Branden Institute and will attempt to block a pending book on psychology by Branden. The people in that room have never seen anything like it, not even on screen, let alone in the studio of the same woman who has founded a philosophy based on reason who has time and again asserted that she never lost control of herself or said anything that was less than a reflection of her absolutely ordered reason.

Q: Sounds like quite a scene. But what do we get out of that, other than that it was a hell of a scene coming from that goddess of reason?
A: Woodroe hears about what happened from his girl friend Leonora, who is close to Barbara Branden—they work in the same office. Leonora finds herself questioning this philosophy of *Atlas Shrugged* that she so much admired, and edges out of the Objectivist movement, quitting her job. Meanwhile Woodroe studies the current issue of the John Birch Society magazine. It features one of those long letters by Robert Welch to the faithful. What Welch is saying this time around is that there is no point in giving aid to South Vietnam in an effort to help the

anti-Communists because our leadership in Washington is so overrun by Communists, the cause would be betrayed. What you had got here is what Sam Tanenhaus, the author and historian, called "the complex ways in which Randism and Birchism formed an unintended interlocking collaboration which looked for a time as if it might pitch the Right into permanent oblivion; instead the crisis was met and mastered into a mature, nuanced conservative movement."

Q: Your book tells how the Republican party—
A: —and the conservative movement—

Q: —I was going to say, how the Republican party and, yes, the conservative movement back then repelled two philosophical and political boarding parties which might have stunted its future development—
A: —and would have left the country bereft of Ronald Reagan and other nice things.

Q: Okay. But you forgot to tell us who General Walker was.
A: To begin with, he was a war hero. But by the time he was given his command in West Germany he got caught up in the Birchite movement and gave his staff to read the stuff the Society was issuing, which suggested that a lot of people were traitors, that kind of thing. He was caught doing this and was removed from his command. That was a big Page One story: DEFENSE DEPARTMENT FIRES/NOTED ANTI-COMMUNIST GENERAL. What he then did was resign his commission, return to Texas, run for governor, and lose. Then he went to Ole Miss and got caught up in the turmoil over the integration of the first black student, was arrested on the explicit orders of Attorney General Bobby Kennedy. He returned to Dallas and a little while later, seated at his desk while talking to Woodroe Raynor, my protagonist, a bullet whizzed just by his ear. It was fired by the same man, the world later found out, who a few months later, again in Dallas, fired the shot that killed President John F. Kennedy.

Q: Does the death of the president figure in your book?
A: Marginally. Just how, you'll have to read *Getting It Right* to find out.

Q: Okay, okay.
A: . . . at your bookstore. Or if you want a signed copy, write to me at *National Review*, enclosing a check for $24.95, plus $3 shipping and handling.

Old School

Joseph Rago / 2005

There is something out of time about lunching with William F. Buckley Jr. It goes beyond the inimitable WFB style: the mannered civility, the O.E.D. vocabulary, the jaunty patrician demeanor. It is also something more than mere age. "Well, I am one day older than I was yesterday," he says, with rather good cheer. Yet if there's anachronism to Mr. Buckley, it is also a sense of being present at a moment of creation.

For all his versatility as editor, essayist, critic, controversialist, and bon vivant, Mr. Buckley is widely credited as the driving force behind the intellectual coalition that drew conservatism from the fringes of American life to its center, with such side-effects as the utter collapse of the Soviet empire. "There's nothing I hoped for that wasn't reasonably achieved," declares Mr. Buckley, who will turn eighty later this month. "Now, I'm going to have a cocktail," he announces, flashing his oblique grin. "Will you join me?"

"My view is unorthodox," Mr. Buckley says of the violence roiling the French suburbs. "It seems to me that a very hard dose of market discipline would distract the attention of the young revolutionaries from their frolics, traditional and otherwise, and my sense is that if they had to worry about how to eat and buy food, they would stop screwing around and face reality. If these people didn't wake up in the morning thinking about what cars to burn—instead of work—they might not be having these problems."

Here, with this talk of young men on the boil, we turn to the episode that made Mr. Buckley's name—the publication, in 1951, of *God and Man at Yale*. His argument, scrubbed down, was relatively simple: that the inner workings of Yale were increasingly hostile to conservative and religious perspectives. It was "the detraditionalization" of a great university. Yet his trim little volume scandalized the Yale administration and Bill Buckley, then twenty-six, found himself subjected to calumnies from every sort of pen-and-inkubus. "A violent, twisted, and

ignorant young man," said McGeorge Bundy. And he was among the more charitable.

"The academic establishment simply agreed that it was a completely forget-
table ideological hour, fit to be ignored completely," Mr. Buckley recalls. "They
were overwhelmed by the fact that such thinking could happen, and they made
fools of themselves—I think." *God and Man*, now regarded as a classic, is worth
revisiting. Its most important consequence was that it "opened up thinking on
several fronts . . . not least being, people became more conscious of ideological
balance, and therefore more sensitive to the overwhelming superiority of the *formalisms* of college life." All these years later, Mr. Buckley remains skeptical of our
higher education. He concedes "a broadening of perspective," but notes that "the
liberal orthodoxy is still pretty secure and it is unlikely that any event—at least in
my lifetime—will dislodge it."

If there has been a signal project of Mr. Buckley's career, it is nicely captured
in his reflection about opening up thought. That undertaking was most alive
in his periodical, *National Review*, founded in 1955. This might seem incom-
patible in light of its famous animus: "It stands athwart History, yelling Stop."
But since the forces of history can no more be resisted than those of gravity, its
capitalization—as History—is a touch that reminds us that Mr. Buckley meant it
to represent the regnant liberalism which *NR* was specially designed to contest.

Mr. Buckley declares without hesitation that *National Review* was his greatest accomplishment. "I brokered it. So I'm very proud and grateful for that. I don't
know if it's possible now to be aware of the number of people who contributed
to *National Review*—their opinions, their historical earning, their grace, their
spirituality—all that made for an extraordinary mix." At its finest, *National Review* seethed with controversy and creative energies, its pages largely given over to
analyses of competing philosophies and politics, balanced by critical introspec-
tion. It was, says Mr. Buckley, "an open laboratory of unhampered thought."

Against this backdrop, it is difficult not to draw correspondences to the world
in which we now find ourselves, and Mr. Buckley evinces a keen sense of disappointment with the fortunes of the movement his journal did so much to shape.
The trouble (if it can be called that) is that conservatism is no longer sutured together by "the galvanizing thread that the Soviet Union provided. And for that
reason I think conservatism has become a little bit slothful. It could be very decisive when the alternative was the apocalyptic reordering presented by the Soviet
Union. . . . But in the absence of those challenges, there were attenuations. Those
attenuations at this point haven't been resolved very persuasively."

Does he believe the war on terror to be the same kind of "long twilight struggle" as the Cold War? "Well," he says, "it lacks the formal face. It's detached from national dimensions. As such, it legitimately inquires into two things. No. 1: To what extent does this society elect to fight it? Because if it doesn't care that much about it then to hell with it. No. 2: Is this society pliant enough to come up with a formula to defend itself that nevertheless acknowledges the ancient restrictions on ideas? If I'm correct, there hasn't been an act of terrorism in the U.S. for four years, and that bespeaks not the absence of will by terrorists to damage but a lack of resources. How much of that is owing to their own institutions or to a sense that resistance is here remains to be seen."

This last is a glancing way of referring to the U.S. enterprise in Iraq, which Mr. Buckley calls "anything but conservative." "Conservatism," he says, "except when it is expressed as pure idealism, takes into account reality, and the reality of the situation is that missions abroad to effect regime change in countries without a bill of rights or democratic tradition are terribly arduous. This isn't to say that the war is wrong, or that history will judge it to be wrong. But it is absolutely to say that conservatism implies a certain submission to reality; and this war has an unrealistic frank and is being conscripted by events."

Mr. Buckley is similarly skeptical of the presidency of George Bush, who, he says, was not elected "as a vessel of the conservative faith." He returns to a formulation he has used before: "Bush is conservative, but he is not *a* conservative." The distinction is not unimportant; it suggests a way of approaching the world with a conservative disposition but having devoted no particularly methodical thought to the subject—perhaps a bit too in thrall to the formalisms of Republican discourse. "There's a certain"—Mr. Buckley pauses mischievously—"*whole*someness to the Republican Party."

Does he think the conservative movement will undergo the same kind of intellectual reinvigoration that *National Review* spurred in its early years? "I don't think there's any way to avoid it," he quickly interjects. "*Mutatis mutandis.* So one point on our side."

Mr. Buckley necessarily declines, however, to speculate on how that realignment will take shape. "I know people who have assured me about what will happen tomorrow, and they'll tell you animatedly about it. I don't have that gift. The happy aspect is that you're never surprised. On the other hand it denies you any claim to prophetic skills. But there's no alternative, and we're lucky there isn't."

Mr. Buckley remains in contagiously high spirits, his world governed by his "cognate aversion to boredom." He continues to add to his extraordinary body of work—largely on account of "the crowning imperative of the deadline." His great enthusiasms have led to thousands of individual pieces of published writing:

close to fifty books, eighteen of them novels, over eight hundred editorials for *National Review,* roughly four hundred essays in other publications, more than four thousand newspaper columns. He tells me his personal papers fill more than a hundred archival boxes in Yale's Sterling Memorial Library. All this, taken as a whole, is increasingly being recognized as one of the richest sustained contributions to American letters of the twentieth century. Most of all, I think, he will be remembered for the promulgation of what he calls "a thoughtful conservatism."

And Mr. Buckley's work continues apace. He canceled his annual writing trip to Switzerland this year after he found he could not ski like he once used to—that would have been "a violation of basic propositions." But he put a book together anyway, another novel. "I said to my gifted son, someone asked me, 'Well, what's it about?' Said I, rather pompously really: 'It can't be described.' Said he: 'Of course it can be described. Anything can be described.' Of course he was right." (I will leave its sinuous premises unsaid.)

"In any case," Mr. Buckley continues, "it's got some readable stuff in it. But I won't test you on that—a year from now you can tell me what you think."

Index